By All Means
Keep On Moving

MARILU HENNER

By All Means
Keep On Moving

with
Jim Jerome

POCKET BOOKS
New York London Toronto Sydney Tokyo Singapore

PHOTO CREDITS

BLACK-AND-WHITE PHOTO INSERT: **1-11:** Author's Collection; **12:** © Patty Beaudet; **13:** Author's Collection; **14:** Author's Collection; **15-16:** JoAnn Carney; **17:** © Silverfilm Productions; **18-20:** JoAnn Carney; **21-24:** Author's Collection; **25-26:** Author's Collection; **27:** G. W. Bailey; **28:** Eddie Frank; **29-32:** Harry Langdon Photography; **33:** Alberto Tolot/LaMoine; **34:** ©1990, CBS, Inc., used by permission; **35:** Author's Collection; **36:** ©1979, Capital Cities/ABC, Inc.; **37-38:** *Taxi,* ©1994 Paramount Pictures. All rights reserved.; **39:** Author's Collection; **40:** *Taxi,* © Paramount Pictures. All Rights Reserved.; **41:** Author's Collection; **42:** JoAnn Carney; **43:** *The Man Who Loved Women* ©1983 Columbia Pictures Industries, Inc. All rights reserved.; **44:** *Johnny Dangerously* ©1984. Twentieth Century Fox Film Corporation. All rights reserved.; **45:** *Perfect* ©1985 Columbia Pictures Industries, Inc. All rights reserved.; **46:** © Touchstone Pictures and Amblin Entertainment.; **47-48:** ©1990, CBS, Inc., used by permission. Photo by Randy Tipper.; **49-50:** Photo by: Lorin Henner; **51:** Courtesy, National Broadcasting Company.

COLOR INSERT: **1-2:** Author's Collection; **3-4:** JoAnn Carney; **5-7:** *Taxi,* ©1994 Paramount Pictures. All rights reserved.; **8:** Melody Henner; **9:** *Rustler's Rhapsody,* ©1994 Paramount Pictures. All rights reserved. G. W. Bailey; **10:** Harry Langdon Photography; **11:** Alberto Tolot/LaMoine; **12:** Still from *L.A. Story.* Used with permission of Carolco Pictures Inc. Motion Pictures ©1991 Carolco Pictures Inc. (U.S. and Canada), Carolco International N.V. (All other Countries). All rights reserved.; **13:** Photo Joseph Kell; **14-15:** Author's Collection; *Double-page wedding spread:* Photos by Lorin Henner; **16:** Courtesy, National Broadcasting Company; **17:** Author's Collection.

POCKET BOOKS, a division of Simon & Schuster Inc.
1230 Avenue of the Americas, New York, NY 10020

ISBN: 0-671-78446-3

To Joe and Loretta Henner, who gave me a life.
And Nicky and Rob, who make me love living it.

Acknowledgments

There are several people whose contributions to this book were indispensable.

Jerry Katzman, the fabulous president of the William Morris Agency, was the person who had the idea for this book in the first place. Jerry also introduced me to my literary agent at William Morris, Jim Stein. Jim was smart enough to put me in touch with the indomitable Judith Regan at Pocket Books. After one lunch Judith became my new best friend, and godmothered this project in its early stages. Judith also played matchmaker in helping me find my literary Mr. Right, coauthor Jim Jerome.

Once the project was under way, I received timely and invaluable assistance from: Eric Kranzler and Gina Rugolo of Susan Geller and Associates, who tracked down photographs and nailed down permissions from studios and networks; Michael Yarish, Linda Keefer, and Frances Cavanaugh in the photo department of CBS; and Dan Melnick for his help with Carolco. Also, my new literary agent, Dan Strone.

A big thanks to: Elena Lewis, who kept my house together; the brilliant Dr. Ruth Velikovsky Sharon, who kept my psyche together; and my nieces Elizabeth and Suzanne Carney, who kept the project together with their spirit and sensibility (especially Elizabeth for all the phoning, filing, faxing, photocopying, and FedExing). Also: Frank Lovece and Jules Franco, whose book, *Hailing Taxi,* is a detailed history of the series; Donna Ericson, the baby nurse/guardian angel sent from heaven by my mother to watch over Nicky and me; my brother Lorin, who helped me reconstruct our family history and whose sense of humor helped provide the funny bone for the book; and, naturally, my patient, understanding husband, Rob, whose main image of me these past weeks has been that of a phone in my ear, pages in my hand, and baby at my breast.

My coauthor, Jim Jerome, demonstrated an extraordinary gift for getting inside my head, stirring things up, and then weaving a life story from 3,000 pages of research. Not to mention that Jim is fun to hang out with and has lots of PF!

Finally, Jim and I would like to thank Amanda Urban, Jim's literary agent at ICM; Jean Brown for her unflagging speed and stamina in transcribing interview tapes; Rebecca Todd, assistant editor at Pocket Books; and, of course, our tireless, irrepressible editor Tom Miller, whose fresh eye was exactly what the book needed in its final stages. Besides, it was Tom who made me leave in all the sexy stuff. Thanks, Tom.

Contents

~

By All Means
Keep On Moving

Introduction

~

Every woman wants to look perfect on her wedding day, right?
Forget it. I didn't have time to care.

But the day I was scheduled to appear on *The Tonight Show* as
Jay Leno's guest alongside Sting—I cared. Oh, did I care. Sting is a
god, one of the sexiest men on the planet. I got in better shape and
paid more attention to my outfit that night than for either of my
two weddings.

I did it all: manicure, pedicure, tweezed my eyebrows, shaved my
legs. I tried on ten outfits with every possible combination of
stockings, shoes, and jewelry. I needed two girlfriends just for the
feedback.

I came out, took one look at Sting, and lost it.

"I *love* you," I said. As millions watched, I ran down all my Sting
Hall of Fame moments. "July 29, 1981: The first time I ever put on
a Walkman I heard *Da doo doo doo, da da da da*. November 17,
1985: I saw *Bring on the Night*. March 21, 1988, I saw you at The
Forum. That was a religious experience."

Sting didn't know what hit him. He had no idea we were on a
date. My husband, director-producer Rob Lieberman, who was
standing in the wings, understood perfectly. He had lived with my
energy and humor for eight years. I was just getting started.

"And your album, '. . . Nothing Like The Sun'?" I told him. "I
wish I could eat the cassette so that it was inside of me." The
mostly female audience whooped, hollered, kept me on a roll.

I told how I'd signed Jay's guest book on the underside of Sting's page, writing: "Please keep this book closed so that Sting is always on top of me. Marilu Henner."

Jay shook his head. "This man will *never* come back here again," he said.

I wasn't finished.

Earlier, during Sting's segment, which I watched from the green room, Jay and Sting had referred to a recent interview in which Sting said that as a result of practicing tantric yoga he could have sex for six or seven hours. *That* got my attention.

"And my husband says," I told Sting, "we'll take the million," a reference to the movie *Indecent Proposal,* in which Robert Redford offers Woody Harrelson and Demi Moore $1 million to spend one night with Demi.

The audience roared.

"Then," I added, "when I heard about the six or seven hours, I decided—I'll give you *two* nights."

Jay, a friend for years, couldn't get a word in.

"You're a mess!" he squealed.

"I know," I said, going limp on camera, "I'm embarrassing myself on national television—and I DON'T CARE!"

The women in the audience cheered wildly. They knew exactly how I felt. Sting has tons of what I refer to as PF. (Actually, it's a phrase my mischievous brothers coined to measure the sexual charge someone gives off, as in "She's not really gorgeous, but she's got incredible PF," or, "Sure, he's handsome, but no PF." F stands for Factor; as for P, read on—and find out why I consider myself an expert on the subject of PF.)

I have never apologized for my sexuality. I love men; I love the way they smell. I love the way they taste, their texture, the way they're built. I'm a big fan of sex. And I'm happy to say that marriage to Rob has only improved and intensified the situation.

My appearance with Sting was the kind of outrageous story that made this book happen. It wasn't something I went pitching all over town. But one night over dinner with Jerry Katzman, the president of my agency, William Morris, and his lovely wife, Carol, I shared all kinds of stories about my unusual early family life, my ever-lively romances as a single woman, my disastrous first marriage, and my fantastic second marriage to Rob. I shared with them some of the homegrown theories and vernacular from my childhood in Chicago. I explained how it was as if my family grew up with backstage passes to Catholicism, since the church and my parochial school were just down the block. My father drove the nuns around on Sundays; my mother took them bra shopping at Vassarette.

Jerry and Carol ate it up.

The clincher was when I told them about family therapy. "My five brothers and sisters and I get together once every two weeks for group sessions," I explained. "We call in from wherever we all are—from pay phones, car phones, air phones, whatever—to our therapist in Princeton, who hooks us up to six speaker boxes." (Over the years I've called in from Rome and Rio de Janeiro, Bangkok and the Albertville Olympics, the Champs-Élysées and the freeways of L.A.)

Jerry couldn't believe this—that adult siblings could remain so entwined in one another's lives. He was intrigued by the fierce intensity with which I seem to approach everything. Casual, laid-back I am not.

I explained how all this family maintenance was connected to the devastating loss of our father and mother when they were in their fifties, the prime of their lives; how their untimely deaths were connected to my fanatical approach to nutrition and fitness; how my obsessive, lifelong quest for perfection was connected to my Catholic upbringing; and how the strictness of the Church was connected to my escape into Hollywood movies and a lifelong dream to entertain. Everything is Connected to Everything.

After I told them all sorts of anecdotes, Jerry shook his head and said, "You've absolutely *got* to write all this down in a book."

So here we are.

Sure, I've had my share of pain and loss and heartache; but I wanted to write this book as a celebration of all the colorful characters—the friends and costars, demons, lovers and family—who have made my life and my career such an incredible trip.

Clearly, a sense of family has always held it together. My life has moved from one "family" to another—from my own Henner menagerie to the nomadic *Grease* company, where I met Johnny Travolta; to being the only "sister" to a garageful of *Taxi* guys like Tony Danza, Danny DeVito, and Judd Hirsch; to playing Burt Reynolds's wife and the mother of four children on *Evening Shade*.

And, just when my *Evening Shade* family was breaking up after four seasons, along came the most thrilling plot twist of them all—the birth of our beautiful son Nicholas, a baby I feared for years I could never have.

The ultimate cliff-hanger!

My husband Rob and I were looking over some photographs for this book. He held up one of me and said I was so ugly as a baby that I was "The Comeback of the Century."

That's an obvious overstatement, but I know what he meant and he's got a point. I was pretty funny-looking as a little kid, but I've hit my forties looking and feeling my all-time best. This book is about the exhilarating journey that has brought me to this wonderful, challenging, adventurous time of my life.

That's why I don't see my story thus far as a comeback.

To me, it feels more like an arrival.

Besides, I've never had any misconceptions about my looks. I've always known that it's determination, tenacity, and a positive outlook that will get you a lot farther in the long run. I've tried to make the most of my opportunities and to practice what I believe is the key lesson behind any setback or triumph: Don't wallow; don't gloat. Assess the situation, deal with it.

And by all means keep on moving.

1

Plan B

~~~

When I was a little girl, my father, who, like my mom, lived life as a celebration of our crowded, close-knit brood, had a game he liked to play with me. He would reach down and grab my hands, then pretend to twist them inward, as if putting me in a wrestling hold. The idea was to see how tough I was, how much I could take. "You going to give in yet?" he'd ask.

The more he gently squeezed and pretended to inflict pain, the more I'd shake my head to say: *No, no, no, I am* not *giving in.*

I loved playing along. Being the third of six kids (two older sisters, two younger brothers, and a younger sister), anytime I had my father all to myself was quality time. With our hands still clasped, we would lock eyes in our playful battle of wills, and again, he'd ask: "Okay, are you ready to say uncle?" And I'd go: "No. Never! I'm *never* giving in, *never* saying uncle."

I wanted him to know I could take anything he had to dish out. Finally, he'd let go of my hands, put his arms around me, and say, "Okay! That's my sturdy little girl," sounding so proud and impressed. "You're my sturdy one."

The fall of my senior year at Madonna High School in 1969 was filled with hope and eager anticipation. I had applied to college and was involved in all sorts of theater and dance projects. I was gearing up to play the lead in my school's senior play, which I hoped would be a famous Broadway musical like *My Fair Lady* or *Carousel*. And there was the excitement of the annual party my mother threw for the 150 or so adult students she taught in her dance studio, which was run out of our converted three-car garage. Our Christmas party was always a major social event that brought the entire neighborhood together.

In our minds we were the Kennedys of Chicago's Logan Square, because we enjoyed some local notoriety. The social, cultural and religious nerve center of the community was St. John Berchman's Catholic Church—its rectory, convent, and parochial grade school —and our house was on that same block, so we had some reflected glory just by sharing an alley with my school. With four kids still living at home between the ages of 12 and 17, we were so in the thick of things that our house became the hub for the gang of friends we all shared.

The Henner name was well known in our community. Most families had either bought a car from one of Joe Henner's showrooms over the years—Ford, Chevy, Cadillac—or had had a family member take dancing with Loretta Henner. My mom's students ranged in age from two to 80—including a stretch class for the parish nuns. Between the driving and the dancing, we had the place covered. The party was a hot ticket along Logan Boulevard.

My dad was handsome in a way that combined Clark Gable, Jimmy Cagney, and former Alabama governor George Wallace. My mom looked like Lana Turner. She never lost her five-foot-six, 115-pound Barbie Doll figure, and my father never lost the mischievous gleam in his eye. She had crushes on handsome priests, while the nuns fluttered girlishly around my dad when he drove them on Sunday errands. At parties, my mom would go from partner to partner on the dance floor, while my father would be off in a corner surrounded by women tossing their heads back in laughter.

But the highlight of the evening was always that magical moment when my mother would vamp her way over to his corner, take his hand, and, in front of his admirers, say seductively, "C'mon, Joe, it's time for the rhumba."

The fall had also been a special time for my father and me. In such a large family, it's often hard to zero in on one-to-one moments. But because I was involved in Chicago's thriving theater scene, with workshops and shows all over town, my father often picked me up at night. I loved this extra time alone with him. We'd talk about school, college, my boyfriend Steve, the family, his childhood, his work, or the many books he had just read.

The car rides encouraged the kind of intimate father-daughter communication that would never have been possible at home. Our house was a lot of things, but a spacious, tranquil place for heart-to-hearts wasn't one of them. My sisters, JoAnn and Melody, then in their twenties, were on their own; but Tommy, Christal, and Lorin were still buzzing around. And I mean buzzing.

And so, when I was 17, it was as if my dad and I got to connect all over again. He was a sunny, magnetic man for whom laughter and wit were like the air and water of his soul. But I sensed a darker, more reflective side: Like me, he seemed at a crossroad, but his was at midlife.

My dad had kicked butt in car sales for nearly three decades to support us. Moreover, he had always sought ways to better himself through speed-reading, memory, and self-improvement courses. He was also the world's greatest efficiency expert. "Daddy, wanna help us with our Christmas cards?" one of us would ask, and in seconds he could turn the entire operation into a fun, Henry Ford–like assembly plant, and we would crank out 400 cards in under an hour.

We were barely middle class, but he had a simple formula for a rich, rewarding life: hard work, a strong family anchor, a knack for re-creating himself and landing on his feet. As I told him of my own master plan for making something out of my life, he got to see how much of his drive and spirit had taken hold in me. And I saw how it touched him and filled him with great satisfaction and pride.

It was clear that things had been getting tougher for him. He was a Type A workhorse who raced through his life with far more stress and far less money than he ever let on. He loved life and he had a wisecrack for every occasion. He used to say, "I don't want to be a millionaire; I just want to live like one."

He was fifty-two, and his swagger had understandably become a little less secure. He was at a tricky phase of his career. He had once been a gung-ho wunderkind, a troubleshooter who could save a failing car dealership by firing up a sales team with his enterprise, showmanship, energy, and charm. Now, the older men for whom he'd worked those miracles were dying off or unloading their dealerships to sons fifteen, twenty years younger than my father. His clout and stature had waned. For the first time, he seemed genuinely depressed.

For years my father had worked as new-car general manager at a number of showrooms around town; but he had recently gone back to commission grunt work with Cadillac, earning $200 a car.

For several years he had been suffering recurrent chest pains diagnosed as angina pectoris. Nobody had any idea what that really meant, so we never attached much drama to it. He took his nitroglycerine pills, but he was far more likely to deny, not dwell on, his problems. Nitro was like vitamins for middle-aged people with a "heart condition." It wasn't like, "Oh, your father can't do this because of his heart condition."

My father liked to say, "People should be blamed for their sicknesses, not pitied"—that you got the sicknesses you deserved, depending on your lifestyle. He didn't seek pity, but he didn't change his habits to reduce the odds of a disaster, either. He still worked long, stressful hours and kept to his killer diet featuring fatty Polish meats with mayonnaise slathered on top. The closest he got to exercise was the rhumba or two every month with my mother. Not even his older brother John's severe heart attack a couple of years earlier while in an amusement park house of horrors had worked as a wake-up call. If Joe Henner was going to stop and smell *anything* to prolong his life, it wouldn't have been the roses, but rather the roast beef sandwich from Eddie's Open Pit & Barbecue.

My father had a special gift for deflecting worry—or perhaps clinging to his denial—with black humor. Sometime between Thanksgiving and Christmas, Lorin, who was twelve, asked my father a hypothetical question: "Would you sign a document guaranteeing you twenty more years of life—till 1990?" My father retorted, "Yes, in a second."

Lorin was taken aback. "Oh, come on. What about till 1980?"

"Absolutely."

"Okay. What about 1970?" Lorin joked. The new decade was barely two weeks away.

"I *hope* I live a few more days," he wisecracked.

My father did slow down long enough to take some pleasure in watching me in our senior production. I was bummed when the theater department announced that our show would not be a Broadway hit, but rather *Somebody Somewhere*—the story of the nun who founded my school. Great! I had the lead role in something that sounded like *The Unsinkable Mother Teresa Dudzek*.

Because it was some big anniversary, the production was moved up from spring to early December to jibe with the school's founding.

It wasn't exactly Plan A, but we had gotten used to adjusting to Plan B at home. Plan A is what your life is *supposed* to be on the drafting table. Plan B is what your life *becomes.* The key to your life is how well you deal with Plan B. The show must go on.

Or, to use the phrase I used later in life: J.F.D.I. Just Fucking Do It.

It was actually an excellent production. My boyfriend Steve had the male lead and played a priest. It was sort of kinky to be onstage together dressed as a nun and priest—only hours after a lusty morning of mortal sin together. I was on a real high.

Unfortunately, at a time when my family had so much to be thankful for—no disasters for almost six months—my parents got into a major fight on Christmas Day about the thing they fought about most often: money. My attempts to referee this one back-fired, and it turned into the only screaming fight *I* ever had with my father. In the heat of the moment, I stupidly blurted out a phrase I had just heard from an older male friend of mine: "Well, maybe you aren't taking care of Mommy's needs." I didn't even know what "Mommy's needs" *meant,* but his blood started to boil. I had never stood up to him this way. Then I really hurt him, when I said I didn't like the necklace he'd given me for Christmas. He coldly wrote me a check, so I could buy myself something else. I was being a brat, and this feud left us all shaken.

We pushed ahead with preparations for our studio party on the 27th, but the house was filled with gloom instead of holiday cheer. I was crushed that my father and I were still not talking or even making moves to smooth things over. The silence between us was heartbreaking.

The war of nerves between my parents intensified the night of the 26th: For the first time ever, he walked out and spent the night at a motel. The party was twenty-four hours away and things were deteriorating. His leaving gave everyone a chance to cool off.

Sure enough, the next evening, in walked my father to make peace. We were incredibly relieved. Because we were in the midst of all the party preparations, he and I never cleared the air face-to-face, but the anger was gone. I now had the whole evening to apologize and make amends.

The party guests showed up and the studio was soon packed and jumping. Everything seemed back to normal. At one moment, I caught my father's eye from across the crowded floor. We gave each other a look, and then a smile. When I caught a slight twinkle in his eye, I took it as an expression of affection and forgiveness—his way of telling me: "We're gonna handle this later, Missy, but everything's okay between us." I was ecstatic.

About twenty minutes later, it was decided that Steve would drive me over to my sister JoAnn's house to relieve her baby-sitter. JoAnn had had to go to a different party for a while, and I was to stay with my two nieces.

We got into Steve's car and, just as he was about to turn the key, I saw my sister Christal out of the corner of my eye as she went dashing frantically from the house to the studio. Seconds later, Christal and my mother went dashing back from the studio into the house. My heart started to pound as adrenaline flooded me with a sense of panic.

"My God, something's wrong," I said. "Let's go inside."

Before I even got in the door, I heard yelling. Once inside, I could not believe what I was seeing. What had transpired minutes before we arrived was this: My father had pulled my sixteen-year-old brother Tommy, who was now drunk, away from the party and into the living room, where my other brother Lorin was watching TV. My dad backed Tommy into a corner and shook him roughly.

"What is *with* you," my father said, grunting and spewing rage, "getting so drunk in front of everybody like that? What is wrong with you?"

Tommy defiantly looked away as he staggered back. This enraged my father even more. "You think you're a wiseguy, huh? You think you're some kind of wiseguy?" As my father repeated this question, he intimidated Tommy by rhythmically poking him in the chest like a gangster. Tommy retaliated by trying to poke my father back in the same manner. This immediately set my father off, and he smacked Tommy hard across the face.

Tommy jumped into a prizefighter's stance. This was outrageously disrespectful behavior. None of us had ever physically challenged my father before. We knew our father had a weak heart.

Tommy threw several wild roundhouse punches, which my father dodged and blocked until he was able to wrestle Tommy to the ground without seriously hurting him. Lorin jumped in to pin Tommy's legs down and helped keep him from getting back up.

At this moment my mother, Christal, Steve, and I ran back in. I saw my father kneeling over Tommy's back, slapping him in the face over and over and screaming, "Don't ever think you can do something like this again, you hear me? Don't you *ever* do this again."

My mother bent over and tried to yank back my father's arms as she screamed, "Joe, Joe. Stop it!" He finally stopped, slowly eased off Tommy, and unsteadily rose to his feet. His face was flushed beet-red.

My father staggered a few steps and collapsed in his orange armchair. Lying motionless with his head back, he suddenly began to gasp violently for air, then lapsed into unconsciousness.

In seconds, the color in his face drained to white and he became still and silent. It was a horrifying sight.

My mother crouched next to my father, massaging his hand, touching his face. She cried his name over and over, pleading with him to come to. I frantically searched for his bottle of pills and ran back to give my mother one. In my mind, if he could just take his medication, he'd be fine. But she couldn't get the pill to stay inside his mouth.

My sister Melody's boyfriend Chuck called for an ambulance. Two minutes later an emergency vehicle and police car arrived. Everything seemed to be unfolding in silent, excruciating slow-motion unreality.

There was still a party going on in the studio. Two hundred party guests were only vaguely aware of what was going on in the living room as the music played on.

The paramedics came in with their stretcher, ripped my father's tie off (he was wearing a suit), opened his shirt, and desperately administered CPR. I saw on my mother's face a look of resignation —as if she already knew that this must be it. As they lifted my father's stretcher out to the ambulance, I followed and glanced over at the paramedics for a clue. In that instant, I feared the worst: While fighting with Tommy, my father had suffered a massive heart attack and he was already dead.

My mother and I rode in the front seat of the police car behind the ambulance, blue and red lights flashing in my unblinking eyes.

This isn't really happening to us.

My father is not going to die.

My father was rushed into the emergency room and my mom and I stood helpless in a waiting area. We didn't have to wait very long.

Moments later, a doctor came out toward us. I felt nothing but oncoming dread.

He looked straight into my mother's eyes. "I'm so very sorry," he said.

We gathered together, numb and empty, in our unbearable grief. An hour earlier my father had been in his favorite blue-gray suit dancing and flirting and full of life. In a flash, we had all been abducted from the safe, cozy chaos of our home and brutally hurled into some other story line in someone else's life.

How do you go on from this, I asked myself over and over, and face this cruel, unknown life taking shape ahead of us? I remember thinking: Wait, why can't we just go back to a few days ago and return to being the people we're supposed to be?

But there's never any turning back. Not in death, not in life. You keep moving.

Daddy's life—and, with it, a precious piece of my *own* life—had been ripped away with no warning or preparation, no chance to say thank you, or I love you, or even just good-bye.

It didn't hit me until later, but, in a way, we *had* said all those things at the end. I came to see what a blessing it was that our senior musical had been moved up several months.

The night my father had seen my performance, I came home later and found him in the dining room. The lights were off. "Come over here and sit down," he said when he heard me come in. "I want to tell you something."

"Hi, Daddy, what is it?" I said as I approached him. It was such a strange sight to see him alone like that in the dark.

"You know," he said, clasping my hand, "you really have to do this. This is what your life's about. This is what you've got to do." It was an incredible moment of connection—one of the sweetest we had ever shared. I knew then that my father totally *got* me and loved me for who I was—and for who I dreamed of becoming. Now, perhaps because he sensed an urgency in saying it, he expressed that love in a way he knew I would get.

"You're really good," he said in a reaffirming tone, "and I know your mother's always wanted you to be an actress. I *really saw* it tonight, too. I know this is the life for you."

Daddy was gone. But I would have the rest of my life to say thank you to him for never letting his sturdy one give in.

2
Everything Is Connected
to Everything

$\sim$

You know you're in for an interesting childhood when your parents choose for one of your godparents a nun, and for the other a department store window dresser who lived upstairs with ten cats, two dogs, two birds, a skunk, 150 fish, a dead butterfly collection, a statue of the Madonna and child, and a longtime roommate named Charles.

Sister Mildred Joseph and my Uncle Dan. My godparents. My God!

My parents knew nothing about yin and yang, about harmony between opposing forces. Still, they managed to unleash plenty of yin and yang energy in my life from day one.

Sister Mildred Joseph looked like a red-haired Grace Kelly. She was absolutely gorgeous, with red hair, red eyebrows, and red lashes. No wonder Daddy had a big crush on her. And my mom was crazy about her, too.

Uncle (everyone, even kids at school, called him Uncle) was a lovably eccentric artist, a true original who served as the neighborhood astrologer, ran a cat hospital on the roof, and owned a black light ten years before the hippies did. My mother's brother, Uncle was an energy center all to himself. He had once designed store windows for Weiboldt's department store, until one day he tried to help a shopper who got caught on an escalator. When he went to her aid, her coat flew open, and out tumbled all the stuff she was shoplifting. She slugged him with her purse and he got a pinched nerve that ended his career in window dressing. He then taught art at our grammar school, and for years he had lived upstairs with his frisky, scampering menagerie.

He taught us to build scooters from roller skate wheels and orange crates; he recycled junk into art. He made old milk bottles and egg cartons into dinosaurs and dragons, used Ping-Pong balls as bulbs for homemade lamps, made reel-to-reel tapes of musicals off the TV for us, and was one of the first people in our neighborhood to have a color TV. He held séances and worked his Ouija board for us to help me bring Marilyn Monroe back after she died in 1962. He and I staged make-believe *Tonight Show* appearances on our front steps, where we would alternate being Johnny Carson and his guest.

In winter, Uncle flooded our fifteen-square-foot area of the backyard with the garden hose and turned it into a private skating rink. In summer, before the large three-car garage was built to house the dance studio, he showed us how to make our favorite roasted potatoes over a bonfire in the backyard. Uncle inspired me through childhood simply by doing as he damn well pleased. My parents vigorously championed and embraced his unconventional ways, which in itself served as a life lesson about tolerance and unconditional love.

My godparents would come to embody the dominant, competing yin and yang forces of my childhood: the rigid conformism of the church and the liberating spark of dramatic self-expression.

When they met as teenagers on a Chicago ballroom dance floor in the late thirties, my parents weren't talking yin and yang, but jazz and swing. They must have been struck by the similarities in their unhappy childhoods, despite the obvious difference: My father's parents were Polish townspeople and my mother's came from a tiny coastal village in Greece. But they both lost mothers very young. Both had fathers prone to erupting into violent rages. Both left home as teenagers to fend for themselves. And both loved to dance.

My mom was born Nikoleta Kalogeropoulos (later changed to Loretta Callis) in 1919, the fifth of eight kids. Her mother, Lucy, died when my mom was about ten, probably of pneumonia—and a broken heart. Her father, Thomas, had been having a long affair with a German woman. At least the mistress moved in and became a caring surrogate mother to Mommy, Uncle, and the other kids until her own death in 1937.

My grandfather was a real Henry the Eighth—he would have five wives.

Loretta was a beauty with auburn hair, brown eyes, great legs, and a dream of becoming a dancer. That dream died early, when her father forbade her to dance or join school activities. Friends were not even allowed in the house, and the phone was often disconnected. No wonder Loretta and her brother, my uncle Dan, six years younger, loved nothing more than sitting together in dark movie houses, clutching their grease-stained bags of homemade popcorn, and escaping their troubles.

The kids endured belt-strappings, spankings, and worse. Uncle tells quite a dramatic story. One day he heard shrieks coming from the kitchen. He ran in to find Thomas standing over my mother, who was about fourteen, and their sister, Lee. His arm was poised in the air, grasping a large butcher knife. My mom was crouching beneath him as their stepmother struggled to keep the blade away from her. No one got hurt, but my grandfather's fury traumatized everyone. Uncle darted out in his underpants and spent the day cowering in the lobby of a movie theater. What had set Thomas off? My mother and her sister had been caught going to a dance.

My mom dropped out of high school and left home to make her way in the world at sixteen—proving to be hardworking and resourceful. She attended a beauty school and was soon running a salon. Now that she was free to pursue a social life, the Merry Gardens ballroom was a natural place to spend her evenings. It was there, in 1937, that Loretta met another Merry Gardens regular, a dashing, witty Polish venetian blinds cutter named Joseph Pudlowski. Joe was a neighborhood kid out to prove he could move up in the world—from venetian blinds to shades and window treatments. Daddy impressed Mommy with his great rap, his quick, self-mocking humor, and his dark good looks. And he was no slouch on the dance floor either.

He was the third of four children, and like my mother he had endured a miserable Chicago childhood. Once a cheerful, wide-eyed altar boy with a paper route, he grew to live in fear of his hard-bitten, abusive father, Michael, a maintenance worker and window washer. The family lived in a fourth-floor, four-room walk-up. Mike was a colorful, but volatile, character who drank hard, danced the *russki gazatzki* hard—and struck hard during his rages. Yet it was emotional, not physical, pain that marked my dad's early years. When Joe was five, Mike placed him, his brother

John, and two sisters in a Catholic orphanage after my grand-
mother, Mary Pudlowski, was sent to an infirmary in southeast
Chicago. Mike could no longer care for them with a wife afflicted
with ALS, amyotrophic lateral sclerosis, later known as Lou
Gehrig's disease.

Life at St. Hedwig's was lonely and miserable for the kids, who
rarely saw each other. Sunday visits with their father were strained
and brief. As much as they feared their father, the kids would cling
to him and beg to come home. He refused.

The kids did get out about two years after they arrived—but
only to attend their mother's funeral in the spring of 1925. She died
without ever seeing them again. Devastated by her death, the
children were finally reunited at home a couple of years later.

Joe, once a sickly kid, turned into a daredevil to impress friends.
One stunt nearly caught the attention of the local coroner. He
climbed an electrical post in an alley behind the apartment and
mistakenly grabbed on to a live wire. The jolt of juice threw him to
the ground unconscious. Only his sister's quick work, when she
heard a terrible thud, saved him.

Joe also developed a knack for salesmanship—and used it to sell
his father on the idea of graduating from McKinley High. His
father saw high school as a waste of time. But Joe was determined
to build a better life for himself and worked diligently to make the
most of his education. He grew into an outgoing, popular cutup.
Unlike his pals, he was no bruiser, but he used his wit and wiles to
talk his way out of jams—and into girls' hearts. He was a rogue
who thrived at playing the field. In his black book he kept track of
schoolgirls who were "too fat," "no fun to be with," or "nice but a
little too tall." He once sent a Valentine inscribed "to my one and
only" to a half-dozen crushes.

Joe was a ham who performed in school musicals. He was also a
basketball player at the Erie Neighborhood House, where a coach
with the German name Henner took him under his wing. After
graduating, Joe worked at Western Venetian Blinds, using Henner's
name to avoid "Polack" jokes and job discrimination.

Daddy also loved to dance, and often found himself with John
and a buddy checking out the action at the Aragon, the Trianon,
and the Merry Gardens ballrooms, where some of the big bands of
the day would perform. The story goes that taller, handsome John,
not Joe, first caught Loretta's eye from afar, but that it was Joe's
lady-killer smile, sparkling eyes, and devilish wit that hooked her
once they all met. They were just sixteen and eighteen and had

never been in love, but they knew the chemistry clicked: on February 26, 1938, they got married in a Catholic ceremony in Joe's Polish neighborhood.

The wedding party was held at my Polish grandfather's house and turned into a real culture shock for both sides. My Greek grandfather went all over the Pudlowski house handing out Greek cookies covered with powdered sugar called *kodumbiades*—while my Polish grandfather followed right behind him with a vacuum cleaner.

Talk about yin and yang! What about northern and southern, hot and cold, oral and anal-retentive? My gene pool was all over the place.

They put off plans to have a family while my father served in the air force during World War II. By 1950, they had settled back home after a stint in San Antonio, and had two girls five years apart, JoAnn and Melody. But it wasn't the dream they had envisioned as teenagers. My father had switched to car sales by then, working for a variety of franchises over the years, usually for a couple of years at a time. He often worked overtime, hoping to make a name for himself in a cutthroat, brutally competitive field. This left my mom feeling increasingly isolated and neglected.

After Melody was born, my mother decided to convert to Catholicism, for social as well as religious reasons. The church soon became the center of her life. She gave dance lessons there, made new friends at Sunday services, and showed off her outrageous hats. My mom loved nothing more than to arrive five or ten minutes late for Mass and make a dramatic, head-turning entrance. The aisle between the pews was her fashion show runway, where she would strut past parishioners twisting in their pews to check her out.

But troubles persisted, and by mid-1951, their dream was slipping away. Around this time, my father suffered a serious business reversal that shook him up for a long time afterward. He was running his own business as general manager of not one, but two showrooms. His two lots, Henner Ford and Loretta Motors, were situated at two choice, high-overhead sections of Chicago. He simply never got up to speed with either, and he lost everything. It was ugly, the way the banks had the locks changed on him in the middle of the night and closed him down. This shattered his self-confidence and dealt a blow to their marriage.

But before the word "divorce" could even come up, my mother

wisely sought counseling with her priest at St. John Berchman's. Father Reardon, who had once urged her to begin a lifelong journey to Jesus to save her soul, was now thinking more in terms of a two-week trip with my father to save her marriage.

The rekindling worked. They fell in love all over again in steamy Miami Beach in July. Nine months later, they had a seven-pound, six-ounce souvenir to prove it: daughter Mary Lucy Denise, born April 6, 1952, named for two grandmothers I would never know.

The fact that I was placed on the altar for my baptism must have been a big deal, since it was often brought to my attention as a kid. My mom had taken a big bite of the Catholic apple, so my baptism symbolized her commitment not only to her revived marriage, but to the Church. Their choice of godparents was their way of honoring God and showbiz, the major influences of my youth.

My parents called me their "love child" because of that hot time in Miami. "You got the best of both of us," my mom would confide in me, and she meant it as a casual, innocent flattery to make me feel good about myself. Instead, being a little obsessive as far back as I can remember, I tortured myself trying to figure out things like: Who's neater, Mommy or Daddy? Who's funnier, Mommy or Daddy? Who's better with money, Mommy or Daddy? There was no end to this. It went all the way to: Who throws their dirty clothes into the hamper better, Mommy or Daddy? I was thus launched on my impossible lifelong quest to be perfect.

But perfection would require order and balance, and order and balance would require obsession and compulsion. By the time I was five, there *was* no order and balance where we lived—my parents would have three more children over the next five years: Tommy, born fourteen months after me, followed by Christal and Lorin.

Now there were six kids spanning fifteen years. Our house pulsed with nonstop commotion, spiked with brief, but seething, eruptions among the four close-knit rug rats. We bickered so much that I began my first Confession: "Bless me, Father, for I have sinned: This is my first confession. I fought with my brothers and sisters twenty-six times."

Meals were a contact sport. My father would drop a huge pizza from Eddie's Open Pit & Barbecue on the living room floor and we'd tear it apart in seconds to claim our prey. Tommy, Christal, and I would polish off our pieces and then circle around Lorin, who would still be gnawing away, his arm protectively curved around his slices.

We were like something out of the movie *Quest for Fire*. As we grew up, we became ringleaders for the block. We could play for hours at a clip, feverishly creating an infinite universe of make-believe. We devised games like Greek and Polish Gods and Heroes (we made up Polish mythology so that our other heritage would be represented) using garbage can lids and broomsticks as swords and shields. Tommy and I were Apollo and Aphrodite, Lorin and Christal were Lubaleski Polonowski and Portki the Polish slave girl.

We had a huge cast of invisible extras, our imaginary friends with names like Icky Winnie and Milky Way, Walko and Walkee, Flora Flushbottom and Laura Alderbuilding. They were so real to us, and our parents were so intent on participating in our lives and letting us be the kids they were never allowed to be, that my father once gladly drove back fifteen miles to a restaurant during a trip when JoAnn freaked out after leaving behind her traveling companions, Flee-Flee and Kongkax.

Money was always a problem. Because my father was floating checks between bank accounts, it was always an honor to be the kid he woke up at two A.M. to go with him to the all-night drop-off slot, where he'd make a deposit that would just cover some check due to come in against his account in the morning. "Just robbing Peter to pay Paul," he'd say with a sly grin. Then, we'd drive out to Parsey's famous hot dog stand for a three A.M. snack.

My mom wasn't any more conventional, especially for a fifties and sixties housewife. Her bowling league outfit was a skimpy top with bare midriff and skintight capri pants. She also ran a one-woman beauty shop out of our kitchen. She only broke even, but it was also a bonding thing with her girlfriends. She had a professional-style hair dryer downstairs and a blue chair rigged with a neck support so women could tilt back and get shampooed in our kitchen sink. She cut, colored, permed, and thinned, so when she cooked her Greek pilaf and American spaghetti, no one minded that the food odors mixed with those of perm solution and color dyes.

My mother's summer barbecue picnics at Sand-lo Beach were big hits for the neighborhood, since she would hire a rock combo so kids could dance by the lake. She herself never went in the water, but still changed into a swimsuit to show off her trim figure and dance with the cute young guys. Meanwhile, my father would roll up his pants to show off his handwalking skills by the surf.

She loved to cook and garden, but her one shot at a typical mom-type hobby was knitting us woolen bathing suits—without bothering to add lining. We did our swimming at the Howard Johnson's Motor Lodge pool. We were members of the HoJo's Motor Lodge Swim Club, which cost the whole family $108 for the summer. That was our country club. (Swimming in our local public pool was out of the question. My mother was convinced we'd get polio. Even though a cure had been discovered a decade earlier, she was sure some strain of it still lived at the murky bottom of Holstein Park pool.)

When we lined up for our Kodak moment at the pool and jumped in, my knitted suit sank to my ankles and within seconds it felt like I was wearing a wet sweater. I popped to the surface yanking my suit up to cover me. Tommy and Lorin were completely naked.

When my mom got overwhelmed with us, she had friends who helped her cope. One was a sweet black cleaning lady named Bertha, who needed all day Thursday to iron the seventeen loads of laundry my mom did every Tuesday. The other was an obese German woman named Lily, a hair salon regular who helped clean house.

Lily was also the enforcer when we acted up. My father was too good-natured—and came home too late—to inspire fear. But my mother could. First it was threats with the strap or the dreaded hairbrush from her purse. Then, when that failed to bring us into line, there was Lily—The Final Solution.

"You want Lily to come over here and sit on you, is that what you want?" she'd ask. "I can get her here in FIVE MINUTES!" We'd scream, "No, Mommy, no!" But we all got squashed beneath Lily's behemoth 300-pound butt one time or another. And for literally being her "sitter," my mom paid Lily in cuts and perms.

With a cast of characters like ours, carving out your own distinct niche was a key to survival—and self-definition. Our quirks and eccentricities flourished under our parents' tolerant, adoring gaze. To them, we were simply colorful.

I was a bed wetter. No problem. JoAnn, with whom I shared a room, let me crawl into bed with her.

I was a biter. No problem. I bit everything in sight—
jawbreakers, Turkish Taffy, Jordan Almonds, my brothers. When I
was ten and Lorin was five, I gave him a huge hickey, which thrilled
him because he became the first Henner kid ever to score points on
the Ann Landers sex test. (One question was, "Have you ever
gotten, or given, a hickey?") Lorin got five points for that hickey.
He scored higher than Uncle upstairs—and he wasn't even in
kindergarten yet.

Other quirks were closer to obsessive-compulsive rituals, a key to
my quest for perfection. Being so insanely anal about my stuff was
really about staking out my own tidy pockets of heaven in a house
of disorder and disrepair.

I had a morning ritual that never varied. I laid my clothes out the
night before, nice and neat. The second my feet hit the floor, I
made my bed, because I would have a bad day otherwise. I walked
into the bathroom and pressed my face up to the mirror with my
eyes wide open in the dark—and flicked the switch. I loved that jolt
of fluorescent light, and watching my pupils shrink as the light hit
them. I stepped over cracks on my way to parochial school. I had to
have perfect pencil cases and book covers. I folded mine inside out;
I didn't want to ruin the front with advertisers like Kosiba's
Hardware or DeVriendt's Funeral Home.

My rituals held it all together for me in a house of "Polish
corners" and stuff that was "hamper." *Polish corner* was the phrase
my mother invented to blame any messy area on my father's
ancestry. It later became a perfect family metaphor for any
lingering, unsettled argument or dilemma (i.e., "Let's not have any
Polish corners in this relationship"). *Hamper* went from a noun for
a dirty-clothes bin to an adjective for anything broken-down or
makeshift, or an innocent lack of sophistication.

Hamper was a family of eight never having a plunger and
sticking wire hangers down clogged toilets instead. Hamper was
thinking normal people couldn't buy hot dog buns because they
were only sold at the ballpark. Hamper was having a record player
with an arm that gave you a shock when you touched it and
therefore using a record to lift it—and taking ten years to get
it fixed. Hamper was a schoolgirl uniform held together by mask-
ing tape, safety pins, or staples. My whole wardrobe was
hamper. Things stayed neglected for so long they almost became
chic.

* * *

One thing my parents certainly never neglected was each other. The energy field around them was sexy and intense. Whether they were doing a rhumba in a dance studio or grumbling in the kitchen over money, the passion that sustained them for thirty years remained potent.

They spoke by phone ten times a day, and when my father walked in the door at night, my mother could count on being grabbed and tilted over in a tango dip. She saw wives whose husbands treated them like their submissive "little woman"; this was so different. Their snappy patter seemed right out of a forties Hollywood romantic comedy. They stayed sweethearts with a feisty sexual energy between them, and my father never learned to keep his groping hands off her. "I ran after her until she caught me," he'd say. Or, he'd brag, "I got married at an early urge." She ate up all this teasing, and even liked to boast: "He treats me more like a hundred-dollar hooker than a housewife."

The urge never died down. I once asked my mother what all the *X*'s and *O*'s were on the kitchen calendar above the silverware tray. I thought they were like signing "hugs and kisses" on a greeting card. She was marking off the days she knew she had to stay away from my father so she wouldn't get pregnant again. That spark never quit firing.

And they never quit fighting. My mother had a relentless Greek temper and a flair for the dramatic that could be scary in its intensity. Occasionally, it was about jealousy ("Why was her earring in your *mouth,* Joe?"), but mostly it was about money. My mother was compulsively frugal. She hid her S & H Green Stamp books in an ice bucket, kept cardboard slots with quarters and silver dollars in her drawers, and moved her savings passbooks all over the place just to keep a step ahead of my father. He was almost compulsively reckless with money. If my mom had controlled the cash flow, we'd have had a lot more of it.

He always owed people money, and he was somehow able to float checks among a half-dozen bank accounts to stay moments ahead of creditors. One day it was: "Lor, I'm a little strapped for cash." The next day it was: "Lor, pack up the kids, we're going to Miami." Or it was off to the nearby Weller's motel for an overnight adventure with the kids. Or to Nippersink, a Catskills-like resort up in Wisconsin, for a week each summer. His philosophy regarding money was clear: "You're a long time in the tomb, so while you're alive—ZOOM, ZOOM, ZOOM!"

This drove my mother nuts. She'd come out verbally swinging, he'd soon be on the ropes, and, as the oldest kid at home, I'd be called in to referee. My father often ended up begging me, "Just do us a favor: Agree with your mother so we can get some sleep."

My mother and father doted on us with tireless attention. It seemed as if our every waking activity was being recorded, Polaroided, home-movied, miked, observed, and generally celebrated. I remember that while walking to school my first day, holding JoAnn's hand, I moved around her tall body and switched hands. This was because the cameras that I imagined were filming this event would get a better shot if she weren't blocking me.

My parents had a big fish/little pond attitude that bordered on snobbery, though our house was far too *hamper* for them to be true snobs. But this "us and them" vision of the world provided a sense of social and economic security.

My mom had a great expression for "them"—"the public." If my father drove past a parking space with a NO PARKING sign, my mother would dismiss it with a perturbed wave of her hand. "Forget it, Joe," she'd say. "Park there. That sign's not for us. That's for the public."

At parochial school, Wednesdays were half-days because "the publics"—Catholic kids in the city school system—used our school for catechism. We'd always find gum stuck under our perfectly neat desks on Thursdays, which was such a "publics" thing to do. If it wasn't the publics, it was the "bummy girls" who smoked after school or the "tunnel kids" who lived on the wrong side of the dark, scary Kennedy Expressway underpass.

As easy as it was to caricature *them,* fine-tuning *us* with our individualized "flashcards"—the term we invented that encapsulated our defining traits—proved more complicated.

Tommy, for instance, got the Accident-Prone flashcard. He was born with an enlarged thymus, and nearly died at birth. His chest received radiation treatments hours after he was born. (When he was twenty-one, he got a letter advising him to have his lungs checked for damage. So now we always joke that Tommy had to have his lungs recalled.) He once went out to get a Tastee-Freez and got hit by a VW van. He fell off his bunk bed and cracked a tooth. Tommy was an accident waiting to happen.

All three of my sisters, who had many other virtues as well, got the Beauty flashcard. JoAnn and Melody were both about five-foot-ten and stunning; Melody was endowed with a spectacular body that drove guys crazy. (With her body and my personality, for sure I'd have ended up in adult films by the time I was sixteen.) While they were dark brunettes, Christal was a blond, blue-eyed, fair-skinned angel, the Miss Congeniality of our family.

The Beauty flashcard was *not* going to be my ticket out of Logan Square. My nicknames didn't exactly suggest drop-dead looks: "Perpetual Motion" (intense, wired energy); "Univac" (computer-like memory, A's in school); and "Braille Face" (that's right).

Even my own *mother* had trouble swooning. In my baby book, she had written, "Well, Marilu . . . people do say she's getting prettier."

But not overnight. I looked possessed; Tommy called it a "wild-eyed glow." I was fiercely determined at whatever I did. JoAnn once gave me a grocery list that had way too many items for me to carry home. But I couldn't let her down. I jammed everything into two bags, and in addition carried two Pepsi six-packs that wouldn't fit. The bottles dropped, and one broke. As I scooped the others up, I cut open my hands, and blood gushed everywhere. But I was not to be stopped. I walked home carrying the heavy bags in my bloody, hurting fingers, singing a song to myself all the way to distract me. My mind kept going: If I can get through this, I can get through *anything.* I was one intense little kid.

I was once standing in the kitchen and the seams of my dress spontaneously broke apart. The doctor said it had to do with my "energy field." All I know is that as a grown-up, I once had a carpet laid and I unplugged my clock radio. Hours later, I plugged it in and it had kept perfect real time, instead of conking out and flashing the usual twelve A.M. Go figure.

A good portion of my immediate energy field was taken up by my teeth, which were so big for my face that when I smiled, it looked like I had a magnifying glass in front of my mouth.

So with my brains, energy, and looks, I got the Personality flashcard. My job at home was to throw off sparks and electrify family and friends. I'd clench my teeth and go, "Okay, I'm just going to take my *personality,* go into the living room, and they're all going to be dazzled."

It was the perfect flashcard for someone who, from her earliest memory, had stars in her eyes and wanted to perform and make people laugh. The first time I took the stage was at a father-daughter church breakfast, where I sang the 1955 hit song "Tweedlee Dee," which I had picked up on the radio. I wasn't even three, but I got my first roar of laughter.

The older girl before me was not an especially tough act to follow, but she was a tall act to follow. I walked out and stared up at a mike stand two feet over my head. After a difficult time trying to adjust it, a man whispered to me, "Why don't I just hold you, Marilu?"

I glared at him and announced, "Get me a chair or I am *not* going to sing."

The audience roared with delight. I was thrilled. I stood on a chair and did my song. Some kids might have been paralyzed by stage fright, or been scared and confused by the crowd's noisy applause, and dashed offstage in tears. Not me. I stood there, jazzed by the power of going over big.

My family couldn't resist teasing me. "Shirley Temple made a *million dollars* before she was five," they would say. "Now you're almost six. How come *you* haven't made a million dollars?"

That only made me more determined. Performing—and being The Personality Kid—became my major focus. It was not only my Master Plan, but my hedge against the dreary, often harsh indoctrination at parochial school.

I had fantasies of being discovered as a child star, but the closest I got was having Sister Leo Joseph ask me to teach holiday songs to the K-through-5 pupils. By third grade, I had my own ten-minute music period at the end of Spelling. I learned to sight-read on piano from a nun who stared out through thick Coke-bottle glasses and whacked you on your knuckles when you screwed up. I mimicked Julie Andrews, for her range; the McGuire Sisters (with JoAnn and Melody), and Ethel Merman, simply because she was so *loud.*

On Sundays, I'd accompany my father as he drove the nuns around on their errands. Traffic jams were my cue to charm the sisters with *"I Could Have Danced All Night,"* and then blow them out by belting, *"There's NO! business like SHOW! business."*

A turning point occurred the year JoAnn enrolled at Loyola University to study theater. I was eight. It happened during a test in Sister Paula Marie's third-grade class, when I linked the test question "How many is in a score?" with "Four score and seven years ago." Out of nowhere, this phrase popped into my head:

Everything is connected to everything. I was thunderstruck. My pencil dropped from my fingers and I stared off. Yes, Math was connected to History was connected to Music was connected to Religion was connected to Math.

My mind raced. This meant that nothing could exist by itself; hence, to be an actress, I'd have to be successful in everything I did. Perfection would assure my future. The entire world seemed to be opening up to me. Suddenly, everything was available for me to be learned, used, made mine.

I was in control of my destiny.

Then I grabbed my pencil and answered the question: 20.

In fact, it was JoAnn's world that opened up to me. She brought me along to classes, workshops, and rehearsals, and I helped her memorize lines. I loved being part of her sophisticated, dynamic scene, and it made me feel older and more mature than my classmates.

In fourth grade, when JoAnn played Anna, I had my face and hair darkened so I could be in *The King and I* with her. I refused to wash off the brown makeup and black hair spray the next morning, just so classmates could envy me. It worked. They all asked what was up. "Oh," I shrugged dramatically, thrilled that they asked, "it's tech week. We're working until ten-thirty at night—you know, getting the technical cues down, like music and lighting." I felt *so* cool.

But this *was* parochial school, and when my life wasn't a cabaret, it was a catechism. I found myself shuttling between the inspiring, creative world of theater and the insulated, repressive culture of Catholicism. Performing demanded that you lose yourself in a fantasy of characterization, song, or movement; school demanded that you blunt and flatten your quirks and rigidly conform to the program's rituals. Obsessed as I was, I wanted perfection in both worlds.

They were worlds destined to collide—and they did. When I was ten, we picked up on a little song at school and sang it in a circle, clapping our hands. Everyone took turns in the circle, shaking her hips, as we sang: "We're going to Kentucky, we're going to the fair; We met a senorita with diamonds in her hair; Oh! shake it, shake it, shake it; Shake it if you can, shake it like a milk shake, then shake it once again." A few weeks later, the nuns outlawed our "Sexy Senorita" song as too suggestive.

But it was Hollywood that best highlighted the gap between church culture and Henner culture. The fantasy world that bonded my mother and Uncle as kids now bonded us kids to my parents, especially my mom. *Everything was connected to everything.* She'd stay up almost till dawn watching thirties and forties movie classics on TV, wired on the sugar and caffeine from swigging Pepsis and puffing on her Silva Thins menthols. This was her only time to relax. When a favorite movie was on, she'd say to us after school, "Hey, kids, take a nap. Lana's on tonight." That way, we could stay up and watch with her.

Mommy could be Mommie Dearest if you woke her before noon. So all the major rules in our house were about being quiet: No flushing toilets, no latching doors, no screaming, no wearing shoes, no sound on the TV before noon. I was an adult before I discovered that *Mighty Mouse* was an opera.

My parents took us to see everything, from *Gypsy* to *West Side Story,* from the Three Stooges to Preston Sturges festivals—and every Elvis picture ever released (my mother *loved* Elvis). Some of these movies would have been rated B for Objectionable by the Church's Legion of Decency ratings. But that's what was so wonderful about my parents: They objected to nothing and urged us to experience everything.

I had all kinds of role models, both from old Hollywood movies that ran on TV and new ones, starting in 1960 with Jane Fonda (*Tall Story*) and Hayley Mills (*Pollyanna*). There were heroes from old movies, such as sexy water goddess Esther Williams, and Cyd Charisse dancing in lingerie in *Silk Stockings.* And then there was red-hot *Ann-Margret.* After I saw *Bye Bye Birdie* in 1963, I practiced tits—*prayed* for tits—and wanted desperately to look like Ann-Margret.

But these sisters in sexual identity were not what *those* sisters had in store for me down the block. Of course, the movies they showed us were *The Story of Ruth, The Song of Bernadette,* and *The Miracle of Marcelino.*

Once my hormones kicked in, no amount of suppression could have squashed my sexual awareness. Even though I was a goody-goody and Miss Smarty Pants at school, I always flirted and had a sexual aura about me that boys sensed. I wasn't the prettiest sister, but I knew early on that being pretty had nothing to do with being sexy. Unlike so many other girls at puberty, I didn't get obsessed with weight, didn't even know what a diet was. I had good legs, too, and I always felt that with good legs, the rest didn't matter. I just seemed to put out sexual energy.

By ten, I was posing for *Playboy*—in front of my mirror at home. At 12, I loved straddling and sliding down the church's wide double banisters. I was never shy when boys checked us out in our plaid uniform skirts with knee socks and white cotton panties. I had no problem with monthly fire drills, either. The boys always hurried out ahead of the girls, but not because they were more afraid of fire; it was so they could stand on the ground and gaze up through the second-floor grates and see right up the girls' jumpers—or, as my brother Lorin used to put it, "catch a little bit of heaven." I always made sure to have on great fire drill underwear.

We never did have a fire, but there was some boy-crazy heat every year. When adorable Tommy Donovan gave me a Valentine in third grade, I almost fainted. Fifth grade was when Rocky DeNicola showed up. He was shorter, darker, and more wiry than most of the other boys; he looked like Andy Garcia. He liked to strut around slapping girls on the butt. It was the hottest, *sexiest* thing any of us had ever seen.

Behind the veneer of asexual purity, no one was fooling me: I saw crushes everywhere—between my dad and the nuns, my mom and the priests, priests and nuns, priests and *us*. One sexy-looking priest actually came on to me during a class trip by train to Washington, D.C. I was sleeping in my seat when I awoke to find him sitting on the arm of my seat with his two hands pressed against my seat on either side of my face. His face was right in mine, as if he were planning to kiss me. I was paralyzed—if also a bit fascinated. It was so bizarre. He had obviously just come from the club car. Thank God, a classmate pulled him away.

I reached adolescence with a healthy, guiltless, assertive feeling about boys and my budding libido, thanks to my parents' open and natural approach to physical intimacy. And thanks, also, to my chats about sex with my two younger brothers.

When we were six and seven, Tommy the expert taught me about birds and bees. "Daddy sticks his wee-wee style in Mommy's wee-wee style," he says. (These were, in fact, my mother's terms.) "What? That's so disgusting!" It just seemed so *messy*. Uncle had explained sex to Tommy, and Tommy, wanting to be a doctor, bragged of knowing "every dirty word in the world *and* the medical term for it."

If I was clueless about boys, my brothers were certainly on to my coming of age. My room was so small I had to keep underwear in a drawer in their room. I was ten and still in undershirts and just starting to develop, when, thinking I was alone, I changed in there. Wrong. Once I was topless, Lorin came flying out of the closet, screaming, "They're *gigantic!*" Of course, what did he know? He was only five.

With Tommy, Christal, and me so close in age, our house literally reeked of puberty. But in my ignorance, I assumed for the longest time that that funky smell in my brothers' room was their three-turtle terrarium. "God, clean that up," I'd say, sniffing around their room. "Whoa, that stinks worse than the cats."

Tommy would give me a sly, amused shrug.

With Tommy in charge of sex ed, I could turn to the nuns for every Catholic term in the world—and the Latin word for it. Though I had my nun horror stories, I loved school, loved to memorize and read. I was much more demanding on myself to get A's than my parents were.

My ability to memorize started when I had trouble winding down at night and couldn't fall asleep. I'd calm down with a mind game: What was I doing exactly one week ago today? Two weeks? Three weeks? and so on, until I could do a full year. I couldn't have known it then, but this memory trick would become the core of what I now see are major anal-retentive and obsessive-compulsive personality traits. Today, I can go back twenty-five years and recall not only every date and its day of the week, but, more important, who I was with, what I weighed, what I wore, etc. Another by-product: closets and drawers that are so perfectly organized they're scary. But I love it. Obsessive-compulsive *order,* not disorder, is what I call it.

For some of the same reasons, the nuns loved me. I was a whiz at catechism and spouting Scripture, but my take on Catholicism was tempered by the same offbeat edge that just seemed to come with the territory. I loved Lent because it offered me an excuse to give up biting my nails; I cherished my holy cards because they had a soft-focus, sexy, rock star–like picture of Jesus and his long-haired, bearded apostles (this is when I became what my Jewish husband Rob calls "a Jew groupie"). I loved my Confirmation because we got to wear nylons and a little garter belt with our pretty white dresses for the first time. And I was sure I saw the statue of Jesus breathe. I'd zone out in the pews at Mass, staring at Jesus' stomach above the priest, sure that at any second he would come to life.

I drew the line at Nun Club on Tuesdays. I wasn't antireligion. But an entire life in those shoes and habits? *What about summer vacation? Swimsuits? Boys?* My religious fantasies weren't about joining the nuns, but freeing them: taking them shopping, giving them makeovers, dressing them like Barbie. And what about the young, beautiful ones? What boyfriend dumped them so badly that they turned into *this?* Besides, Sister Florence, who ran the Nun Club, told me to go home with the boys. "You get out of here," she'd say playfully, "you're not going to be a nun. You're going to be a star."

I did observe the holy days—Hollywood style. All Souls' Day is a major event on November 2. You prayed for all the souls in purgatory to get out and go to heaven. Dying with venial sin on your soul got you to purgatory, but you could still plea-bargain your way into heaven through contrition. Dying with mortal sin on your soul—murder, sex before marriage, sex *outside* marriage— was a ticket to hell; end of story.

On All Souls' Day, we competed to spring as many souls as possible from purgatory. The way we did it then was like a kids' game show on Nickelodeon today. Six Our Fathers, six Hail Marys, and six Glory Be to the Fathers would free a soul—and the race was on. You'd gasp as you said your prayers, then dash outside the church with your lunch box clanging, book bag swinging, bumping into statues, knocking into the holy-water fountain. Then it was a race to exit the building and enter again, to start the Hail Marys and Our Fathers all over again.

Some kids wanted the honor of freeing local parish people after they died. Not me. I believed that anyone you got into heaven this way could be your guardian angel. So I got Marilyn Monroe out of purgatory. I freed all of my favorite dead movie stars. I got Clark Gable out for my mother. I was there from morning to night, giving up *lunch* to get movie stars out of purgatory.

But it was Marilyn Monroe, the sexiest movie star bombshell and role model of them all, whom I chose as my guardian angel. Marilyn and I did everything together. We had pajama parties, I told her about my boyfriends, she helped me pick out clothes.

Marilyn was so great for me that I decided that all my brothers and sisters should have movie-star guardian angels, especially my accident-prone brother, Tommy. To me, there was no better choice in all of purgatory than Curly from the Three Stooges. I was so proud that I provided for Tommy his very own guardian angel and, as Tommy used him, scapegoat: To this day, Tommy still blames most of his mishaps on Curly.

By the end of grade school, I needed a guardian angel like Marilyn Monroe to protect me from some of the nuns. My seventh-grade sister was a psychopath. She was scary. She looked exactly like Richard Nixon in a habit. Kids were getting smacked around every day. My hair got yanked regularly for nothing.

She wasn't alone. When a kid in Christal's class got roughed up by a bully, he asked the nun to go home. She refused. He threw up and complained of pains all day, but she made him stay. That night, he died of internal injuries. A scandal ensued, and the nun left the convent later that year.

It wasn't uncommon, either, for me to look out the classroom door and see Tommy pushing chewing gum down the hall with his nose, his hands tied behind his back, or being paraded around with a bow in his hair, a pacifier around his neck, a rattle in one hand, and a sign in the other that read, I AM A BABY.

The nun who looked like Nixon was constantly touching her face as she'd ramble on about her hygiene fixations. Every few days, she'd go, "Okay, Row 1, smell Row 2," and Row 2 would lift their arms so Row 1 could sniff their pits for B.O. Then 2 would do 1's pits, 3 would do 4's, and so on, as she patrolled the rows for stinky pits. This was just what you wanted to do before lunch.

I heard she was eventually put away in an institution.

By the end of grade school, I came up smelling like a rose. I was in a theater program during two summers at Loyola which JoAnn helped run, and was named best actress after the second summer for my role in Jean Giraudoux's *Apollo of Bellac.*

Everything *was* connecting to everything.

Even in the one area of my schoolgirl life that lagged behind the more daring girls, I was about to get into gear.

By then, I was so ready to connect it was ridiculous.

3

One Small Step for Man, One Giant BLEEP for Mankind

~

My high school years coincided with the height of the Vietnam War and the sixties counterculture of free love, LSD and pot, miniskirts, acid rock, and velvet bell-bottoms. The world just beyond our sheltered, conservative enclave in Logan Square had become an intellectual war zone where traditional values and institutions were under attack, or simply crumbling.

It was also a time when the sheltered, idyllic family life we took for granted was shattered by the stunning reality of untimely death and life-threatening disease.

Our first encounter with tragedy occurred in May of 1965, when my oldest sister JoAnn gave birth to a son born two months prematurely. The baby's lungs were too weak and he died a day later. JoAnn and her husband Bob, who had a beautiful little daughter named Lizzy, were devastated. I was thirteen, and I remember seeing JoAnn, who had virtually raised me as a child, lying on our couch, sobbing about Robert Joseph's tiny casket.

But Bob and JoAnn, whose childhood nickname was the Powerful Katrinka for her supreme competence and classic, statuesque beauty, rebounded and had Suzanne a couple of years later. But tragedy struck again in August of 1968: JoAnn gave birth prematurely to Nicholas Christopher, who died that day. And incredibly, Bob's father passed away the same day. It was a profoundly sad time for all of us.

The nightmares were far from over. Just before Christmas that year, JoAnn was carrying Suzanne, then twenty months old, out to her car. A fierce gust of wind off Lake Michigan tore loose a sheet of masonite from the twenty-fifth floor of a construction site on Lakeview Drive. The masonite struck JoAnn, knocking both her and her baby unconscious. JoAnn's head oozed blood in the snow; miraculously, Suzanne was thrown into a snowbank, but her tongue was split in three.

Bob rushed them to Columbus Hospital, where the newborns had died. JoAnn had part of her head shaved and took thirty-two stitches. Her face swelled up like the Elephant Man. Suzanne's tongue healed quickly, but in the days that followed, she kept falling down for no apparent reason. When JoAnn and Bob brought her in for tests, they were stunned to learn that her brain was hemorrhaging.

She was rushed into surgery. Five holes were drilled into her head to drain blood and fluid and reduce swelling and pressure. JoAnn's baby girl was hospitalized for nearly two months. It was so sad to see her there day after day, hooked up to an IV, her shaved head covered by a turbanlike bandage. For me, this was almost more upsetting than losing the boys, because Suzanne was my godchild and already a major part of my life. Plus, we sweated out whether there would be permanent aftereffects. (A few years ago, Suzanne won a modest settlement from the involved parties. Today, she and Lizzy are gorgeous knockouts in their twenties.)

We were barely past that calamity when, in the summer of 1969, suddenly it was my mother's cue for hospital drama. She became gravely ill after complaining of feeling bloated and heavy. After undergoing all sorts of tests, doctors found a massive, ten-pound tumor in her uterus. She immediately went in for a complete hysterectomy.

Not even this could diminish my parents' spirit. As they were wheeling my mother into the operating room, my father leaned over the gurney and French-kissed her for good luck. She looked up at him and said teasingly, "Sex, always sex."

The mass was benign, and she rebounded beautifully, returning to her dance classes with inspiring spunk. My mother, who was always sexy and a little vain, was definitely back to her old self when she said, without trying to be funny, "Thank God it was just a tumor. I thought I was getting a little *fat.*"

By then, we were all getting used to—and better at—laughing our way through life-and-death crises.

* * *

Perhaps because of these family ordeals and my own serious career pursuits, I managed to miss the druggy-dropout part of high school during the heyday of the sixties counterculture. The closest my family came to a sixties radical was my sister Melody, who was at the University of Wisconsin at Madison at the time. Her idea of "revolutionary" was buying a stinky llama coat. It's a good thing she wasn't into bra-burning, since that would have definitely caused the second Chicago Fire.

I was far too theatrical to be a radical. Besides, when I was in high school, it seemed kids in college were doing drugs; when I got to college, kids in high school were doing drugs.

Then again, I didn't need drugs in high school to experience mind-blowing head trips and consciousness-raising growth. Sex worked just fine all by itself. If I wasn't perfectly virtuous, I was a lot less imperfect than many of my classmates: At graduation, seventeen girls at school were pregnant.

In ninth grade, the church still had a lot of impact on our lives. For instance, I would have killed to be in the S.D.S.

Where we lived the S.D.S. did not stand for the radical anti-war Students for a Democratic Society, but rather for Supply the Demand for the Supply fashion pageant, a ludicrous Church-sponsored anachronism doomed to become a casualty of the war era. It was a pageant designed to show all-American flag-waving retailers like Sears that there was still a wholesome middle-of-the-road youth market in fashion.

More than a thousand wanna-bes tried to be crowned the S.D.S. Fashion Queen of All Catholic Girls Schools. The runners-up were elected to the Queen's court. Twenty girls from each school were selected, and that group was cut to sixty-five finalists. (Many stayed on to model for the fashion show, held in a tacky downtown hotel.) As a freshman at Madonna High School, I took my shot at the crown.

Amazingly, the House of Henner boasted not one, but a pair of royal flushes: JoAnn, who was everybody's idol throughout her school career, was crowned Queen her senior year; and, perhaps more amazingly, Melody, the queen of all Catholic cleavages, managed to hide hers well enough to make the court.

Undaunted, I stepped to the plate—and struck out. I failed to even make the Madonna High cut of twenty girls, and I never got another crack at it; the pageant was closed down that year. I was demolished. To console myself, I kept thinking that if I had just weighed 125 pounds instead of 130, I'd have at least made the court. This started the diet phase of my life.

In my head, those extra five pounds had done me in.

Yeah, right. Never mind that both my sisters outweighed me and won. Never mind that for the audition I had bad skin and wore a slut dress. My tryout at school was hysterical. I wore a god-awful orange knit dress that featured major VPL—visible panty line—and so much static cling that there was an audible crackle coming off me as I strutted past the judges. I had grabbed the dress from my mother's closet thinking it made me look sophisticated. But I had forgotten a slip.

It was a stinging defeat, but I got over it—with a vengeance. Fashion modesty wasn't for me, so I moved on to modeling underwear. A photographer shot my first composite and I nailed my first TV commercial as a dancing teenage bra and girdle. This was a test teenage version of a famous national spot, and I was paid a whopping $120. I wore a white bra and girdle over a black leotard and tights and danced in front of a black background with a black hood over my head. All you could see on TV was the white dancing underwear.

I got the job through the choreographer of our school plays, Donn Manning, a flamboyant, cultured, committed theater coach who had a big influence on my high school life. Because of Donn, I was a featured dancer—and the only freshman—in the senior play that year, *The Unsinkable Molly Brown,* because dancers for his productions were often supplied through my mother's studio. Donn saw my tunnel-vision intensity, and got that I was hellbent on making it. He knew a commercial producer, and that got my foot—and the rest of my 130 pounds—in the door at an ad agency.

Hanging out with Donn made me feel like I was really in showbiz. He was the first man with a hairpiece I ever saw up close. His acting classes were held at the apartment he shared with his lover in a funky part of town. He had outrageous flash, arriving at night rehearsals with his big fur coat and sunglasses. He exuded knowledge of that exotic world of Broadway.

That was not the *only* exotic world he seemed to know. Some of his male students also danced with my mother, and I'd occasionally hear one at the studio say, "Oh, I was over at Donn's house and he measured me for my costume for our next play." And I'd think: *Uhhh, what costume? Which play was that?*

Actually, if Donn dangled *anything* in front of these young guys, it was probably nothing more than the dream of stardom.

He dangled it in front of me, and I went for it. I moved on from bra-and-girdle sets to an industrial film for Armour Star, and, in my sophomore year, was a featured dancer in the seniors' production of *The King and I.*

High school made me realize that my dream of getting out of the neighborhood and having a life as an entertainer was within reach. My new idols reflected some fine-tuning of that dream since my Ann-Margret phase: Barbra Streisand, Chita Rivera, Shirley MacLaine—women who performed with awesome, and utterly feminine, power and grace. In addition to my acting, singing, and dance classes, by junior year I was resident choreographer for a small theater called Center Stage. I did *The Roar of the Greasepaint, The Smell of the Crowd; Carnival;* and *Once Upon a Mattress.* I got to apprentice with the Illinois Ballet Company. I rehearsed plays after school, and worked with JoAnn when she choreographed shows for schools and colleges. I did homework on the fly, often on city buses after dark. Whatever time I had left was taken up with being one of the ringleaders at school—president of the Political Science Club, vice president of the Math Club and Student Council. I was on a roll.

I never got an allowance, but I had always been one enterprising, industrious kid, following my mom's example. Even before I was allowed to teach with her in the studio from the age of fourteen on, I was always working, stashing away my coins and dollar bills. I loved the independence that came from having my own money— and I made it from baby-sitting when I was seven, or carrying groceries for people, or going around selling "chances," like raffles, through a church newsletter. My father even gave us a penny per page to go through a huge phone book from Motor Vehicles and check off names of people who had bought Fords and Chevys, so he could contact them and pitch the idea of buying a new model.

But turning fourteen was a major rite of passage at home, because it meant you got to work closely with my mom, teaching ballet, tap, and jazz at our studio. I taught there two afternoons a week and all day Saturday—earning a dollar per student.

The big bucks would have been in selling dance class tickets to my horny brothers. Something about ballerinas in leotards drives boys wild, and Tommy and Lorin were always trying to sneak peeks at my nubile teenage girls at the barre, doing their splits and pliés.

Not surprisingly, the personality of each Henner kid who taught dance was reflected in their students' styles. Every spring, we put on a recital with different themes and costumes to match. JoAnn's students were classic and ethereal and didn't even look at you when they danced. Mine were totally "on," with jazzy, exaggerated, in-your-face Broadway moves. But when Lorin, the best dancer in the family, got his own sweet young things at age fourteen, his girls were decked out in lingerie, garter belts, and titillating tutus. Lorin was Bob Fosse waiting to happen.

Our dancing genes came, mostly, from my mother, by far my most influential source of strong, assertive female energy and identity. And humor. My mother was one of the most naturally, and unintentionally, funny people I've ever known.

But she was also tough and independent in the way she ran her business, which was particularly rare for a mother of six. She was comfortable with the way she looked and never hesitated to dress that way. She radiated an infectious knack for connecting with people through dance, which to her was, above all, social and noncompetitive. She could turn anyone into a dancer. She used keen instincts and observations about people—to break down their inhibitions and put them in touch with a more risqué and exuberant piece of their souls.

As she always said to my father, highlighting one of their basic differences, "You're book-smart, and I'm people-smart."

Though being the best mother in the world meant more to her than being the best wife or dance teacher, she possessed an amazing gift for creating "chemistry" among people by making them move and sweat together. Her Friday evening teenage social dance classes also included such sixties dance crazes as the jerk, twist, frug, and hullaballoo—bumping, grinding, and thrusting that sent everyone's raging hormones to high tide.

Things were so humid in the basement (where the studio was originally housed) from the stifling mix of Canoe, Yardley, Brut, and damp teenage pits that I wasn't even allowed down there until sixth grade. Before then, I'd sit on the stairs, daydreaming through slow dances. There was a primal, tribal energy emanating from the basement that was beyond sexual. Dancing was chromosomal, in the blood. I'd lose myself in the pounding rhythms and heavy footwork that made the whole house shake, and felt that pulse beat along with my heart.

Once I was introduced to slow dancing, I felt a different kind of pulse beating a lot closer to my hips. Some boys would lead by pressing against the girls, pelvis to pelvis. It felt so strange at first, and then I began to wonder: Why do these guys all have rolls of quarters in their pants? Where are they going after this, to do laundry?

My mother was more than a teacher; she was a nurturer-therapist who saw dance as a great equalizer. It didn't matter whether she worked with insecure, outcast eighth-graders or thuggy troublemakers with slicked-back hair and motorcycle jackets. She got through the facades that people put out to the world and, using dance as a mirror, held up a new, improved reflection of themselves.

She was at her best at orphanages, old people's homes, and veterans' hospitals. Once we visited a VFW hall where almost everyone was a Korean War amputee. We performed a few dance numbers, and for the finale my mom had each of us go into the audience and bring someone out onto the floor. My mother was p.c. long before it was hip: She didn't see these vets as handicapped —just choreographically challenged. And Mommy loved the challenge. She felt that even people in wheelchairs should dance, and they were delighted when she gave them the opportunity to do so. When she looked beyond whatever disability they had, the result was astounding. "They still have arms, they still have rhythm," she'd say. "They're dancers. So get them to dance."

On Saturdays, she would sneak me into the fabulous Madison Dance Club. I was fifteen, sixteen. The building was hideous outside, but then you'd walk upstairs and get swept up in a fantasy of fountains, chandeliers, and dramatic lighting. The music was taped, but there was a sense of magic in the air. Charles and Rosemary Madison were about the oldest couple I'd ever seen, but remarkably well-preserved. They taught dance instruction all week, and then on Saturday night it was Strictly Ballroom at the Madison.

The women wore petticoats under full, ballerina-length skirts that would swirl around as they kicked and twirled. The dance pairs were always gearing up for some competition or another.

The Madison attracted some of the most eccentric people I ever saw. There was an almost scary underside to the place, like those wartime German cabarets in the movies where everyone had his or her own smoke-shrouded freakiness.

One unforgettable character was Wally, a terrific dancer everybody wanted to dance with. It didn't seem to matter that Wally had no arms. He had thalidomide-type stubs; you couldn't hold his hands, and his stubs obviously couldn't get around your back. But you could always tell who had danced with Wally. Wally would poke one finger into the dress material behind your shoulder and twist the material until it was hooked securely enough around his finger to get a grip. Then he could dance with you. In other words, if you were wearing a backless dress—no Wally. It was both heartbreaking and wonderful to watch Wally glide with such graceful ease—and then see each of his partners with the same bunched-up curlicue on their dresses where he had held them.

Many of these people were probably insurance salesmen and wives who sold cosmetics door-to-door. But on the dance floor, the women, with their forties Joan Crawford hair and makeup, and their gowns, and the men, in their tuxedos, coupled up in the exaggerated, dramatic sensuality of the tango, were transformed into fantasy Freds and Gingers. I loved that about dancing, and about my mother.

Around that time, I was learning a brand-new dance myself that would lead me into some fantasies and transformations of my own: I had my first boyfriend. Steve and I "met" when a bunch of girlfriends at a pajama party started making crank calls and one of them said, "Oh, what about this really cute older guy I know who goes to Weber High?" I had no idea who he was. She dialed his number, let it ring—and jammed the phone into my hand as he picked up. I freaked. The challenge was you had to stay on the line for five minutes. I kept him on for twenty minutes, and we identified ourselves only by our zodiac signs.

A couple of days later, when a girlfriend pointed him out to me at a dance, I thought he was adorable. I went straight up to him and introduced myself. "Hi, Leo, I'm Aries." He was dumbfounded.

I was a huge flirt, and, though I was far from a knockout, my feeling was that if you kept on moving fast, they never noticed the flaws or the funky angles. They just picked up on the flash, the spark.

I dated Steve through the end of high school—though we were always "clicking off" with each other and dating other people until we'd click back on. I remember my first big kiss with Steve, for two reasons: one, because it was exactly like the "sloppy, smacking sound" I had described so vividly in a creative writing exercise at school; two, because, just as Steve left, my heart pounding with the thrill of that first kiss, I thought I caught my bratty brother Tommy sneaking out from under the hallway staircase. This totally broke the spell for me. I was furious.

The next day, I picked up the phone to call a girlfriend, only to hear Tommy on the phone upstairs, dishing with his pubescent buddy: "Man, you shoulda seen 'em goin' at it. My sister's a total make-out queen! They were really swappin' tonsils."

"TOMMY!" I squealed into the receiver. I slammed it down and wanted to *kill* the jerk.

I was a quick study, but I still took my time. There were *plenty* of venial—and, thus, pardonable—misdemeanors to drive me up the wall before I ever got to the mortal sin of penetration, which earned you a one-way trip to hell. In my Catholic-girl mind, the venial stages were all fine to explore with gusto. A little knee-to-knee contact in a darkened movie house, a hand brushing my thigh—these were enough to make my eyes roll up inside my head. There is nothing as hot as that teasing, tortured, make-out-session buildup.

It wasn't long before I saw venial acts not as "sins" but milestones: first French kiss (hallway at home); first time petting above the waist (back door at home, wearing a man's dress shirt, unbuttoned); first oral sex (dance studio, Steve's birthday, my gift). I threw myself completely into this side trip on my life's quest for perfection. The first time I ever saw a naked erection, it was just the most shocking, fascinating thing I had ever seen in my life. I was, like, *How does this happen?* I studied it for hours. Oral sex was something that had never even crossed my mind. I thought Steve had invented it. But, then again, sticking things in my mouth as a kid was always a great source of pleasure. And this was so much more interesting than a Tootsie Pop.

I saw myself as a lusty, aroused, curious, open-minded Catholic girl who loved having older guys in my life who were willing to teach me. I never felt threatened by guys and sex, because of the rapport I shared with my father and brothers. I felt I understood men's behavior, attitudes, and urges.

The mysteries of intimacy were revealed in strange ways. I used to baby-sit for a couple named Pat and Doris. Doris was the hottest woman any of us had seen: like Angie Dickinson, with her outrageously sexy body. I loved hanging out at their place. I felt sexy just being there.

Years later, sexpot Doris's equally sexy husband Pat was kind enough to share with us the secret of their long and happy marriage: "Every time I look at her," he said, "I wanna fuck her brains out."

Tommy and Steve ranked delectable Doris at the top of their E.O. list—i.e., their Eating Out list—of women. It was the highest honor they could possibly bestow.

With major role models like Pat and Doris, it was only a matter of time before guys would pick up on how much I loved being around them. But they always treated me with respect and caring. And because I didn't drink or do drugs, I felt totally in control. My parents trusted me, trusted that I could handle it. And to use today's word, I played things *safe*.

What was *un*safe was forgetting to call my father by two A.M. if I were going to be later. No call and forget it—my father was like Mr. Clean standing at the door, arms crossed, out of his mind with worry. More than once, I made it just in time for the bed check, hustling under the covers with my clothes on.

In senior year, Daddy almost caught Steve and me once in their bedroom. (I liked my parents' bedroom. One reason, I suppose, was that there was always so much sexual energy in there from, as Tommy would say, using one of his *non*medical terms, all the "frolicking" they did. Also, the beds were pushed together, so there was more room to roll around.) I was home sick from school and Mommy was out somewhere. Steve had cut school to be with me. We were fooling around when I heard a knock in the middle of the afternoon. Thank God, I had locked the door. We were half-undressed, taking our time. We freaked out silently, like crazed mime actors. Steve slid under the bed and I opened the door, putting on an Oscar-caliber display of calm and fake fatigue. "Oh, Daddy," I said, stretching and yawning on cue, "I was just napping in here 'cause it's so *bright* everywhere else in the house, you know?"

I got awfully brazen and took some outrageous risks. If I baby-sat for my nieces at JoAnn's, Steve stayed overnight in the same bedroom. We also used the dance studio, which was great because it had music and a rug and you could lock the door. We rarely needed to use Steve's car.

Maybe I'd have felt more Catholic guilt about my sexual escapades if I were pulling B's and C's. But with a straight-A average, my healthy sexual adventures clearly weren't hurting my GPA.

In July between my junior and senior years, on the night of NASA's first lunar landing, I made some history of my own: While three astronauts were taking one giant step for mankind and bathing in immortal glory on the dusty desert surface of the moon, I was showering in mortal sin in a steamy, soapy bathroom near Lincoln Park.

One of my mother's big sayings was, "Always have a spare," which applied to boyfriends as well as dresses and job opportunities. That summer, my spare was Buddy, a cute, smirking, seductive actor several years older than I. Steve and I were in a "click-off" phase and I had met Buddy at a theater company I was working with.

People warned me over and over about Buddy's Don Juan complex, but there was nothing complex about it at all: We just started going out. One night we were strolling through Lincoln Park and he suddenly scooped me up and wrapped me around his body. Buddy was like that—a spontaneous, passionate, sexy, slow-motion montage. He told me he was going to take me home, that it was a good time to cool off. That summer I was answering phones at a tacky encyclopedia company, and was going out of my mind. I was in an advanced state of readiness. After one especially torrid weekend of "everything-but" with Buddy, I remember feeling so wonderfully spent that I just couldn't imagine it could get much better than that.

Wrong. The night Buddy carried me part of the way home we started making out, and next thing I knew we were practicing the venial taking-a-shower-together. But once our bodies got all soaped up and slippery, I got to a fever pitch of fondling and pure sensation and was ready to explode. I just couldn't wait any longer. If this meant I was going to hell, at least I was showing up all clean and scrubbed.

Buddy then pressed me against the wall of the shower, and it happened. It felt so slippery, so natural, so inevitable, so *good*. And yet, for all the buildup and fantasies, it wasn't nearly as big a deal as I had imagined, probably because I'd already made it about 96 percent of the way there during other sessions. And, I felt some sadness that, while I *had* showered before with Steve, I hadn't been with him for my "first time."

Or my second. Or third. When we were finished, and drying off, I said, "I guess we've done it."

"Yeah, I guess so," Buddy said with a smile.

"So why don't we get out of the bathroom and go into your bedroom and do it right?" I asked.

He had no argument there. We went to bed and made love two more times.

Afterward, all Buddy seemed to want to know was whether I had had an orgasm.

All I wanted to know was whether the nuns would look at me and be able to tell.

Summer ended and I clicked off Buddy, clicked back on with Steve, and turned my energies toward the senior production and getting into the University of Chicago.

"Find something you love to do, then find someone willing to pay you to do it," my father always liked to tell us. To him, that was the secret to success. It was a theme we had touched on time and again during our talks in the car that fall. It was part of living like a millionaire. Doing what you loved in life—and getting paid for it—was worth millions in the human currency of contentment and joy.

As the Christmas season drew near, I was feeling on top of the world, still guided by my life's Plan A. It had been an amazing few months. I'd found something I loved to do (and would soon find people to pay me to do it). I'd come to know my father better and received his heartfelt blessings to pursue my dream. I had committed—or was it *discovered?*—mortal sin, and had loved every minute of it.

My passage into womanhood had begun, and it was all going to be smooth sailing ahead.

It simply never crossed my mind that my life wasn't always going to be this wonderful.

4
This Too Shall Pass

~

A death in the family not only tears away a loved one; it gives death a face, a presence in your life, and it confronts you with a sense of your own mortality. In five seconds a life can end before your eyes. If that doesn't smack you upside your head to take better care of things, of yourself, and to appreciate what you've got while you've got it, nothing will.

Coming as it did for me at a time of transition—the end of childhood, the beginning of my sexual identity as a woman—my father's death set me off on a shakier trajectory than I might have anticipated when I left home to live on my own.

Certainly, Daddy's death became a presence in our lives, marking the end to a perfect family life as we knew it, a farewell to our private Camelot on Logan Boulevard. In its aftermath, we all went through our own brutal little dramas. The most anguished, of course, was Tommy's. My father died twenty minutes past midnight on the morning of December 28. When we got home at about two-thirty in the morning, my mother, sobbing through her grief, remained composed. She was more concerned about poor Tommy, who had disappeared in anguish when we left for the hospital.

Christal was washing dishes and cleaning up. Lorin looked at us the moment we walked in and fell apart, collapsing under the kitchen table in heartbreaking sobs of pain. When Tommy materialized, he looked forlorn and wasted. "Did he die? Did he die?" he asked.

We had to hold Tommy down and comfort him as my mother broke the news. In her protective, maternal way, she lied and said that my father had rallied at the hospital just long enough to tell my mother to make sure Tommy never blamed himself. It was a *second* heart attack sometime in the night, she said, that killed him. Tommy was an adult before he learned the truth.

The next three days we were all sobbing and sharing warm memories among family and friends. The curtains and shades were down; there was no sense of time. Friends from the neighborhood brought huge pots of pasta and a baked ham to keep us going. My girlfriends paid condolence calls and I went through the motions of being gracious and strong, though a voice-over in my head kept saying: "This isn't real, this isn't happening." I was living someone else's movie.

Two nights later, my boyfriend Steve, who was like family by then, was so distraught he had chest palpitations and thought *he* was having a heart attack. We went to the same ER my father had been brought to, where Steve, aged nineteen—my first, but hardly my last, hypochondriac—checked out fine.

Twelve-year-old Lorin was so upset he had been prescribed tranquilizers that weekend. He had to leave the house on Monday for a dinner theater rehearsal of *Oliver.* Steve and I drove him and watched as he sang "Where Is Love?" while sitting in a casket in a funeral parlor. The timing was perverse, and I felt my heart rip open again, knowing we would leave the theater and drive straight to Daddy's wake at the funeral home.

My mother fell apart when she found the pieces of a card from my father that read: "All my love, Joe." He had given it to her in the midst of their big fight just before he died, but she had ripped it up in his face and flung it at him. I knew how she felt. I was so thankful that I had not cashed the check he wrote me on Christmas Day, because he had signed it. For my mom and me, just seeing his handwriting made us cry.

Even the wake seemed unreal. My father and Christal could both shut one eye without squinting and keep the other one open, like a doll. The joker in him had loved to do that while driving, so if you were in the passenger seat and he shut his right eye, you would think he had shut both eyes. And you'd scream, "Daddy, wake up! Wake up!"

Seeing him at the wake, I prayed for one eye to pop open like a doll's—for it all to have been a crazy Daddy prank.

We buried him on New Year's Eve day, 1969. In the dead of the Chicago winter, the ground was frozen rock-hard. I took my first limousine ride, with the seven of us and Uncle John packed inside. He had us all in teary laughter as he regaled us with tales of what my dad was like as a little boy. We had to compose ourselves as we rode up to the church, because we looked like we were having a party in there.

We held a funeral mass at St. John Berchman's. In keeping with church ritual, all forty-seven cars in our procession, a major turnout, filed past the house and the church before mass. The natural-born showman in my father would have been thrilled to know he drew a standing-room-only crowd. The funeral was the ultimate tribute to Joe Henner: If true wealth is measured in love, respect, humor, and joyful remembrances, he had not only lived like a millionaire, he had died like one, too.

As reality began to set in, the pain became unbearable. Whenever the phone rang, or I heard someone come upstairs, I couldn't help thinking it might be Daddy.

And yet, on the surface it was life-goes-on at home. My mother put up an incredibly strong front. She began working as a bank clerk in January, something she had decided to do before my father died. It was not only therapeutic; she needed every penny of it to clean up some $20,000 in debt and bills that my father—the high roller who liked to say, "Now don't you worry about money, Lor"—had left behind. Twenty grand was what he *earned* in a year—the best of years.

I had no idea how dire our financial situation was. We didn't even know my father had taken out a $25,000 life insurance policy on December 10, two and a half weeks before dying. But the day after he died, an insurance agent called and told me about the policy, and that it had kicked in the day before his death. "When he came in," the agent recalled, "he said, 'I want to do this for Lor and the kids.'"

I had sensed something was up while applying to the University of Chicago in the early fall. That had been part of my dream all through high school—if I was going to take my 3.65 average anywhere for college, it would be there. But when my father helped fill out the financial part of my college application, he refused, curiously, to let me look over his portion. "I don't care how much you say you make," I told him, figuring that was his concern. (How much aid you received was determined by need.) I just wanted to make sure the form was properly done. He said no and I mailed it in.

Sure enough, the form came back after he died, with a letter requesting my parents' ages. Because my mother always lied about their ages, I hadn't known what to fill in. Now, I looked it over. My father had indicated his income for 1969 was $20,000; for 1970, $10,000. Eerily, he had marked a small asterisk next to the $10,000 figure and written: "Expect decrease in salary because of decrease in health. Angina pains are more frequent and severe."

Given that he would have gladly signed a deal granting him twenty more years of life, it all started to add up: My father must have known, in some psychic way, that the end was near.

The $25,000 insurance payout and my mother's money-handling skills cleared things up. But behind her courageous, forging-ahead facade, things were clearly not the same for her. I moved into my parents' bedroom until I went off to the University of Chicago nine months later. My mother could not deal with sleeping there alone.

When he died, she was almost fifty, but looked thirty-five. With the love of her life gone, she began to age overnight. It was shocking to watch. I was almost out of the house and, within a few more years the three younger children would be gone. In a haunting—and unnecessary—way, it was as if she too had started to read the end of the script. She lost her vibrant joie de vivre. She didn't go out, didn't see another way to live her life.

She had had mild arthritis before this; now, her sadness and the mercilessly frigid Chicago winter made it worse by the day.

Three months after my father died, spring arrived, leaving the cruel, endless winter behind. If I wasn't exactly living in denial, I did my best to stay in avoidance. Staying busy helped distract me. I got to perform with Steve in a Chicago production of *The Fantasticks,* which was a great challenge. I got accepted to the University of Chicago, the only college I had applied to. If I had gotten rejected, Plan B was to head for New York and be an actress, wait tables, whatever. Money could have been an issue, but I won four scholarships. That sealed it: I'd stay in Chicago, be near my mom, and go to the university for free. Out of all the high school juniors and seniors in the state, I was named Outstanding Teenager of Illinois, and was presented with the award at graduation by Governor Ogilvie. I was also salutatorian of my class of 352 girls. It was everything Joe Henner had wanted for me, and I felt that he was up there making it happen.

* * *

After graduation I got a summer waitressing job at the Nippersink Manor resort, where we had spent many summer vacation weeks as a family. Nippersink was about sixty miles from Chicago in Genoa City, Wisconsin, which I call the Midwest Catskills. It's in a gorgeous area of lakes and streams, woods and rolling lawns. It was straight out of the movie *Dirty Dancing*. For years I had helped waiters and waitresses during our visits, dreaming of the time I could become one myself. They all lived in dorms, which seemed like the most glamorous thing in the world.

I loved waitressing. I was sassy. I loved impressing guests with my memory. I'd recite the menu and remember everybody's orders without writing anything down. That was my trick, my claim to Nippersink fame, and it got me great tips.

One thing I never had any trouble remembering was to eat. Looking back, maybe a large resort dining room/kitchen wasn't the healthiest environment for me that first, emotionally vulnerable summer away from home after my dad died. I worked like a horse, and I ate like one. I put on thirty pounds. I was cross-addicted to dairy and extra rare roast beef, the bloodier the better. I blew up to 160 pounds. As a teenager my idea of a diet was keeping to 1,600 calories a day, and getting them all from a pound of Jarlsberg. I was also really good at having a cheese omelette and calling it protein, or eating my way through a package of processed cold cuts.

This was years before I discovered that food doesn't have to kill you to taste good. I made no connection between heart disease and a high-fat diet, or between cheese and bad skin and chronic constipation. The connection I did make was between overeating and my father's death. I was, simply—if unconsciously—eating my feelings. Without knowing it, I was still fighting off feelings of loss and abandonment. But at least my extra poundage was evenly distributed, so I merely had a bigger version of my shape.

I just looked like the Beefy 19 girl. Beefy 19 was a Chicago hamburger joint way up on Western Avenue, and its logo was a zaftig dance hall girl holding a tray, wearing fishnet stockings and built like she'd invested heavily in beef and pork futures. I was Nippersink's Beefy 19 girl.

Another reason I stuffed my face was exhaustion. I started working breakfasts at five-thirty in the morning and finished dinner shifts at ten at night, seven days a week. If you needed a day off you had to pay someone to take your station. I wish I had known about food combining and eating properly, because it was all right there. Instead, I went for meat, dairy, and garbage like beef Stroganoff and chicken à la king.

Even my love life that summer became just another reason, after depression and exhaustion, why I porked up to 160. It was ten pounds for my father, ten as a reward for working too hard, and ten for the turmoil of a new affair. I looked like I'd been fattened for the kill.

His name was Jim and we were assigned to the same dorm, working and constantly hanging together. He was four years older and had just graduated from college. I was intrigued by the idea of an affair with Jim, who was handsome in the way that the slightly neurotic-looking Tom from the Barbie game was handsome. (Ken was too good-looking in a straitlaced and uptight way, with absolutely no PF—probably because, in his anatomical incorrectness, poor Ken had no P.)

I immediately figured Jim for my big summer romance. We seemed compatible and he seemed into it, especially after two make-out sessions in the cool summer-night air. Steve and I had come to Nippersink together, but as soon as I saw Jim, I clicked off Steve. Clearly not the most stable period of my life.

If I was self-conscious about gaining weight, it didn't diminish my sexual appetite. I'm not sure the weight or body type exists for me not to love sex. Sure, I feel better looking my best—that dance-around-the-room-bare-ass-naked-to-a-great-tape feeling. But the gusto factor, my sexual energy, is a constant, even across a forty-pound span. Just turn down the lights and put me in black lingerie. I have never been one to wait—or lose weight—just so someone could give me permission to feel and act sexy.

All women, no matter how they look, have to get this message through their heads. What "looks" sexy is far too subjective: A man's definition is different from a woman's; and every man's definition is different from every *other* man's. Plus, "sexy" for too many women is what society *tells* them it is, depending on the seasonal marketing strategies of retailers, designers, and Madison Avenue. Whether you're a waif or a waddler, life's just too damned short to wait for your look to be "in."

Being sexy and lusty is more a state of mind than a specific look, and I always felt that, no matter how thick or thin I was, I was bringing something to the party. Besides, overweight's no excuse. As I like to say to uptight women: Stop obsessing that you're not sexy for your man because you hate the way you look. Sexuality isn't just visual. It's in your mind, in your touch. Besides, *you've always got your mouth.*

One night Jim and I had plans to meet, but he never showed up. A friend of his came by to tell me why: Two of Jim's college buddies had been killed that day in a car accident and he was so devastated he was getting drunk by himself in his room.

I could relate. I went over there to comfort him as best I could. The effort, the investment, paid off. We made love that night. We felt closer and I instantly bought into the idea that some "spiritual" connection now existed—an I-was-there-when-he-most-needed-me bond that upgrades you to Girlfriend status.

It was the first time I was totally wrong about a guy. He was the first prospective boyfriend who was not from my social or theater circle, where guys always treated me as someone special. I had never been mistreated or roughed up emotionally.

The fact that we had slept together was simply no big deal to Jim. Things just sort of petered out after that. I didn't feel devastated, just empty. I had always felt special to myself, with an unshakable self-esteem that had never been diminished by my relationships. Now, though, I was forced to ask myself what I had done wrong, how I had mishandled things. I was blaming myself. But I learned a major, *major* life lesson: Never sleep with someone who doesn't make you feel special. It was up to me not to make the same mistake again.

At summer's end, when I walked through the door, my mother was so shocked to see my Beefy 19 look that she recommended I take up smoking two or three cigarettes a day to curb my appetite. I couldn't be bothered.

In September, I moved into my college dorm with an old girlfriend I'd known since I was five. After twelve years of Catholic education, I absolutely loved the free-thinking intellectual climate and the magnificent Gothic architecture at the University of Chicago. You felt smart just walking the grounds. I declared a major in Political Science, mostly because I loved my Political Science professor. But all I wanted to be was an actress. It would just be a matter of time—and breaks—before I'd get there.

My favorite building was Ida Noyes Hall, the fine arts center. It had a basement bowling alley and one huge sunbathed room for a dance studio with floor-to-ceiling windows. I hung out mostly at

Noyes Hall. Once I told him about the sunny dance studio, my brother Tommy was a regular there too, sniffing around, keeping me company.

I loved the campus, loved the feel of academia. But I was always looking for that break. During the last weeks of my senior year at Madonna, I had begun readings at a community theater workshop for a hugely ambitious, intriguing project written by a man I had known for a couple of years. Jim Jacobs was a writer at an advertising agency I had met when I performed in the play *The Boy Friend* during my sophomore year. He was outrageously creative— he also had a memory like mine—and he had been trying his hand at acting when we met.

He had contacted me in my senior year when he wanted to get his script into production. Jim was ten years older than I was, and his work was a reconstruction of virtually everything he could remember about his fifties high school era. This was the fall of 1970. The Vietnam War was raging; ponytailed, drugged-out, dropped-out hippies ruled the youth culture. After the tumultuous sixties, the relatively pristine Eisenhower-Nixon fifties was ancient history even for anyone who could remember them. Jim's only problem was that, in his fond, nostalgic tribute to his class of 1959, there was nothing he could *forget*.

The readings were at a converted trolley barn called the Kingston Mines Theater. Jim's script was immense, a veritable Bible of fifties vignettes. He had written twenty-seven songs for Act I alone. But in its loosely structured, four-hour-long form, his hilarious sketches lacked a concise through-line. He had a locker room scene, a book report nightmare scene, an air raid drill scene. Our readings were intended to help him streamline and mold the material into a musical. It was amazing. It was like: Okay, here's a song, is this in your key, great, you sing it. Or, Okay, your character'll do this song—no, that one. It was very free-for-all, very hamper. But I loved doing the read-throughs.

If you haven't figured it out by now, the name of the play was *Grease*.

I was just starting at Chicago, and he called to cast me in one of the central roles, a tough, curvy bombshell named Marty. Marty was the ultimate bummy girl, the kind of chick I'd crossed the street to avoid all through childhood. Now, my fame and fortune depended on my ability to *become* a bummy girl, one who put razor blades in her hair, ran her nylons, hiked up her tight skirt as she wiggled down the hall, and thrust her breasts out at you in her big angora sweaters.

After Nippersink, I must say, the casting was perfect. In the fifties you could be a porker and get away with it. Who cared then? Those styles made you look fat anyway and it was still years before Twiggy. I looked perfect for a time that celebrated my guardian angel Marilyn Monroe as the ultimate sex goddess. In truth, right behind a plow is where I looked like I belonged, but I was able to get away with the weight because my legs always stayed in shape.

We worked hard, honed the show, hit our marks, and opened to terrific reviews on February 5, 1971. The buzz and excitement were thrilling. This was a first-rate production for community theater, and we were all flying high.

Five days later, I came frighteningly close to crashing and burning. The first year I was away from home seemed like I had borrowed Tommy's Accident-Prone flashcard—four major car wrecks in a half-year tear. I learned how to drive and took my test all in the same day. If I had been eating my feelings unconsciously at Nippersink, now I seemed to be driving them.

One day a few college girlfriends and I cut school and drove up to Nippersink in a winter snowstorm. They were interested in working summers there, so I offered to show them my old stomping grounds. I was way too cocky to be driving, and still only had a temporary license. I had absolutely no business taking the chances I took.

Somewhere just short of the Illinois border, some guy at an intersection hooked a sharp left turn into my path and I skidded to avoid him, but clipped his rear right side. There was minor damage, but it was terrifying to lose control and spin out like that at 50 miles an hour—especially when you hadn't been driving more than a few days.

Five days later, I had another brush with disaster. Steve was driving on Kennedy Expressway, I was in the front, and Lorin was in the back. A driver raced into traffic from an entrance ramp, cut diagonally across the lanes of traffic, and all hell broke loose. I saw the crash coming up ahead and braced myself with my foot up against the glove compartment and my knee against my chest. We hit a four-car pileup with unbelievable impact.

I was shot forward into the windshield and opened a major gash

on my forehead. Lorin was hurled forward into me with such force
that my shoe burst apart. My foot swelled up like a balloon. It was a
disaster scene, with helicopters, police cars, fire trucks, and ambu-
lances all over the place. The accident and resulting traffic tie-up
even made the evening news.

Amazingly, I was the only one of us hurt. An inflatable boot was
delicately slipped around my foot to reduce the swelling, and I was
rushed to a hospital for X rays. No fracture, but every muscle in my
foot was torn.

I was stuck hobbling on crutches for six weeks. But after missing
two weeks of shows, I was back—although in pain. At that stage of
my career, nothing was going to stop me from going out there. I
managed to gimp my way through *Grease* with a soft cast on my
foot.

I left the show in June, though it enjoyed a successful run
through September. I was thrilled for Jim Jacobs and his writing
partner, Warren Casey. For me, it was a longer run than any of the
fifteen shows I'd done previously. I had learned some critical things
about my craft, about creating and changing a character night after
night. I was doing what I loved and getting paid to do it—bus fare
and about ten bucks per show. I loved the cast and the whole
creative energy of the troupe.

Jim Jacobs was the funniest person I had ever met in my life. He
still is. His gift for machine-gun, hallucinatory caricature was
amazingly fast; he was like a vulgar Robin Williams with a Jack
Nicholson delivery. I once threw a huge party for the cast in my
house, and I asked him, "How's the party going downstairs?" He
snapped back: "Oh, it's great, a typical Henner party: Your
mother's peeing on some Italian man's face and your brother's got
his dick in a vacuum cleaner."

By then, the big news for Jim and Warren was that *Grease* was
going to off Broadway's Eden Theater. Producers had been watching it closely since we had opened and the Broadway buzz on it was
incredible. But I didn't see it as a lock to become a smash hit. I felt
it was too Chicago, too scummy for Broadway.

Another huge Chicago show called *Warp* had just gone to
Broadway and bombed miserably. I was afraid the same fate might
well await *Grease*. It still felt like a pipe dream. I had so little
experience that I didn't understand what Broadway could *do* with
good material, in the right hands and with enough money. I

dreaded the idea of leaving school and home, then finding myself a college dropout/out-of-work actress/waitress.

Moreover, I didn't feel ready to leave my mom behind and go to Broadway yet. It had been a very rough year and a half for her since my father had died. Also, because of my accident, I had taken an incomplete for two courses and couldn't imagine leaving school not in good standing. And with my most recent success, I was now in a position to earn up to $200 a week choreographing shows and teaching dance.

So I decided to spend another summer at Nippersink and make up my university work. As carloads of cast members packed up and split to pursue their Broadway dreams, I stayed back, wished them all the best—and said good-bye.

It was almost a very long good-bye at that. In September, I had two more near tragedies in cars. I offered to drive the car of a Nippersink friend named Roger, who was returning to his college in Washington, D.C. For some reason, he had bought an old sixties Mercedes stick shift without knowing how to drive it. In fact, he didn't even have a license. I had the idea that I'd go along and drive—and that Tommy would tag along.

I drove through the night, and at around seven A.M. on the Pennsylvania Turnpike outside Harrisburg, I got drowsy, my eyes began to glaze over, and I drifted off behind the wheel. The car must have lurched because suddenly I heard Roger screaming: "Lu, wake up, wake *up!*"

I came to and freaked out just as the car veered left, veered right, shot back left across the turnpike, mowed down two standing reflectors, and jumped the grassy median, coming to rest perpendicular to oncoming traffic.

It was horrifying. Thank God there *was* no oncoming traffic. If it hadn't been seven o'clock on a Saturday morning, we would definitely have been smoked. Roger's car had to be towed and repaired. We bused the rest of the way to Washington. I was traumatized—and immortalized. The state highway whatever ordered me to pay for the two busted reflectors, which I said I would do, provided they put my initials on the new reflectors. I was only joking, but they promised they would.

Three days later the car was ready, and we bused back to pick it up. This time Roger, not trusting my driving, insisted on taking the wheel. Never mind that he still had no license, and no experience with a stick.

We took off in a wicked rainstorm and got on the turnpike heading west. All of a sudden, Roger's car veered out of control—right, left, right, left—and did three 360 spins before all four wheels popped off. Lightning flashed and there we were, bouncing around in a Mercedes stick shift box, heading for the shoulder—and a steep 100-foot drop into a ravine.

"We're going to DIE!" I screamed. The car finally lost its momentum just short of the edge of the shoulder.

At least he hadn't lost his sense of humor. "Lu," he said, "tomorrow I go to D.C. and buy a bicycle." The next day, Roger bought his bicycle, and I bought my first pack of cigarettes.

I made up my grades in the fall, but couldn't erase some nagging regrets about my decision to stay in Chicago. In March 1972, I had taken a trip to New York to see Jim Jacobs and the new production of *Grease,* which had opened on Valentine's Day at the Eden. It was awe-inspiring. Director Tom Moore had come in and helped Jim give the show structure, pace, story—real production value. Now, it was like the *real* Broadway shows I grew up with. I thought to myself: *Shit, you were wrong.* I got excited about the show all over again—and went home torturing myself over the decision I had made.

Grease moved to Broadway in June. Around Thanksgiving, the big news in my theater community was that the show was doing so well in New York that a national touring company was being auditioned. I couldn't *believe* this. How could I have been so wrong? It was eat-your-heart-out time for me.

I was on campus when I got the phone call.

"We haven't cast Marty yet, and we'd all love you to do it," Jim Jacobs was telling me from New York. "Rehearsals start tomorrow. I've made sure nobody else has gotten your part. Henner, you were *born* to do this part; you should do this."

I was clutching an armload of heavy library books—and thinking. Remembering. The last person who had told me that—in almost the exact words—was my dad, just days before he died.

"I have two papers due tomorrow," I said, wincing, biting my lip in the freezing morning air. "I just don't—"

"Trust me," he cut in, sounding even more emphatic, almost

impatient. "You're going to be kicking yourself in the ass for the rest of your life if you don't do it."

I hesitated and agonized. "I'm sorry, Jim."

And I hung up the phone.

I started off toward the library, my heart pounding, adrenaline flowing, my free hand pressed to my head. *What have I just done? Am I out of my mind?*

I slowed down, stopped, looked back at the pay phone.

"FUCK IT!" I screamed.

I threw my books in the car and raced to the phone. I got Jim Jacobs right away. "What is it?" he asked warily. But he didn't hear any hesitation in my voice this time.

"I'm coming."

5
Greased Lightning

~

SHOWTIME!

After I hung up the phone, I ran to my car, drove (carefully) to the airport, and flew to New York for the audition with nothing but the clothes on my back. No way I wasn't going to be in the national tour.

I auditioned for the role of Marty and when it was over, Tom Moore, the director, said to me, "Can you come back in two hours for the choreographer?"

No problem. That audition went great. "You're fabulous and we want you for the part," Maxine Fox, the producer, told me. Then, after a pause, she asked, in a lower voice, "But we'd like you to lose some weight. Do you think you could do that?"

"Sure, no problem," I said quickly.

"Fine," she said. "Then be at first rehearsal tomorrow."

I was elated. I called home. "Mom," I said, "I'm dropping out of school. I'm in New York."

"What?" she said, stunned.

"I just got offered the national company of *Grease* and I'm leaving school and I'm going to do it," I said excitedly.

Some mothers would have been upset by the news, but my mom, always supportive of my dream, was thrilled. "Wonderful," she exclaimed. I'm sure she had mixed feelings about my leaving Chicago, but she knew there was no stopping me, and that this was my big chance.

That night, I stayed on a couch in the one-bedroom apartment Jim Jacobs was sharing with his beautiful model girlfriend on West

Eighty-fifth Street and West End Avenue. The next day I had my first rehearsal and met everyone in the show. Then I had fifteen hours to go home and wrap things up at school, get ready for a new life and career in New York, and be at the next rehearsal at ten A.M. the following day.

It was the most hectic, thrilling twenty-four hours I had ever known—to leave my old life behind, become a professional literally overnight, sign my Equity card, earn a living, work with fabulous people. My spirits were soaring.

I flew in, went straight home to see my family, and hosed everybody with manic Personality flashcard exuberance. I breezed in, breezed out, kissed everyone good-bye, and split. I didn't have a second to waste or get sentimental. I broke the news to my two shocked roommates, packed up my stuff, spent the night at the place of a guy I had been seeing named Doug, woke up, scribbled an I'm-outta-here note to the bursar, which I ran over to his office and slipped under the door, and caught the next plane to New York. I left my 3.5 GPA behind—but I wasn't looking back.

After landing, I headed straight to the rehearsal at the Ansonia Hotel on Broadway at West Seventy-third Street. The Ansonia is an imposing Beaux Arts knockoff that looks as if it were lifted off the Champs-Élysées and set down on Broadway. It's famous for its studios and creative tenants—world-famous voice coaches, ballet and modern dancers, pop and classical recitalists, opera divas, theater actors. It was so totally Broadway, so mind-boggling. I walked past the crusty old New York-type guy who sold egg salad sandwiches and newspapers right in the block-long lobby—the Ansonia had a smell all its own—and rode the elevator up. I stepped into a vast, loftlike space with bad lighting, the clanging of folding metal chairs on bare hardwood floors, and a pair of prop tables on either side to simulate walking onstage with makeshift props. The set and its props were all marked with tape on the floor. The company had rented out a suite of rehearsal spaces—one for songs, one for dance numbers. I should have been exhausted, jet-lagged, anxious, but I wasn't. My heart was pounding with the rush of it all as I took it all in.

The guys were adorable. Each one was more handsome and intelligent-looking than the next—a far cry from the hoody, pockmarked guys from the Chicago company.

I later learned that one of my costars, Jerry Zaks, took one look at my voluptuous figure and told Michael Lembeck, another actor,

"With tits like that, I'm not gonna fuck on this tour?" When I heard the story, I loved Jerry for that. Today, Jerry's one of the most distinguished and successful Tony Award-winning directors on Broadway, with credits like *Guys & Dolls, Six Degrees of Separation, Anything Goes,* and others. He was the resident therapist-confidant for the group, and a very funny guy. Jerry went to Dartmouth, so every time he used a multisyllabic word like "specificity" to explain some fifties greaser thing, the cast would bust him and go, "Whoooaa, 'spe-ci-fi-ci-ty'?" And he'd go, "Hey, I fuckin' wenta college." That became one of our great lines. Whenever someone busted you for saying or doing something lofty, we'd say, 'Hey, I fuckin' wenta college.' "

The truth is I very much wanted to have an affair with Jerry. But he had a gorgeous girlfriend who did TV commercials, so I didn't push it. I was quite hot for Jerry—absolutely crazy about him— and he knew it. One night, in Philadelphia, we got a little buzz on from a few too many Black Russians, and there was some heavy flirting. If nothing happened, it wasn't because of me. He was just faithful to her, and decent enough not to exploit my young-actress susceptibility, either. A real mensch. If he had made a move, I'd have gone for it in a second. So my teasing line with Jerry when we've seen each other over the years is always, "Ooooh, our Black Russian night in Philadelphia—what might have been!"

That same day I met a hunky, shaggy-haired New York actor who was on his way to do the London production of *Grease*. He was as gorgeous as he was unknown. His name was Richard Gere and he and Jim Jacobs and I went out a couple of nights before Richard left to play Danny Zuko, the lead role.

That day I also met another young, unknown actor who immediately struck me as soulmate potential. He was sweet, wonderful, beautiful, and, like me, insanely curious, pumping me for all kinds of inside stuff on the original Chicago shows. His name was John Travolta. Though he was from New Jersey and Italian, and cast out of L.A., we had a lot in common. We both grew up in strong Catholic families; we both had two brothers and three sisters. His mother taught theater, my mother taught dancing. His father sold tires, my father sold cars. Like mine, his home was the center of a neighborhood, with its offbeat, hamper qualities.

As the two youngest cast members, we were the kids and everyone else the grown-ups. It was spooky how intense and powerful that spark was. Once we started talking, we never stopped laughing. It was like rediscovering a long-lost sibling. Johnny, as we all called him—and as his friends and family still do—had the role of the goofy, innocent kid named Doody, and he was perfect for it. Before the first day of rehearsal was over, we were linked, we were buddies.

The other cast members included Jeff Conaway, who had the Danny Zuko role (the part Johnny later played in the movie with Olivia Newton-John). Jeff had the spoiled-child quality of a child actor, which he had been. But he was lovable and had a big heart. He had all the working-actor *stuff,* all the accoutrements: a gorgeous leather shoulder bag, a beautiful suede fringed coat, an actress girlfriend (Carole Demas, who played Sandy in the Broadway cast). He had scripts, books, and a slew of vitamins, special herb teas, and vaporizers. Yet he was always sick anyhow and required daily wake-up calls. He had the most experience, the most money, and was one of the wilder personalities. I'd look at Jeff and wonder: Do you need all this stuff in order to be an actor?

I adored two girls in the cast: Judy Kaye, who played the lead, Rizzo—Judy has an extraordinary voice—and Ellen March, who played Frenchy. She was my dressing room partner because we both smoked; neither of us does now. (I had taken my mom up on her suggestion to help lose a few pounds.) It was a time of tight bonding, and Ellen, who is now a psychotherapist in Manhattan, remains one of my closest friends.

The company's contract minimum was a little under $300 a week and I was getting $325, a huge amount of money for me. During the three-week period we were in New York, Jim Jacobs let me stay at his place for free. Then, in December, we packed our bags and hit the road for our thirteen-city, twelve-month barnstorm.

First, we did three days of dress rehearsals and previews in Boston before opening night, December 23, 1972. Part of our last-minute preparation was watching every fifties movie we could find, like *Rebel Without a Cause,* and reading the Time-Life books that chronicled the fifties. As thorough as we were, that week over the holidays was an insane disaster. Everyone was sick, and we all had to take each other's parts in tech rehearsals as they put the set in. It was the kind of separate-the-men-from-the-boys time I loved, when I could be the one with a cool head who rallies the troops and thinks on my feet as everyone else is losing their heads.

1. My father (far left) at seven in 1925 with his brother John and sisters Bernice and Stephanie. . . . Apparently my dad was a big fan of Moe from *The Three Stooges.*

2. My stepgrandmother Agnes, my dad, and my grandfather Michael during World War II

3. Clockwise, from upper left: my grandfather Tom, "Uncle," Aunt Lee, a friend, Aunt Joan, my mom, and cousin Geri during World War II

4 and 5. My gorgeous mother, Loretta—no wonder Mommy and Daddy got "married at an early urge."

6. My father and mother (who was pregnant with me) in Florida, with my two older sisters, JoAnn and Melody. A content, happy, normal family, completely unaware of the obsessive-ompulsive little demon who was about to invade their lives. . . . Nice trunks, Daddy.

7. Our house on Logan Boulevard in Chicago. No one would believe that this innocent-looking house had a dancing school in the garage, a beauty shop in the kitchen, eleven cats, two dogs, two birds, a skunk, 150 fish, ten humans, and a cat hospital.

8. I hate this picture of my father, but I love it for the rest of us. Clockwise, from upper left: Melody, JoAnn, my dad, Christal, my mom, Tommy, and me.

9. I used to tell new boyfriends that if they could find me in less than sixty seconds they'd get thirty minutes of "your wish is my command." I knew I'd marry Rob when he found me in one and a half seconds.

Saint John Berchmans GRADE 1 (1) 1958   PHOTOGRAPHY BY THE PALOMAR STUDIOS CHICAGO

10. The only kid at a wedding—I wore my hair up to look like a grown-up. From left: Melody, our friend Rosette, Mommy, me, and Daddy.

11. This is my favorite picture of me as a child. I loved that tutu so much I even wore it to bed.

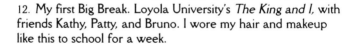

12. My first Big Break. Loyola University's *The King and I,* with friends Kathy, Patty, and Bruno. I wore my hair and makeup like this to school for a week.

13. No, it's *not* the Mamas and the Papas. That's me— the Dairy Queen—with my friend Jim Canning. Even in those days I did a lot of work modeling—for the face on the Kool-Aid pitcher.

14. One of the later Broadway companies of *Grease*—clockwise, from upper left: Ray de Mattis, Ellen March, Mimi Kennedy, Timothy Myers, Karen Dilly, Barry Tarallo (on the hood), Treat Williams driving, me as a blonde, and Matt Landers

15. Doing my Betty Grable number on Broadway in *Over Here*

16. With Lloyd

17. I played a stripper in my first movie, *Between the Lines,* here with Lindsey Crouse. I was wearing this makeup—including false eyelashes—when I flew first class to England to shoot a ring-around-the-collar commercial.

18. Between shows of *Over Here* with Johnny and Jim Canning

19. Kissing at Johnny's favorite place—the airport

20. At Lake Tahoe

21. The night we left for Europe, 1978

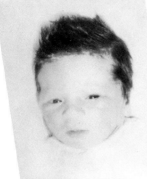

22. One hour old and already finding the lens

23. Awww. . . . I look so cute with my beaver teeth and hamster cheeks.

Marilu Henner
ACTRESS — SINGER
DANCER — MODEL

24. My actress-singer-dancer-modeling composite. I was fourteen and trying to look like my idols—Jane Fonda and Hayley Mills.

25. With my seventies do

26. My lucky 1978 headshot that helped me get *Taxi*

27. What do you *mean* they preferred Sharon Stone?

28. My tough leather jacket—windblown—foxy lady shot. Every actress in the early eighties had one.

Boston set the tone for the entire tour. We played over two weeks there. One Saturday, between the matinee and evening shows, we all went out to a famous seafood joint called Durgin Park, whose specialty was New England lobsters. The place had delicious lobster and terrible lighting. (I've never understood why great seafood always goes with bad lighting.)

One of us didn't finish his lobster. That night in the lunch scene during a moment when one of the guys is supposed to take out a tuna fish sandwich from his paper bag, he reached in and pulled out a lobster instead. The lobster made an appearance in various places throughout that performance, finally ending up in a locker for the rest of the weekend. From that point on, people were doing outrageous and crazy things onstage.

I had a moment in the pajama party scene where I take out my wallet and all the plastic-wrapped snapshots unfold. I'm supposed to look at my boyfriend Freddie and talk about him before singing, "Freddie My Love." Invariably, someone would get to the prop table first and slip in a photo of a naked man or a boyfriend with his head cut off in a devil costume. Anything to crack me up and throw me off. People were spraying shaving cream inside things so when you reached into a bag or behind something you'd get all messed up.

Johnny had an absurdly huge souvenir comb from Disneyland; he once used it to slick back his hair, and it cracked the audience up.

In the scene where Sandy, the sweet, innocent girl, calls Frenchie and asks her to bring over her makeup case, it's clear she's going to try to turn herself into a vixen. Then she sings a really sad song into the phone. Our sound guys had it wired up so that we could get on the line and breathe and say all sorts of nasty, wicked things into her ear as she sang into the phone.

Our cast was accident-prone, too. We got to know the emergency rooms in every city we visited. I did my ER time in Detroit in May 1973. Johnny was across the hall at the Leland Hotel and, when I told him I needed to nap before the show he promised to wake me up. The idea sounded so good to Johnny that he decided to nap too—and overslept until six-thirty. The curtain was rising in a half hour.

We scrambled out and sprinted through the lobby toward the revolving door. I angled my body through but left my hand behind me, and it got crunched by the door. When we got into the cab, I held my limp hand up and said, "Johnny, it's broken." We started laughing, because bone was practically piercing the skin. "Uhh," I added, "I'm like dying here."

When we arrived at the theater, they took one look and sent my understudy into action. I went to the ER and wound up with a cast on my hand for weeks. I missed the next week and went home to Chicago.

I got generally good reviews, except in Baltimore. The part of town where the hookers hung out was called The Block, and the reviewer said I was built like a girl from The Block. (I imagine he wrote that on good authority!)

Johnny got good reviews, too. There was no doubt that he was going to be big. He had such striking features—those big, plush lips; big, melancholy, warm blue eyes; big, distinct nose. And he was an incredible talent. Women loved his character Doody, a vulnerable puppy-dog, sad-sack type.

Not all shows sold out. Small-city matinees were killers. We had some tough audiences. In Columbus, I was given a matinee off so my understudy could log some stage time—a practice that applied to all of us. It was a huge 3,000-seater. I was sort of disappointed not to play to this crowd—until I came around from backstage to get my seat and got a good look at it.

About 300 people showed up. They immediately reminded me of that famous shot of a movie house full of people staring up at a screen wearing 3-D glasses. Every kid in town was at school, so we had 300 elderly ladies with blue hair, bad eyes, and oversized eyeglasses. They probably couldn't even hear the show.

By the time we got to Philly, Johnny was my best guy friend on the tour. We were always going out to eat, catching movies, or just sitting up all night talking. This is one of the payoffs for a girl who grows up with brothers: Your comfort level around guys tends to make friendship and communication much easier.

Johnny told me a great story about going to a gypsy fortune-teller on a whim as he was going to the theater. She was the kind who took your hand, stared at it, then said in a croaky voice, "Ahhh, I see you leev in a house, you come from a woman, you are a male . . ." But her rap went one better: "You have terrible curse on your head, you have bad spirits all around you. And I get reed of curse for you, eef you bring to me two boxes linguine, three cans Contadina tomato paste—not watery kind please—and Parmesan cheese." She was obviously cooking Italian that night. He left, determined to face his spirits and curses by himself.

In the early weeks of the tour, we were throwing ourselves so fiercely into the show that there was little or no intra-dating. Besides, the guys were all taken. I had been dating Doug in college, but after he spent a weekend with me in January of 1973, that sort of faded.

There was much excitement, between waiting for the reviews, being a working actress on tour, the road experience of arriving in strange cities, staying in new hotels with these new friends, exploring restaurants and sites, playing this character I knew so well by then, doing a dance number in city after city on local morning talk shows. And no more worrying about term papers or incompletes. (I had finished the incompletes months before.) I was five or six years younger than many of the actors in our cast, who were just getting their big break. So I felt that much farther ahead of the game. It was an extraordinary, fantastic time for me. I felt so alive.

Despite the warnings about my weight, I was still struggling—and no wonder: I had the worst eating habits. My idea of gourmet dining was a Reuben sandwich. I judged restaurants—entire *cities*—by their Reubens. That was my thing. Staying fat and having pimples and being constipated was also my thing, but at least I always knew where you could get a wicked Reuben sandwich. Corned beef, Muenster cheese, sauerkraut—and grilled in butter on rye bread. Whoa! Talk about an evil curse on your head. I wore *that* curse right on my face and butt.

Johnny and I were both still under twenty-one, so we were the only two actors who still had half-fare student standby cards. We were always plotting trips on our day off. When we were in Columbus, we took off for an overnight visit to Chicago. From Detroit, where we were holed up for three weeks and once had Sunday and Monday off, we flew off to L.A., just for the night. Johnny was like a little kid in one adorable way: He just loved airports, even before he started flying his own planes. We loved hanging out and eating in airport restaurants.

One thing that allowed us to get so close so fast was that we had none of the romantic issues to hang us up, since while I was unattached, Johnny had a lovely girlfriend, Denise Wurms. I met

Denise when she came out to visit once from L.A., and again when we took that overnight to L.A. And Johnny met my family when we did Indianapolis in early 1972.

If they had broken up early on our tour, we would have been having a hot and heavy affair. Our platonic friendship baffled more than a few people. One time when my sister JoAnn picked us up at the airport and met him for the first time, she said, "My God, why aren't you madly in love with this guy? He's so gorgeous, so darling."

"Who, Johnny?" I sounded shocked. "Don't be ridiculous. Johnny's my pal." I was almost insulted, because I never crossed that line if there was a girlfriend or wife in the picture. I've always respected those boundaries. In fact, whenever I've been attracted to a married or involved guy, I try to meet the woman right away. It personalizes the situation and cuts the attraction. Then I have two reactions. If she's great, I say, Well, no wonder he's with this great girl. If she's a skank, then it's, Thank God I *didn't* have anything to do with him. It's like she lowers his property value for me.

Denise, though, was a doll. It made sense they were together. She and I became pals. Though I sensed that things were becoming iffy in their relationship because of the separation, they were very much involved in each other's lives. And I was involved in their lives. They had grown up together. Denise's brother was Johnny's best friend. Johnny's sister Annie was understudying in the company. And I was delighted to feel part of this extended family.

There was very little of the jealous backbiting and bitchiness you often find in road companies. With a core ensemble of five guys and five girls, the dynamics of the show could only work if we were tight and supportive offstage. None of us was vying with anyone else for his or her attention. There were always intrigues and cliques, and some girls dated musicians in the orchestra. But there was no mean-spirited, cat-scratch action tearing us apart.

Whenever I had a show in the Midwest, I tried to go home. When I did, Johnny always asked me to bring back a fresh Uno's pizza. This was a year after the deadly Munich Olympics, and metal detectors were everywhere to guard against acts of international terrorism. Security agents never believed me when I told them I had a pizza in there. It's too bad the X rays didn't help to keep the pizzas warm, since I always had to pass the pies through the detectors.

Lorin came and visited us in Toronto. It was the first time he had flown alone. He called in advance, concerned about whether or not his blackhead extractor would get through the metal detectors. Imagine a fifteen-year-old boy being held by authorities as a terrorism suspect as they examine his blackhead extractor! (That alone would open his pores pretty efficiently, I would imagine.) This thing looked a lot more dangerous than a slice of pepperoni and mushroom. It was more like a crochet needle with a small eyelet at one end. You pressed it hard against your facial skin until blackheads and pimples popped. It was truly gross. Sometimes you missed and kept digging for oil for hours, leaving marks. But it was like Lorin's Pimple American Express card: He didn't dare leave home without it.

I knew I had come a long way in my self-assurance as a working actor when Lorin arrived. In fact, I almost got myself thrown out of the show over it. I was thrilled to have him with me for a whole week. But because I was going to be tied up at a rehearsal all day, I instructed Lorin about going through customs and taking public transportation to the theater. When he arrived he was so exhausted, he fell asleep in the audience.

By this time, we had a new stage manager on board who was out to prove to the company how tough he was. So he picked his first battle over my sleeping teenage brother. But he picked on the wrong kid—and the wrong sister.

He shook Lorin and told him he wasn't allowed at the closed rehearsal. This was a ludicrous power trip. I flew into what we called in my family "snorting snot" fury—spewing and raging and almost hyperventilating. I threw my first and only backstage fit.

Nobody crosses my family, and *no* show is worth performing in if you pay that kind of price. I was inconsolable and ready to risk everything.

"If you push me on this," I screamed, "I'm leaving the show. You want to get off on throwing someone out of here, try throwing *me* out of here." He's lucky Lorin didn't whip out his deadly blackhead extractor.

Once my close allies, writer Jim Jacobs and director Tom Moore, got involved, it was no contest and that was the end of that. But I learned something crucial from that incident—a complete intolerance for the injustice and humiliation that often seem to come with some people's bullshit star trips. I get crazy when I see people throwing their weight around and treating people like shit. This guy was a prick *from the start,* although he mellowed and we became friendlier later down the road.

Lorin settled in and we had a wonderful time together. I was thrilled to watch Lorin and Johnny, both the youngest of six children, hit it off the way they did. Lorin ended up staying an extra week, then hitched a ride on the cast bus from Toronto to Detroit before the three of us shared a teary good-bye at the airport when he flew home.

Johnny and I were by then so in sync we could pick up and fly off somewhere at a moment's notice. We became such close pals that we always booked single adjoining rooms, and neither of us made a move without the other. At two A.M., he'd knock on my door and say, "Can't sleep, let's go out and do something."

The amazing thing is there was, at this point, no sexual energy, no push in that direction whatsoever—and it worked beautifully just that way. We weren't like some priest and nun. We definitely *got* each other's sexuality. We took naps lying on the bed next to each other. We had all-night conversations *about* sex. I'd never known anyone I could talk to until sunrise without a break. It was that, and not sexual conquest, that was always at the core of our connection.

Romance was not an issue at this point. I was a confidante who was in on everything going on with Denise. I gave advice. More than an urge for seduction, there was profound comfort and exhilaration in knowing we would be in each other's lives forever.

I was, in fact, one of the least wild girls in the company; winter and spring had been a very long, very dry spell. But then, at the beginning of June, when the company did a week in Denver, I hooked up with Foster. And not a moment too soon.

Foster was a great affair. I had met him when I baby-sat my two nieces and Foster, a friend of JoAnn's, came over with his wife, a gorgeous Swedish girl named Natasha who was a ballerina or ski champion or international spy—something like that. I took one look at Foster—who, at twenty-eight, was twice my age—and swooned. Wealthy, extremely handsome with his Omar Sharif mustache and dark, sexy looks, he drove me up the wall.

Cut to eight years later: JoAnn tells me he and Natasha have divorced and he's living in Denver.

"Give him a call," she told me. Most people dial 911 when they need an emergency rescue. I dialed 411 for mine.

"Do you want to come see the show?" I asked him. He did, then took me to dinner. Now thirty-six, he was still gorgeous and darling and easy to be with. And nothing happened.

I spent my day off with Foster. He drove me up into the mountains around Boulder and pulled over for some breathtaking vistas. I was just *dying* to be seduced. I didn't have long to wait. We drove back to his place in town, and I stayed over—thus commencing an absolutely ideal weeklong affair.

Back in those days, when affairs and flings and spontaneous urges weren't the life-threatening events they've come to be, you could have a perfect, anxiety-free affair. All you needed was a mutually acceptable context. The context—the limits—framed your little work of sexually gratifying art. Once you were in that frame, and knew your limits, you could fill your canvas with the greatest, richest time imaginable. Foster and I did just that for the week we played Denver. We both knew it wasn't going anywhere, but it didn't matter. We vowed to stay in touch. I was off to L.A. for our three-month summer run. Our week together had been well worth the wait.

In L.A., *Grease* was one of the hottest tickets in town. All the stars came to see us sooner or later and stopped by to say hi backstage.

Lorin flew in and had a summer job as usher, doubling up as softball pitcher for the weekly cast-crew games in Rancho Park. Lorin could have been an eagle-eyed Secret Service trainee the way he'd scan arriving hordes for two of his idols, Goldie Hawn and Groucho Marx. His whole summer was waiting for Goldie or Groucho. Goldie did show up, and Lorin almost lost it. He took an empty seat behind her and just stared at her the whole show.

During intermission, he went up to her and said, "I've been waiting for you and Groucho Marx all summer," and offered her the sweaty yellow *Grease* T-shirt off his back. She passed.

I got a one-bedroom apartment in Westwood for the summer. By early July, it was clear that Johnny and Denise were on the outs. He was back at his place at the Larrabee Apartments in West Hollywood, between Sunset and Santa Monica. I certainly had not been watching their impending breakup opportunistically. He and I did everything together, had dinner all the time, stayed up until the middle of the night talking. We had traveled a dozen times together as buddies. Now, I could offer consoling, perspective-enhancing support; but it wasn't like I was going to make a move to jump in. Plus, I had just had my wild week with Foster.

Still, Johnny and I were best friends. There was no one else I could talk to and laugh with like him. There was simply no reason to change our relationship and run the risk of ruining everything. It was a classic *When Harry Met Sally* conflict, except that I had no conflict. I was clear in my mind: The status quo worked perfectly for both of us, and there was absolutely no reason in the world to jeopardize it.

Except for one small detail: Johnny didn't see it that way.

After the second weekend of July, on Monday the 9th, our day off, we went to Disneyland and had a blast. We had already made plans to go to San Francisco on one of our getaways the next weekend and low-road it at a Ramada Inn or Travelodge. As far as I figured, it would be like all the other trips we'd taken as best friends. Just because it was over with Denise didn't mean anything had changed for me.

But somewhere between Fantasyland and Adventureland, Johnny stopped, faced me, and hit me with a question that sounded right out of our greaser show: "You know, Henner," he said, "when we go up north this weekend, what do you think about *it?*"

It was as if Doody had finally gotten his nerve up and was laying some fifties line on me.

"What do I think about *what?*" I asked. I wanted to make sure I wasn't hearing strange things through his vagueness.

He shifted his weight nervously. "How about we get together." I instantly thought: *Us? Are you kidding me?*

Then I thought about it some more as we walked, and a voice-over in my head said: Us. My God, yeah. Right. *Why not?*

6
When Mari
Met Johnny

For years one of my favorite phrases has been "figures prominently." It always came up while playing with my eight-ball as a
kid, and, later, while reading horoscopes. I later found that it
applies perfectly to the movies—and to life as well.

Imagine a key scene in a thriller where a jealous, suspicious wife
confronts an unfaithful husband who's come home as she's opening the mail. If the director then cuts to a close-up of her
razor-sharp letter opener, you can assume it "figures prominently"
in the climax.

When we rewind the movie of our life, it's fascinating to see what
behavior, incidents, or props end up figuring prominently in the
plot twists. Even though we are all both star and director in our
lives, we can sometimes miss our own clues and telling details.
Sometimes, the person you cast for romantic lead ends up a
walk-on, cameo, or extra. And vice versa.

When Johnny and I left for San Francisco, he was nervously
awaiting the outcome of his audition for a key role in a movie with
Jack Nicholson, *The Last Detail*. Once he'd arrived in L.A.,
Johnny's career had taken off. He had an aggressive manager, Bob
Lemond; he was seeing people all over town about TV series and
movies; and there was an industry buzz about him.

In our movie, his career would "figure prominently" in the ways
our relationship was about to change.

For romantic settings, you can't do any better than San Francisco, and so our night together around Fisherman's Wharf and at
the Travelodge was absolutely incredible—tender, open, passion-

ate. It wasn't some big now-it's-time-for-me-to-seduce-you thing. Our slide into intimacy didn't have a dramatic movie-score-montage feel to it. But it was hardly disappointing. It was natural and effortless, more like: Oh, we're going to sleep over like we used to, but now we get to play doctor, too. There was a comfortable, exploratory feel to it, and I felt closer to him than I ever had before.

The next night, Johnny checked in with his manager and found out that Randy Quaid had gotten the part. Johnny's life would probably have been quite different had he gotten that role. He would have had his breakthrough with a dopey-misfit persona instead of a Brooklyn stud with raging PF. But this was no time for sulking, and Johnny was never one to wallow anyway.

"Let's go to Vegas," he said, just like that. Johnny's idea was that when you're disappointed, don't throw a pity party, get out of town. Throw a new reality into the mix. Get stimulated.

We were together, off on one of our adventures, and I was getting a big lesson in Plan B strategy: When in doubt, travel.

After a week together back in L.A., and another weekend trip two weeks later, I felt we had definitely blossomed from friendship to genuine couplehood. He and I were never ones to miss our cue for passion. One hot rendezvous spot was a tiny first-aid room backstage at the Shubert Theater. It was just down the hall from where musicians entered the orchestra pit, and had a cot and a lock. That was all we needed for the fifteen or twenty minutes between the first and second acts. To some, such obstacles would have meant "Intermission Impossible." Not us. We decided to accept our mission. We did this more than a dozen times that summer and somehow never got caught.

Backstage looked just like high school—all ugly cinder blocks and bad lighting. It was fun to pretend we were being kept after school for being bad—and getting even worse in the nurse's room. The ultimate detention fantasy for a pair of good Catholic kids.

I couldn't help but put a typically feminine "hearts and flowers" haze on things. Johnny's thinking was more typically guy stuff, like: "Hey, we're still buddies, only now we have sex." In the aftermath of San Francisco, we were obviously fumbling our way through, and not expressing real needs and wants—beyond, of course, first aid at the Shubert.

What I needed was lots of intimacy and affection. My switch had been flicked. Having taken the plunge from platonic to passionate, I felt incredibly alive and sexual and vulnerable, so turned on to romance, to being in love, to being made love to. I had waited a long time to feel this way.

Meanwhile, Johnny was spending more and more time with his career. He was busy with auditions and meetings, and less available than I had hoped. I wanted a love affair with picnics in the afternoon. What I got was guys picking up my very-out-there sexual vibe and zeroing in. Everything was connected to everything. As my mom used to advise: "Always have a spare."

I found myself not with a spare, but a pair. And brothers to boot, two adorable guys I met through the cast softball team. They were sniffing around all summer long, and I ended up in a heavy flirtation with one of them. Johnny and I managed to muddy things up in a hurry after the clarity of the Travelodge.

One issue was simply that my feelings were too intense for the kind of relationship we could have at that time. Another was that the show was scheduled to go to Chicago, and me with it, while Johnny was looking for a career move that would keep him in L.A. When we were together, he was, like, "Oh, God, I love you, love your body, love sleeping with you." But he was also going: "I have to worry about my career; we're still technically on the road and who knows what's going to happen in September?" With L.A. feeling like home to him and like the road to me, he slammed on the brakes.

Once in Chicago, I moved in with my former college roommates. It was a sweet homecoming for me. I was so glad to be close to my mom and my siblings; I also got back into teaching dance to preteen girls. I visited Johnny a couple of times a month and we had our usual marathon phoners twice or three times a week. But the momentum of romance had been broken.

I had tried losing weight through the summer, with little success. I didn't obsess over it, but after one of our Chicago shows the message came through pretty loud and clear—and from no less a connoisseur of the female figure than Pat, the husband of Doris, my sex-goddess idol. Pat and Doris came to a show and stopped backstage afterward.

"You've got star quality," Pat told me, "and you were incredible onstage. But I'm going to tell you this only because I love you and have seen you grow up. If you want to be a star, you have to lose twenty, twenty-five pounds."

I was shocked. I had never seen myself as that heavy, and I

thought my fifties wardrobe hid much of it. Pat's comments came out of nowhere, but I took them to heart—and to hip.

I began investigating various diets and fads. Starvation was always a surefire way to drop a quick five in forty-eight hours. It didn't exactly make performing more fun, but I was suddenly on a semidesperate kick to trim down. Pat's comment marked a turning point for me. My weight-loss lightbulb went off, and soon I went on Weight Watchers.

During one of my visits west to see Johnny, in October, he and I went to the home of our *Grease* director, Tom Moore, for dinner. Tom was now planning to do a Broadway musical with the Andrews Sisters called *Over Here.* He played us some of the tunes for the show, but said, rather apologetically, "There's really nothing in the show for either of you." We were like, Hey, no problem. Neither of us was dying to be in it anyhow.

Figures prominently.

In the first week of December, I took a trip to New York. I missed my old cast buddy Ellen March, who was in the Broadway company of *Grease,* so I arranged to stay with her Sunday night when I arrived.

The next day, she had a singing class, so we decided to meet at the theater. I went a little early to hang out with a bunch of the *Grease* people. When I got backstage, I realized some were there to audition for Tom's *Over Here* cast.

I had recently cut my hair short and dropped twenty pounds. I looked really different. Many of my former road company pals backstage barely recognized me. They assumed I was in character for a role. One of the guys said mischievously, "Tom's out front. Why don't you just go out onstage and I'll announce you."

We came up with a fictitious name and I put a beret on. I slowly entered the stage with my back to the seats and started kicking some little steps. A cigarette dangled from my hand.

"Excuse me, excuse me," I heard some of the people out front yelling angrily. They had no résumé or glossy telling them who I was, and had no idea what was going on. Usually, auditions are rigidly controlled and intimidating, but I knew these people. And there was nothing at stake. I was doing this on a lark, and I was completely loose.

Suddenly, I stopped, whirled around to face them, and blew smoke out with a vampy flourish.

"Marilu, oh my God," Tom screamed. He was beaming. "You look terrific. I can't believe this. What're you *doing* here?"

"I'm waiting for Ellen."

"Are you here to audition?"

"Well, no, Tom. Remember, you told Johnny and me there were no parts for us." Tom, his producers, and his casting people quickly leaned their heads together and huddled in their seats.

"Marilu," Tom said, "why don't you sing something."

"Are you kidding?" This was ridiculous. There were a dozen people waiting to audition and I was just screwing around. Now, I was auditioning for a Broadway musical cast.

"Do you know anything from the forties?"

"I know 'Goody Goody.' "

"Okay, great."

I knew the set and stage, and Tom was a pal. I felt surprisingly at ease. I just let it rip and belted out the song with no rehearsal. "That was great," he said when I finished. "Can you read something for us?"

"Sure." No problem. It was the part of Donna, the waitress. They had apparently made some script changes, I had made some weight changes, and it seemed as if the character had just found me. As I left for Chicago the next day, I kept thinking: God, could this work out? Maybe I shouldn't get too attached to the idea.

Johnny called from L.A. with amazing news. "You're not going to believe this," he said, "but there might be a part in this musical for me. I've already auditioned for it."

"What show?"

"Tom's new musical—*Over Here.*"

"What? You're kidding," I shrieked. I told him what had happened and we were both in hysterics thinking we could be working together again for a year—and on *Broadway!*

"Can you imagine," I gushed, "our spending another year together? This is unbelievable, this is fabulous. Okay, four things can happen," I said, trying to be rational. "We both don't get it; we both get it; you do and I don't; I do and you don't. Oh, please God," I went on, "I'm really gonna tweak on this."

That's what I call it when I beam intense psychic energy on something to influence events. I truly believe certain people can tweak and make stuff happen, and not just the Uri Geller–teaspoon-bender types. If my energy field can keep an unplugged clock radio going for hours, why not tweak for stuff?

Johnny and I had certainly defied labeling, and that had been one of our strengths. It was friendship, it was lust. It was distance, it was intimacy. The danger was that he and I simply wanted different things. Yes, we could have an extraordinary time together, adore each other, get each other, party and have great sex. I once had this vision of our connection as this long, long corridor, with all kinds of colorful, adventure-filled rooms off to both sides as you walked down. Some doors led to incredible trips together, others to wild and fascinating parties; some took us on weekends with close friends and family.

But the door you walked into straight ahead at the very end of the corridor was the whole-rest-of-our-lives-together door, and it was the one that led to what I felt might be the danger zone. That was the door I'd open when I fell totally, madly, in love with Johnny. I wasn't ready for that one yet. But there were still all kinds of other doors for us to open—and I was tweaking hard that week that one of them would lead us to Broadway.

Over the weekend, my telepathic powers helped me navigate my way through a trip—and not the kind that has anything to do with travel.

After our matinee on Sunday, December 9, we had a cast party at a friend's house, and I was, naturally, starved. I spotted a plate of thick, yummy brownies and tore into them like there was no tomorrow. As a result, there almost *was* no tomorrow.

After my fourth brownie, someone who noticed me eating came over with a look of concern. "You *know* what's in those brownies, right?" he said ominously. I gave him a naïve shrug, and his pained grimace told me all I needed to know. I froze.

"You're kidding me," I said.

"Uh-uh."

The idea of hash brownies was totally insane—I *never* did drugs. The idea of *brownies* was daring enough, since I never even liked chocolate as a kid; I even had licorice Easter bunnies. But I was hungry. Plus, shouldn't there be Surgeon General warnings on hash brownies saying they could severely fuck up your mind for days? I had been worried about getting fat; now I was worried about not getting home alive.

This experience had some serious special effects. I was sure I was paralyzed. Everything moved in slow motion. I saw a tiny rock singer on a stage giving an entire concert—in the *fireplace.* Some guy who had been coming on to me sat next to me on the couch and started talking, but I couldn't be sure he was actually there and real or not, or if any of it was happening to *me.*

Then it got *really* weird. My actress friend Rebecca was talking to a musician from the show. Suddenly, I saw in my mind a Little Rebecca inside Rebecca and a Little Marilu inside me, and these tiny clones were crawling down endless, narrow ladders inside our gigantic bodies. They got to the last rung and met in the middle of the room.

Little Rebecca said to Little Marilu: "Please get me out of here. I'm going to give you a fight, but I want you to get me out of here. I cannot stay with this guy. You must do this for me."

Meanwhile, I was still in a conversation with the guy coming on to me, who must have had second thoughts when I blurted out to no one in particular: "Oh, all right, Rebecca, come on, let's go. We have to split right now." With that, Little Marilu and Little Rebecca crawled all the way up the ladders and straight back into our minds.

Rebecca leaned over and said: "Marilu, what are you talking about. Are you kidding? We're leaving?" She put up a huge fuss, which I'd known she would.

"No, trust me," I insisted. "I know what I'm doing."

Outside, Rebecca sighed. "Oh, thank God you did that for me. I don't know *how* you knew. I thought you were out there in your own world, but it's incredible you picked up on me and that guy. He's *married.*" Rebecca was thrilled I had rescued her from herself.

I got in my car—a brand-new Mazda—and soon realized I wasn't driving anywhere. I felt like I was sitting underwater. My foot couldn't find the gas pedal. My entire nervous system had closed down for the night.

I explained to Rebecca what had happened. We got out and hailed a cab to go to her place. Once we got there, I had to eat. I felt hollow and crazed. Soon I was slapping together peanut butter and jelly sandwiches from a jar of preswirled peanut butter and jelly. I didn't care. I was in the throes of a major munchie seizure. The food helped bring me down—eight hours or so after the brownies. I made it home and called Johnny in L.A. and talked to him for three hours. It was one weird, tough, scary episode. Not once since that night have I ever had any trouble just saying no to drugs—or to brownies.

* * *

I came down just in time. Monday night, Tom Moore's casting director phoned me to ask if I could fly in Tuesday morning for a callback for *Over Here*. "You're kidding," I groaned. I was still in recovery.

"Well, let me put it this way," she said. "You have a really good shot at this. But if you don't come in you're not going to get it. So you might as well take the chance."

I flew in Tuesday morning, did the audition, turned right around, and went home for Tuesday night's show in Chicago. I was flying. Late that night, Johnny called to tell me he got the part. He was out-of-his-mind excited. *This just has to work,* I kept thinking.

On Wednesday, during the matinee intermission, the company manager got a call and waved me over to break the news. I tried to stay cool, but my heart was pounding like a jackhammer: "You got it," he said, "and you're leaving this Sunday."

I started screaming and jumping, and everyone gathered around to congratulate me. The notion that I was about to *originate* a part on *Broadway* was almost more than I could grasp.

Because the same producers did the two shows, I was released from my *Grease* contract and signed on for *Over Here* as of December 17, when rehearsals started in New York. Johnny and I were jazzed. We stayed with his family in the New Jersey suburbs and bused in to the Port Authority every morning, going over our lines and sheet music together like two giddy kids looking at each other's homework on the school bus. We had a great cast: the dancer Ann Reinking, in her first big Broadway role; Treat Williams; the Andrews Sisters. This was to be the most expensive Broadway musical ever, we were told. And the payoff, of course, was that Johnny and I were reunited.

After I spent Christmas in Chicago, we took the show down to Philadelphia for previews and to work out the kinks before opening on Broadway. The first time I heard the show in a large ballroom with our full twenty-eight-piece orchestra, my head almost blew off, it was so thrilling. The show's whole look, sound, feel, and body language was pure forties—lush, romantic, stylish. It was a period I had always loved in the movies, more than the fifties and sixties. Plus, I fell madly in love with my character, Donna, a good-hearted waitress who is obsessed with old movies.

Johnny and I had a blast during our month in Philadelphia. For fun, he and I went to the same fortune-teller, who once again gave him a grocery list—this one called for ingredients to whip up a Chinese meal—to rid him of his demons and curses.

We stayed in a funky, cheap dive called the Morris Hotel. While I was out on our day off, Johnny got ambitious and cooked what he called "guacamole especiale"—tuna fish and guacamole heated up together. The only thing that was especiale was the fire he started when he dozed off and the pan caught fire. I came home to a street roped off for fire-fighting equipment. But at least Johnny had a new recipe for tuna melt.

We should have known right then and there that we were in for a rough ride. It was an enormous show, designed to take place on a train, with a three-level stage (the big band rising in a band shell at the back of the stage like at the Hollywood Bowl), and a treadmill that moved people across the stage. It had to work like a Swiss watch, but it came together more like Swiss cheese.

Things were completely falling apart left and right. If Johnny's two-alarmer wasn't foreboding enough, Tom Moore fell into the orchestra pit and nearly wiped out. I loved being the organized one amidst chaos. I knew from dance and choreography that sometimes things have to come totally apart before real creativity—and some happy accidents—can emerge.

Two weeks before we opened, almost the entire show—script, songs, choreography—was changed. There were things now we had no time to learn; other numbers we had spent hundreds of man-hours to get right were scrapped. We felt adrift, with no focus, no cohesion. We tossed everything but the kitchen sink at every problem. One of the big numbers, "Scuttlebutt," opened the second act. Treat and I had a blast with it, because we were caught kissing in different places all over the stage. It was a cute, special moment for me. But the audience didn't get what it was about *at all* and it was pretty lame. The number was scratched, just like that.

One day, it was decided that for one song, the guys would hold up sticks with Frank Sinatra masks on them and the girls would wear formal ball gowns. It was something they had obviously come up with in desperation. Johnny came up with a classic line. He brushed in front of me clutching his Sinatra mask and quipped, "Gee, I hope the PTA likes our show."

That was so dead-on. No matter how big and important the job is, behind the scenes is always so hamper. But it was an invaluable learning experience. I witnessed the making of a Broadway musical, and I got to create a character, and you learn you might open and close in one night or become part of a classic. You never know.

Johnny's big show-stopping number at the end was an outrageously complex sequence that required three treadmills, the orchestra rising on its hydraulic lift, and lots of precise commotion onstage and frantic costume changes offstage. Johnny was especially excited that night because we had heard Bette Midler was in attendance. With very little rehearsing, though, the climax was wired for disaster.

It should have worked. I go around the stage and take everybody's dream order and they get acted out like scenes from a Busby Berkeley production. Mine was winning Miss America. I turn my back on the audience and unzip my gown. Underneath I've got a white Betty Grable outfit and I peek back and do a forties cheesecakey smile.

Then I go to him, "Okay, that's one Esther Williams, one Sonja Henie, one Miss America. So what's your dream?"

"I don't know," he says.

"Well," I answer in a sassy tone, "if you're going to dream, dream big." Johnny starts tapping on the table and singing, "I'm Dream-Drumming." He wants to be Gene Krupa. At this moment, his little tune turns into an extravaganza with a complete set change. The orchestra gets treadmilled across the stage, playing sequined instruments, and the Andrews Sisters come over the top level, also sequined.

Within seconds, it broke down into frenzied chaos: Folding chairs and music stands toppled; people missed their marks and collided; Johnny started improvising, trying not to look totally lost and embarrassed.

The audience loved the show. But Johnny was devastated and vanished afterward. At two in the morning, he called from the airport. Despondent and humiliated, he said he was quitting the show and flying that night to L.A. I talked him out of it. It wasn't that hard: There were no flights out and he had no money.

"Could you wait up for me?" he asked forlornly. "I don't have any money for the cab fare."

We fine-tuned the show for Broadway and opened on March 6, 1974. In the two months we'd been in New York, Johnny and I had taken an apartment together and then decided to get separate places. Although we were very close, we both wanted to start dating other people. I got a fourth-floor, one-bedroom walkup in a West

Eighties brownstone near Central Park. Great way to keep your legs toned.

My mom, two brothers, and sister Melody came in the night before for the opening. The Henners Go to Gotham!

Knowing I would be at the theater when they taxied into town, I instructed them to go to my address, ring the first-floor tenant, who would buzz them in, and go up and wait. Simple.

Because my mother's arthritis had become increasingly painful, traveling was an ordeal. So was traveling with Tommy, who decided he had to shower less than an hour before takeoff. That, plus my mother's slowness, had Melody, who was already at O'Hare, going crazy, urging gate attendants not to close the door.

Finally, my brother showed up, pushing my mother in a wheelchair they had grabbed to pick up speed. Now, these three crazies and a crippled lady were trying to get to their seats, seething and cursing in front of a cabinful of weary businessmen and travelers— "You cocksucker," "Yeah, well, fuck you, too, asshole," "Goddamn motherfucker, you're always late." All of this delivered in Linda Blair voices from *The Exorcist*—the passengers from hell.

They got uptown, rang the buzzer, got upstairs, and waited. And waited. Finally, a woman walked to the fourth floor and froze when she saw four strangers with luggage parked at her door. "Hey, howya doin'," Tommy said. "Where's Marilu?"

"Who are you people and why are you at my apartment?"

My brother had turned my address—48 West Eighty-second Street—into something like 28 West Eighty-fourth Street.

Hamper, Manhattan style.

Johnny and I both earned strong notices on opening night. The show improved technically through the spring and summer, and so did our relationship. We could have terrific times together with no commitment. That may even have been the key: No questions asked.

The montage from our *Over Here* time remains vivid and wonderful. We spent whole days off going from movie to movie to movie to catch up. One time we sat at the fountain by the Plaza as I taught him the James Taylor song "Long Ago and Far Away." He once proudly waved a $181 commercial residual check in my face and vowed to spend every penny of it with me that night. One time he decided to drink two beers—the only time I had ever seen him drunk—and he became quite frisky and seduced me.

"You should drink more often," I told him.

Johnny left the show in September to pursue film and TV series work. I missed him terribly.

Once after he left, without telling me he was coming to town for a week to shoot a commercial, Johnny popped out of a bathroom stall in the girls' dressing room. I jumped into his arms, screaming like a lunatic. We had a whole week together at the Warwick Hotel, doing the usual Johnny things we loved doing.

I stayed with *Over Here* through the fall. By then, things were poppin'. I had all kinds of agents looking for projects and I was offered what was then an amazing contract—$650 a week, up from $375—to take the show on the road. I was psyched.

Always one to keep a spare, I did find someone who helped fill the void after Johnny left town. He was an extremely intriguing mentor figure twice my age who was separated from his wife. Johnny knew the guy—we had all spent some evenings together. I never mistook this for a torrid romance.

What I got mostly from him wasn't romance, but confidence in coping with my own emotional and psychological issues. As a good, self-reliant, intuitive Catholic girl, I found it striking that so many of New York's artistic people were in therapy. This brilliant guy had his devils, to be sure. But he inspired me by facing them, chasing them. Through him, I found myself increasingly drawn to people—whether at a party, at the theater, or with girlfriends—with an introspective, analytic side to them. I tended to gravitate to people at parties who were in therapy and had that sort of *searching* intensity. Similarly, this man spent a good deal of time sharing with me how therapy was helping him—and urging me to give it a shot. I mulled it over.

It was timely advice. At Christmas, the bottom dropped out. Two weeks before I was supposed to go on the road, the producers pulled the plug. The Andrews Sisters had apparently failed to work out some of their sibling rivalries, so that was it. Having counted on the road company, I now had nothing to do, nowhere to go.

But as I had learned with Johnny: When in doubt, travel.

In January, Tom Moore, a friend, and I decided to drive cross-country, getting to Chicago just in time for my mother's birthday on January 10. Tom and I had become very close, platonic friends. It turned out to be an extraordinary adventure—Minneapolis, Des Moines, Cheyenne, Aspen, the Grand Canyon, Vegas, and on to L.A. for two weeks. We stayed in decent motels, taking two double beds. It was no big deal for Tom and me to share a bed. In L.A. I stayed at Johnny's because he was out of town shooting *The Devil's Rain.*

I had my own devils to face. Having eaten my feelings and driven my feelings, I learned that a cross-country road trip allows you to eat and drive your feelings *at the same time.*

The farther west I got, the more depressed I became as it sank in that my big-time contract had fallen through. Tom and I pigged out on road food. I indulged myself, didn't care, lapsed into vacation mode. About every 200 miles, I put on another pound. I hadn't been out of a job in two years. I just pigged out and ballooned up, from coast to coast. It was sad: After all the discipline and hard work to drop all that weight, I now had an extra layer of padding.

By the time I got back to New York in mid-February, I was literally eating my way to unemployment, and stopping at any number of gourmet pit stops that lined the route. I was fat, depressed, beet-red from sunburn, and out of work. I had hit my first true dead end.

You know you're in bad shape when you cancel all appointments on account of fatness.

I couldn't bear to be seen by an agent looking like that. I made up that I had horrible conjunctivitis just to get out of auditioning.

My mysterious eye infection—and porker self-pity—cleared up instantaneously in the first week of March. The cure: a call from the *Grease* producers, who asked me to take over as Marty on Broadway.

I had four weeks to get it together and lose fifteen pounds. I felt saved, and threw myself into feverish conditioning.

But the show hardly proved to be a panacea. I was working, yes; trimmer, yes. But happy? Hardly.

In July I went home for Melody's wedding and got so rip-roaring drunk on vodka gimlets that I sent the food back to have it weighed—as if this were some Weight Watcher's spa wedding. I didn't even *like* vodka gimlets, but then again, a wedding isn't exactly the best place for a single woman in her twenties when she's feeling alone, desperate to fall in love. In those days I called myself a P.O.W.—a Professional Other Woman, because I was meeting nothing but married, taken, or otherwise unavailable guys. When was *my* partner going to find me?

Johnny was committed to L.A. He had done the pilot for a new upcoming fall '75 show called *Welcome Back, Kotter* and was on the brink of superstardom for his brilliantly sketched Vinnie Barbarino. He had also been dating a stunning dark-haired actress from the devil movie named Joan Prather. We talked and he'd visit when in town, but we were in friend mode.

Joan was deeply committed to the Church of Scientology and turned Johnny on to it. Johnny loved Scientology, and said it made a tremendous difference. We talked a lot about Scientology and, though I saw its beneficial impact on him, I felt, simply, that it was not for me at the time.

Not that I knew what *was* for me. Happy as I was to be working, the Marty role had worn thin after playing her for four years. It was time to move on. My heart wasn't in it anymore, and I obviously wasn't fooling anyone close to me.

Lynne, the show's stage manager, confronted me one day: "What's wrong? You look like you're in a fog these days," she said. Her intuitions were right on. I knew there was more compassion than accusation in her voice, and I liked her. Still, I was stunned. "It's not affecting your work, somehow," she went on, "but you just look really *numb*. You're clearly not happy, not in touch."

She got *that* right—and then she gave me a number to call.

In late July, I picked up the phone, and, for the first time in my life, I heard myself utter the words, "I need help."

7
The Incredible
Shrinking Woman

I knew it was time for therapy when I took the subway downtown to the Psychoanalytic Institute.

I lived at Eighty-third and Broadway, so I walked to the Seventy-ninth Street station and boarded a local. My destination was Fourteenth Street, an express stop. As complex as New York life is, it all sometimes comes down to one burning issue: express or local? It's always a gamble to get off a poky local to wait for an express at junctions like West Ninety-sixth, Seventy-second, and Forty-second streets. In a city mind-set where minutes, even seconds count, the number 2 and 3 expresses are New Yorkers' answer to bullet trains. Timing is everything.

The number 1 local got to Seventy-second Street and the doors opened just as an express barreled into the station across the platform. I'm thinking: Should I make a run for it, or stay put? Make a run for it; stay put? I was frozen in indecision.

Impulsively, I darted out across the platform, but the express train's doors closed just as I got there. I slammed my palm against the window in frustration. Then I wheeled around and dashed back to the local as *its* doors closed.

There I stood, running late, in the middle of the platform with both trains whizzing by me, going, "Now I know why I'm going to therapy." When you manage to miss the train you're *on,* and miss two trains *at once,* you're ready to make some changes.

I was missing my cues, not hitting my marks. Glimpsing, then missing, opportunities. I wasn't using all my resources. I was sinking into one of the darkest periods of my life.

After calling for my appointment a week earlier, I had made up my mind that in the week to come, I would heal myself, get in touch with my feelings. I wouldn't say no when I meant yes, stuff like that. Then I'd breeze into the doctor's office and she would size me up and say: "You don't need therapy; let's have lunch." Then we'd breeze out, we would become new best friends, do lunch, and go shopping. I had it all worked out.

And then I missed two trains getting there. That's how together and sure of myself I was.

I walked in and instantly disliked the therapist who interviewed me. She was too intense, too serious, too old to go to my pajama party. Maybe this wasn't such a great idea.

"If I decide to go ahead with this," I hedged, "who would be my therapist?"

"I might be," she said.

"Well, I wouldn't like that."

"Why?" she asked.

"Well, I'm not sure I want to work with you."

"Well, I'm not sure I want to work with you."

We were really getting somewhere now. I was outraged that someone might not want to work with me. I felt challenged.

I went to Lynne, the stage manager, for sympathy, but got a reality check: "She sounds *exactly* like someone you should work with," she said.

The issue was making commitments—to projects, to myself, to relationships. I was getting lazy as an actress. I wasn't disciplined when it came to food and exercise and regimens, or to agents and workshops. It was time to draw the line, so, despite the near-instant animal dislike that flowed so effortlessly between us, I began seeing Dr. Ruth Velikovsky Sharon.

Sure enough, things started changing immediately. That year would be a major time of transition as I laid the groundwork for future moves.

Two major changes: Commercial work started pouring in, and I began an intense love affair with a man I believed I was meant to be with my whole life.

Great sex will do that.

The commercial jobs—amusing, often mindless, always lucrative—were amazing. In the next two years I did twenty-eight of them and made well over $40,000 a year, a ton of money for a theater actress.

The first one marked my comeback in a Playtex bra, ten years after my dancing bra and girdle gig. It was four office girls going, "It's got sass, it's sheer and seamless support!" In another, I declared, "I'm what you'd call well-developed. But my support bra—here, let me show you." Cut to a plastic mold of the bra superimposed on me as I go, "See, now look at this."

What a weird shoot. My silk blouse had to be completely smooth. TV bras not only didn't accentuate your bust back then, they flattened it. I had a woman under my dress whose job it was to lie down on a board with rollers like a car mechanic and tug on my blouse to keep it wrinkle-free. Mighty embarrassing. (With all the guys in the world who would *volunteer* for that kind of work, why pay a woman to do it?)

From there I became the Ponderosa Steak House Girl, and played Helen Keller's teacher Annie Sullivan in an Exxon "Bicentennial Minute" aired during the '76 celebration. We shot fifteen scenes in two days out of town, all based on *The Miracle Worker*. It was a beautiful piece of work, and the ad and I both got nominated for a Clio award.

I became a "body parts" model. I did hands for Wisk and Joy detergent, I flashed my teeth as a Little League mom for Gleem, and I can only guess what body part they were featuring for Reese's peanut butter cups. I even earned some money on my back—I spent one whole day lying down in panty hose for Fruit of the Loom. All you saw was my legs sticking out of a giant apple in heels and panty hose.

Then there were my shoots for Playtex panties. You waited around in a room full of gorgeous women in leotards and swimsuits. (A true bonding milieu—cutthroat competition intensified by feeling like a piece of raw meat.) Then they snapped a roll of crotch-shot Polaroids in a room full of guys. The photographer leaned down and in to crop you just right, then asked you to turn around so they could shoot your butt and thighs and see just how tight your gut was. It was done more matter-of-factly than lasciviously, but there was no way to avoid feeling mildly exploited.

When it rained it poured.

One of the men in my *Grease* cast, Lloyd Alan, an understudy for the Danny Zuko role, had a huge crush on me. He had asked me out a couple of weeks before I started therapy. I said no and he got so upset that later he started kicking around chairs at home. A real catch. He acted like a jerk around me all the time. I never imagined anything could develop.

But when he filled in, we ended one scene together in a freeze, with his arm around me as the stage went black. He took that moment to get to know me, and to tell me how attracted he was.

Lloyd was rather adorable, in a smirky, curly-haired, Jimmy Caan-as-Sonny-Corleone way. Once he took over the role, it was amazing: He *was* Danny Zuko. Women stormed the stage to get to Lloyd. He drove them nuts with a combination of macho bravado, vulnerability, humor, and sexiness.

After two therapy sessions, I said yes to a dinner, and felt emboldened enough to spell things out plain and simple for him. "Basically," I said, "a lot of bullshit games have brought us to this point. If it's not going to be honest from now on, then let's forget this. If it is, then I'm making a date with you right now for tomorrow night."

"I'm not going to be like that," he said sheepishly.

With the ground rules in place, we hit it off beautifully. We went out the next night, and two nights later, on his birthday, August 15. By Labor Day, we were a couple. I began to get the feeling that, finally, Lloyd was the boyfriend I had been waiting for all along.

The news was not universally hailed. When Ken and Maxine, our producers, found out I was dating him, they actually hung up on me. They couldn't believe that this asshole with the attitude was now dating their darling little friend.

But dating him I was. Timing was everything. Two months earlier, I would have been too brittle and self-defeating to put up with any of his bullshit. Two months later, I would have been too healthy and self-respecting to take him on. But Lloyd slipped through just as I was opening myself to Dr. Sharon.

Often when someone on a self-help program finds success or a relationship—or both—while in some transformational, or 12-step "process," it's tempting to believe that it's all linked by cause and effect. Thus, it's difficult to give up a relationship tied to your therapeutic "process," or a "process" tied to your success. Each starts to justify the other.

Lloyd was quite a character. I used to say that he woke up at the crack of noon and moved through life at a notch above death. Lloyd slouched through life with what I called a misguided, self-defeating "I'll show me" posture that hurt no one but himself. He put his feet up on a casting agent's or producer's desk and didn't put that together with rejection. You only get to do that kind of stuff in show business when you've earned a reputation and your talent has made you a valuable commodity. People were dismissing him, which was sad, because I think he was a talented guy who was just scared inside. With early signs indicating that I would outgrow Lloyd, though I was crazy about him, I made sure I didn't by getting him into therapy six months later.

What I never imagined outgrowing was the outrageous sex. I know he adored me, and being madly in love with one another, we became exquisitely tuned in to each other's bodies. It was like taking toys out of a toy box. One at a time, we could focus on body parts and just get stuck on an exploration for an hour. It was the kind of animal passion—smell, textures, raw desire—that thrived regardless of how much we were fighting or hating each other in the moment. I almost never didn't want to jump him.

I was freer sexually than I had ever been. Lloyd loved for us to act out sexual fantasies. Actors are usually so desperate for work that they're inclined to create fantasy improvs. Lloyd and I had some pretty hot ones.

One was a teacher-student act where he made me stay after school and then seduced me. Sometimes the student seduced the teacher. We never did heavy S & M stuff, but detention often included a few over-the-desk spankings here and there, just to keep the student in line.

Another favorite was Lloyd as a hot teenage basketball stud and me as his Mrs. Robinson character, a lusty, older friend of his mother's who lived downstairs and liked to watch him and would invite him in for a glass of water.

Or we would go separately to a bar and pretend we were meeting other people and then try to pick each other up as strangers.

Maybe his rich fantasy life had something to do with the reality of where he lived. Lloyd had a one-room crash pad in a hovel of an apartment building on Forty-fifth Street and Eighth Avenue, diagonally across from our show at the Royale. I had bounced around, from West Eighty-third to a quaint landmark building in the East Thirties, to an adorable rooftop tower apartment one block north of The Dakota over Central Park in the Seventies. And I often house-sat my producers' fabulous three-balcony duplex on Thirty-eighth near Park, feeding their chihuahua Tiffany. But, because I was spending most nights after shows at Lloyd's one-room place anyway, I eventually just moved in with him at his building, the rather ironically named Camelot.

It would be hard to imagine two people being more in sync sexually and less compatible domestically.

I was compulsively fastidious; Lloyd was an incorrigible slob. I'd go away for a few days to feed Tiffany crosstown and come back to tumbleweeds blowing across the floor. His one chore was tossing out garbage—gathering bags in our kitchenette, opening the door, taking a few steps to the incinerator, and throwing them down the chute. If he did that, the deal was, I'd keep the rest of the place clean.

Even that sometimes proved too much. Once I yelled: "Fuck you. There are ten bags of garbage here; you can't even do your one fucking job!" He had just come out of the shower, so all of a sudden, he ran into the kitchen, grabbed up all the garbage, and went out the door to the hallway—naked. This was Lloyd's "I'll show me" streak rearing—no pun intended—its ugly head.

That was my cue: I locked him out and started laughing hysterically as he pounded frantically on the door, "Mar, Mar, c'mon, all right? Open the door." He was furious.

Then I heard the elevator arrive and a male voice going, "Hi, how are *you* doing tonight?" It was our neighbor, the nighttime drag-queen pharmacist, eyeballing butt-naked Lloyd.

Lloyd freaked. "Marilu, I'm going to KILL YOU!" Oh, was he furious that night. But it was the only way to train him.

There was, however, nothing I could do about the rest of this hellhole. It was crawling not only with cockroaches, but with $20 Eighth Avenue hookers, and with men you'd see leaving with an attaché case in the morning and coming home in a chiffon dress late at night.

We once thought there was a body rotting on the floor of our building because of the stench in the hallway during an August heat wave. We never saw anyone either leave or enter this apartment, although the tenant was supposed to be a typesetter at the *New York Times*. We called the super, who called the police. They knocked and blowtorched and screwed around with locks for a half hour until a frail voice called out from behind the door: "Can I help you?"

The tenant cracked open his door, revealing an apartment totally in darkness. Pasty-faced and disheveled, he wandered out into the hall and put on his socks, while the police went inside. (Bare feet in the hallway was the least of this fellow's problems.)

My pharmacist neighbor was fluttering up and down the hall trying to peek in. When he spotted some gift wrap near the door, he screamed: "Oh my *Gawd!* That's my wrapping paper from last Christmas. This just isn't *normal.*"

Not even close. The two-bedroom space was filled with floor-to-ceiling, wall-to-wall garbage, with tunnels cleared just enough to get around. The food garbage was caked and rotted; mountains of newspapers had yellowed and stiffened. What's more, the guy had a second apartment one floor below that was *completely* filled with trash.

They hauled the guy off to some hospital as six massive men in gas masks spent three days scraping, peeling, and disinfecting the toxic waste dump down the hall at the Camelot.

Fortunately, I always had my own sane and sanitized corner of reality. I loved my small, charming apartment in the Langham on Central Park West. James Taylor and Carly Simon, Mia Farrow, Liv Ullmann, and John Schlesinger all lived there. My apartment sat atop the building like an ornament and was tiny, with a stair winding to a loft bed, from which I had fabulous panoramas over the park. For $210 a month, it was quite a deal.

But so was Lloyd, I thought, and we spent most of our nights at the Camelot.

I left *Grease* in April 1976 and immediately wound up as one of the chorus girls in *Pal Joey* on Broadway. I was glad for the work, but disappointed not to have gotten the bigger role of Gladys Bumps. I was getting restless.

What I hoped to do was make the jump from stage to TV work. Doing comedy before a live taped audience seemed natural and appealing. I had gone up for several auditions at CBS, where I had a real guardian angel, Jean Guest, the head of casting.

At "Black Rock," CBS's notoriously pristine corporate tower, the word was that a strict code limited what employees could put in their offices. Plants, for instance, were out of the question, for fear of bug infestation.

One day, while sitting with Jean, a surrogate-mother figure to me, out of the corner of my eye I spotted a juicy, well-fed cockroach—more like a palmetto bug—on her empty white wall. Her eyes followed mine, spotted the huge insect, and she went absolutely crazy. She was mortified. She called Black Rock's roachbuster squad, but before they could get there with acetylene torches and smoke bombs I stood and calmly smashed the sucker.

Jean was horrified and wouldn't stop apologizing. I kept going, "Oh, please, come on, not to worry. I always heard this could be such a *problem* in New York, for, you know, *everybody.*"

I could afford to be cavalier. There was no question that this free-range cockroach had been a stowaway from the Camelot in my dark, comfy purse.

Despite the fact that I'd violated Jean's airtight, sanitized climate with the insect equivalent of the Andromeda Strain, CBS offered me $1,200 a month just to stay away from the other networks while they tried to come up with a pilot for a series.

One night I had a terrifyingly real dream in which I was visited by my mother, who was in a white outfit and with a white animal that looked like no other animal I had ever seen. It was a mind-blowing vision—a mythical beast of some sort. It was freezing-cold in the room and she came to me and sat on the bed and we had this surreal conversation. She told me that she was going to pass away, but that she was going to be okay. I shouldn't worry, but should take care of myself and the family. It was so much more powerful than a dream. It was some other kind of psychic experience.

The truth was that when I went home to see her after this dream, she was in the best shape she had been in in ages. She was on an arthritis diet—no red meat, dairy, sugar, or nightshade (eggplant, potatoes, peppers, tomatoes)—that was designed to ease her pain. It was working wonders. Those are four killers for arthritis sufferers, and giving them up brings miraculous relief. I thought to myself: *What a stupid dream that was.*

In the fall I ended up back in *Grease,* but I got my first film work in October. I was cast to play a stripper in an offbeat movie about an underground Boston paper being bought out by a tycoon. *Between the Lines* featured an incredible ensemble of then-unknowns: Jeff Goldblum, Lindsay Crouse, John Heard, Steve Collins, Bruno Kirby, and Jill Eikenberry. And me.

I decided to research the part by hanging out at the Metropole and talking to topless dancers. I already had one piece of the research down: the body—slightly fleshy in the stomach, but sexy. The research helped me create my stripper's "back story"—the background that helps define what happens onscreen. That got me into character. The insight I had about her was that she had no compunction, no hang-ups about ripping her clothes off. So I got into it.

The movie location was a sleazy bar right in my West Forties backyard. The first thing I was asked to do was take my clothes off for a hundred or more extras. No matter how cool or how much of a trouper you think you are, it's still a camera, you're still stripping down to pasties and a G-string, and those are still a hundred guys out there whoopin' and hollerin'. It was a shock, and maybe not the easiest transition to the big screen, but what the hell. Keep on moving. J.F.D.I.

Then in one of my takes, my pasties went flying, which left me really exposed. I could have used one of those sassy, sheer, and seamless numbers from Playtex right about then.

I did solid work, and gave my character a real "arc," as they say. Nothing ended up on the cutting-room floor. I had found it easy to throw myself into this character who was so foreign to me.

Then it was on to the next foreign place—Europe. The moment I wrapped my scenes, I raced to the airport and flew British Airways in first class, dressed as my character. I still had glitter nails, glitter eyes, fake lashes, and a trashy outfit. It was my first trip to Europe, and I went as a stripper.

I was flown to Venice via London for seven seconds of a ring-around-the-collar commercial. A second-and-a-half mood shot of Venice, a close-up of a gondolier singing "Of love I sing, tra la la la . . . for you've got ring around the coll la la," and a pan to me saying, "My powder didn't work." The rest of the spot was shot in America. It was wild. Three days in Venice for seven seconds. Then I was off to Paris for the weekend.

I loved Paris. I spoke some French, and felt like I had been there before. I hung out the whole time with this cute Brit named Danny, who approached me at Notre Dame hours after I got off the plane, and said, "You're an American." I couldn't believe it was so obvious. The Adidas running shoes gave me away, he said—this was before running shoes went global. Danny was a poor, starving, eighteen-year-old film student at the Sorbonne who sold the *International Herald-Tribune* on the street to survive. Classic. I had never met anyone quite like him. A sexual fling was out of the question because of Lloyd back home. He showed me sights, turned me on to shopping bargains and cheapo Left Bank dives, and exuded a great "street" feel for Paris that shortcut me around a lot of tourist nonsense.

As great as Paris and Danny were, I couldn't wait to get home to Lloyd. Even though I was on a European adventure, I missed him after a week away. Then, the moment I got home, I walked into a potent reality check: Lloyd, staring at some dumb football game, twisted around and mumbled, "Hi, honey," as if I'd gone to the deli for a bagel and a soda. And I had just nursed him through pneumonia before my big trip. It was exciting to be on Broadway together and all, but just how terrible he was at being a boyfriend was beginning to sink in, and figure prominently.

The low point was when he and I briefly split up in 1976 and I caught Lloyd fooling around. I was needing some space, so I agreed to house-sit for an upstairs neighbor in the Camelot. But we still did things together, like visit the bungalow colony where his family had a summer place in the Bronx. While there, I overheard Lloyd on the phone making plans for that evening.

She was an older woman Lloyd had been eyeing all summer, a lusty friend of his mother's who had enormous tits. Now it all fell into place: *I had been playing her part in our basketball fantasies all along.*

I was furious, and took control. I told a cute buddy of mine from one of the stage companies to come by and we'd go have an early dinner nearby. Then I called Lloyd's number and left an upbeat message he must surely have found reassuring: "Hi, it's me, I just wanted to pick up some clothes I need for an audition, but, uhh, it's okay, I can come by tomorrow. See ya."

When my platonic date walked in, he never knew what hit him. I revenge-fucked him like nobody's business. Premeditated, cold-hearted, hot-blooded revenge. Handed him a glass of wine, started kissing him, and moved in for the kill. This was my way of steeling myself for what I'd be facing an hour later. If I was going to get suckered into the Tortured Girlfriend game, I was going in empowered, playing to win.

I had it all timed. We dressed and went out to Joe Allen's, a restaurant popular with performers. Over dinner, I begged out of meeting his friends later, as planned, so I could hustle back to the Camelot and catch my hotshot hoopster slam-dunking Mrs. Robinson.

I tiptoed to the apartment door, heard nothing inside, and let myself in with the key. Once in, I peeked around the wall where the bed was and—there they were, scrambling like maniacs to get their clothes on in the soft glow of the sleeping alcove. I said something like, "Oh, excuse me," and slammed the door.

Minutes later, Lloyd was pounding on my door, begging forgiveness. I wept and sobbed and read him the riot act. He pleaded for mercy. I'd won. "Now," I said, "let's just go to bed and do it right." I tortured him over this for months.

By the end of the year, Lloyd and I had both left *Grease* for good—finally. He went on to a Chekhov play, *The Seagull,* and I wanted more time to focus on getting TV and film jobs.

We almost left each other for good, too. Little things had started to bug me, like cat allergies. When we visited Chicago at Christmas I couldn't even stay with my mom because of his allergies. I saw his allergies as part of his mommy-wipe-me wimpiness. Lloyd would wash one dish and slice up his hand. He was always sick. I saw the inside of the ER at St. Luke's-Roosevelt Hospital on Eighth Avenue more times than I care to remember.

Other warning signs: We took a romantic beach weekend in Montauk, Long Island, and tried our "strangers in the bar" improv. It backfired. The character he "played" at the bar was so obnoxious that I refused to go home with him. He totally turned me off. The weekend was shot; we slept in separate beds.

When we went to the Bahamas, I managed, with no help from Lloyd, to wangle a terrific deal for us on Paradise Island after our travel agent had booked us in a Nassau dump. True, I had pulled off an incredible Plan B coup; the bad news was that the trip underscored the major difference between Lloyd's energy and mine. Johnny and I used to constantly bounce off each other and make things happen. We were the world's greatest frustrated travel agents. Like me, Johnny saw instigating trips and mastering logistics as an art form requiring passion and precision. One side effect of being on life's quest for perfection is having no tolerance for botching plans and squandering energy on damage control. I missed the zeal for planning and execution that I had shared with Johnny.

These feelings rose to the surface in the spring of 1977, when Johnny moved to New York to begin preparing for his *Saturday Night Fever* shoot. Johnny's work on *Kotter* had established him as a genuine star, and he was just slipping into gear. He and I were now in "maintenance"—not seeing each other much, but having warm, if sporadic, long-distance phone contact.

I was dying to play opposite Johnny as his dance partner, and I let him know it. Johnny wanted me to play that part, too. But it got touchy. Even though this was his huge break, he kept going to bat for me with the director, John Badham, slipping my picture into Badham's casting files whenever he pored over them. I did interview, but most likely as a courtesy to Johnny. The story I heard was that I never had a shot: Badham was madly in love with an actress named Karen Lynn Gorney, who got the role—even though she was clearly not a trained dancer.

Johnny, meanwhile, had fallen in love with the actress Diana Hyland, who played his mother in the 1976 TV movie *The Boy in the Plastic Bubble.* Diana was in her early forties with a young son, and Johnny was just twenty-three. When he showed up in New York in March, I wasn't working much, so we had a great opportunity to hang out and get back into each other's lives. But there was no issue as to the ground rules: We were back where we had started—the best of friends.

I was happy to offer Johnny my friendship and caring. God knows he needed it. Diana was back in L.A., fighting for her life against breast cancer. I didn't know Diana, but I certainly felt Johnny's love for her and the pain they shared. His career was about to explode, but what mattered most to him was flying home every weekend to be at her side through her suffering.

Johnny's spirit and courage were astonishing. We tried to keep things light and fun, and it was great to have him back in my life. We'd stay up all night talking and then go for breakfast. We had a ball doing wardrobe research for Tony Manero's costumes, checking out places in Brooklyn, Queens, and the Village. I was with Johnny and Patrizia von Brandenstein, the great movie costume designer who had worked on *Between the Lines,* to buy the legendary white three-piece flared suit that Tony wore for his Odyssey 2000 dance contests.

After living with Mr. Notch-Above-Death, I got a welcome lift just being around Johnny's energy. It was amazing to see his dream unfolding just the way we had planned it when we were starting out. Johnny was already famous, with bigger and better projects and me and a dozen of his friends on a chartered DC-3 to his sister's wedding in New Jersey. It was a classic Johnny trip: He printed up his own customized tickets and had souvenir T-shirts made. This unpressurized prop plane flew so low it felt like we were hovering over America in a floating living room. We had to stop three times for refueling.

A month later Johnny hosted a lovely Thanksgiving dinner at his apartment, with everyone cooking and bringing something. Then a dozen of us piled into cars for a ski trip in Mammoth. It was my first time on skis, and just getting *in* the skis was miserable. (I've since gotten the hang of it, and I can now fearlessly rip down black runs, an accomplishment ranking way up there with giving up dairy.)

In early December Johnny invited Lloyd and me to the premiere of *Saturday Night Fever* at Grauman's, a spectacular and lavish "A-list" Hollywood event. I put a little too much energy into my outfit that night, a Moorish Laise Adzer–wanna-be number with a turban, a billowy blouse, and flowy-drapey harem pants. It was one of those what-was-I-thinking numbers.

I read a showbiz column item mentioning that a new sitcom was being developed by Jim Brooks, who had been the driving force behind *The Mary Tyler Moore Show,* and that it was going to be called *Taxi.* I made a mental note to check it out, but I had a hunch. I thought: *I'm going to do this one.*

I visited a psychic to get a beat on what was going on in my life. He mentioned nothing about my landing a major TV series job, but did tell me, rather cryptically, "The lady in pain is going to be out of her misery."

It made me incredibly nervous. I was afraid he was talking about my mother and her worsening battle with arthritis. I had to know how she was doing. The psychic's remarks also brought back from my strange dream of the lady in pain. With the move and countless auditions and screen tests, I had hardly seen since the Christmas before. So, as the holidays rolled around, and I visited my mom in Chicago.

My visit with my mother was a huge letdown, for many reasons. Lloyd and I were definitely not getting along—again. Of his allergies, we had to stay with Christal, which pissed but more important, the winter was rough and my mom. She was understandably crankier than usual. Her life

coming his way. I was evolving along my own path, and ready for a breakthrough.

Looking back, it seems both of us were destined to endure painful losses to achieve our dreams. That was a big lesson we would both learn over the next year.

In the spring, Diana died in Johnny's arms. It was absolutely devastating for him.

We often sat up in the weeks that followed and talked of how it feels to see, and hold, a loved one as he or she dies. I had gone through that with my father. I tried my best to offer what comfort and perspective I had to give. Watching someone die, we both felt, wasn't like witnessing some external *thing* that arrives and takes over a person, but rather experiencing the strange sensation of life leaving that person.

One of Johnny's most poignant and personal scenes in the movie was shot around the time Diana passed away. It was when Tony Manero describes for his girlfriend his dream of crossing the Verrazano Bridge into the city and his determination to build a new life for himself on the other side. It was a telling, and hauntingly prophetic, moment. The movie, of course, went on to become one of the biggest blockbusters of all time and made Johnny a hugely popular, "bankable" movie star. But he had paid a terrible human price in crossing his bridge.

I didn't know it then, but, like Johnny, I was about to cross a bridge of my own, and to build a new life for myself on the other side.

8

Waiting in the Wings

～

In April 1977, after a great audition with director Robert Mulligan for a part in the movie *Bloodbrothers,* a drama based on Richard Price's novel, I flew out for a screen test. I was thrilled and nervous. By then, Lloyd and I were back on track in our roller-coaster relationship, and thinking of moving to L.A. if I got the job.

I was up for the role of Annette, a three-fingered cocktail waitress with a heart of gold. She's the woman in the life of Stony, who has two crazy parents and who'd rather work with kids in a hospital than go into his father's construction business. I loved the character and felt I could do a great job with her.

I stayed in Johnny's one-bedroom apartment at 100 South Doheny, in Beverly Hills, because he was still in New York shooting *Saturday Night Fever.* My screen test with the actor considered to be the front-runner for Stony was a softly lit bedroom scene. I wore a man's shirt, panties, and no bra. It was a sweet scene, and the actor, wearing only his underwear, was understandably a little uptight. After some dialogue, we started kissing and making out, as the scene called for.

Two days later, I got the call I so anxiously awaited: "You have the part, but we're still looking for Stony, so you're going to have to test with another guy next week."

My new screen test partner was a guy I had met at my very first *Grease* rehearsal at the Ansonia years before: Richard Gere. Richard was just about to break big with *Looking For Mr. Goodbar,* which hadn't been released. Screen chemistry? No problem.

I got into my man's shirt with panties and no bra and slid into

bed with Richard. He promptly whipped open the covers, revea that he was bare-ass naked, grabbed my breasts and said, "Boy is a real woman." Richard certainly knew how to throw hi into a love scene. I was shocked and amused. Whatever m this was, it worked. Richard was star material—brash, out and brilliant.

His gutsy, visceral approach rubbed off. Richard seemed no hang-ups or inhibitions, which helped me deflect self-conscious "How should I look?" questions and foc work. In some scenes I'm shocked at how good I looked. looked fat and way too made up and ugly. But I didn' that interfere with my "finding" the character.

That shoot was a turning point in finding myself. was still looking for a TV series for me, I felt much that my future would now be in film.

Lloyd and I found an apartment in West Holl summer. Johnny was back in L.A., and on an amazi just wrapped *Saturday Night Fever* and was about t Olivia Newton-John before going back to *Kotte* loved to have a part, but I was again disappoint with *Bloodbrothers* and couldn't get a "stop producers, so I wasn't free to work on *Grease.*

I did go up for a movie called *American Hot* didn't get the part (the fabulous Fran Dresche up with a close, adorable friend, a young, u named Jay Leno. I met him on one of the six back to do for *Hot Wax.* We hit it off performing often at the Comedy Store and show. Jay got a part in *Hot Wax,* and there he would make it big. Soon, he and his gi Adele, were double-dating with Lloyd an

In September, after I wrapped *Blood* another blowup which ended it. I walke Hollywood and stayed with Johnny for

Johnny was like a jack-in-the-box— moment's notice. I'd turn the crank a coming," and this fun little person w

Johnny took me to an awe-ins Olivia's house in Big Rock Canyon fist-sized shrimp and a phone in th His dedication to friends was ti had changed drastically in the past couple of years. She participated in Parents Without Partners and novenas at the church, but wasn't getting out as much anymore. She stayed in her robe more than she bothered to get dressed. We still had great talks, and she took enormous pleasure in my successes. But she was more weary, sedentary, less sunny. Life seemed to have become more of a struggle. She had lost her glow.

Still, her spirit remained tough and vibrant. My mom had fractured her hip in a fall in 1972, and when she got a walker for her recovery, she had wheels bolted on so she could still teach the cha-cha at the studio. Somehow, she never felt pain when she danced. But she no longer stuck faithfully to her arthritis diet, and so her hands, feet, and joints would swell and virtually cripple her.

That winter had already been especially hard on her arthritis; the cold, combined with chronic discomfort from her broken hip and the lingering sadness of losing my father, had aged her twenty years.

Still, I refused to see it. When Lloyd mentioned that he thought my mother resembled a soap opera actress, I assumed he meant one of the gorgeous blondes; but when he pointed to a gray-haired grandma type, I was shocked. To me that was never my mom. She was still a radiant Lana Turner Barbie doll.

My mother had sustained other emotional blows. She had always looked forward with excitement to the back-to-school autumn energy down the block, as she sent around a flyer to sign up new kids for the dance studio. It was a Henner family ritual. But that year, after her visit to school, the principal, Mr. Zengara, announced over the P.A. system that the school did not endorse and would no longer be affiliated with the Henner Dancing School.

That was like taking away part of her soul. Zengara had been ordered to do this by Father Shotkowski, the pastor of the parish. The idea was to avoid what Catholicism calls "the near occasion of sin." The idea of boys and girls dancing together was apparently too hot to handle. My mom was crushed. Lorin went crazy and marched over to school and threw a fit in front of the principal, to no avail.

Another setback for my mom was seeing her sister Marge and other relatives from Phoenix that fall. She had always talked about rejoining her brothers and sisters in sunny, dry Arizona when the kids were all grown. My parents never imagined themselves growing old and dependent. They would go somewhere warm and retain their youthful life-styles. Half of that dream died with my father.

During Marge's trip, I believe my mom realized, deep down, how different her relatives' values and lifestyles were from her own. The years apart had turned them into strangers. To her, Phoenix sounded like a terribly provincial place. She lost her Plan A vision of where she would spend her twilight years, and when her dream of going west died, part of her simply gave up.

The whole secret to Plan B in our family—in all families—is in constantly reinventing yourself, adjusting, moving on. Deal with the equation in front of you. Not making the adjustment from Plan A to Plan B can ruin your life. Believe it!

Then, in November, Lorin, who was nineteen, moved out of the house. Now, her baby was gone. With the nest empty, my mother was more alone than she had been since she married as a teenager. I hated leaving her in Chicago after the New Year.

The truth was, I wasn't doing so hot myself. After moping through January, I was relieved when Lloyd landed a February theater gig in Florida. It was time for me to confront the futility of our situation. Too much resentment had built up in me, too much professional jealousy in him.

A pilot for a David Susskind series about a country-western singer fell apart. I auditioned for a new series spun off from the hit movie *The Paper Chase* and assumed nothing would ever come of it. I was never even given an entire script, but only read the "sides"—the relevant pages for my character.

That night, I was sitting in a Chinese restaurant on Pico Boulevard with Johnny and Lloyd, feeling blue, when Johnny said he was leaving for Rio de Janeiro the next day. "Why don't *you* go?" Lloyd said to me. "I could use the space." Thrilled, I hitched a ride. We left Wednesday and got there Thursday night.

Of course, I had hardly unpacked when I got a call from L.A. "Why did you leave town?" It was the *Paper Chase* producer. "We want you." It wasn't the well-bred, preppy law student Lindsay Wagner played, but the role of a pizza waitress. I wasn't wild about the part—and even more reluctant to leave Rio.

I told him I wouldn't do it as a regular character, but only as a guest star. "No way I'm going back now," I said to Johnny.

My agency called back with the news that I could, in fact, do it as a guest star. "Shit," I screamed. "They want me and we start work on Monday." I booked out of Rio and made it back in time for the CBS pilot of *Paper Chase.*

A month later, I shot a pilot called *Leonard,* playing a perky, just-out-of-college secretary, the brains behind Leonard Frey's lawyer. Shooting the pilot honored my CBS contract. Now it was wait-and-see until they market-researched the projects and decided my fate.

In the meantime, I had a Schlitz beer commercial lined up for January, but no other commercials for the winter. Residuals from commercials done a year back and before were beginning to dry up. I had never been out of a job for more than two months, but now there were no stage prospects. It was so strange. I was going up for movies but not getting them. In February, I got called back for a screen test and got my hopes up to play opposite Jimmy Caan in a terrific movie, *Hide in Plain Sight.* But I was too young and Tuesday Weld got the part. Lloyd was now in Florida doing a play with Paul Lynde. And my sweet deal with CBS was up; I had honored it with *Leonard.* I was so broke, I had to borrow money from Johnny for groceries.

He was an absolute sweetheart. *Saturday Night Fever* was a blockbuster, establishing him as a superstar. Johnny was nominated for an Oscar as Best Actor—a remarkable coup, given that this was his first big feature role. We rode his Oscar-nomination euphoria into a whirlwind week together all over town that lifted my spirits sky-high. All I could think was: *This is crazy. I'm with the wrong person.*

What was really happening was I was falling in love.

At the end of the week, he asked: "Do you want to go to Palm Springs for the weekend?" When in doubt, travel.

Before we got on the I-5 heading east, Johnny did something I had never seen done before. He said, "You know something, I want to buy a new car." With that, he pulled into a Jaguar showroom, made some very quick, easy arrangement, and drove off in a new white Jag. That was cool.

I felt Joe Henner smiling down on Johnny for that one.

We drove through the heaviest rains L.A. had had in years. Canyon roads were collapsing and flooding. It didn't matter. We spent a magical, wonderfully intimate weekend at the Ingleside Inn. The Inn looked like a thirties hideaway for stars of

Hollywood's Golden Era—a plush, cozy, romantic place with old hardwood floors and throw rugs, wide wooden beams, and antique iron-framed beds with embroidered linens.

We were like two utterly new people starting over. So much had changed. If I hadn't officially clicked off from Lloyd yet, the weekend proved that the end was near.

After Palm Springs, things felt increasingly messy and undefined —given our underlying three-way friendship. Lloyd and I had had our share of tearful reunions, but when he came back in late March, I was torn and miserable and not focused on our relationship. There was way too much going on to deal with it.

At the end of the month, though, I got a boost when I saw casting director Joel Thurm, a friend from the *Grease* auditions, for a *Taxi* audition. I did a strong monologue as Elaine Nardo, the ensemble's main female role. *An Unmarried Woman* and *The Goodbye Girl* were both big movies at the time, and the independent single mother was becoming a Hollywood staple. My audition was a monologue, a phone conversation with my twelve-year-old daughter, who I'm picking up at the airport from her visit with my ex-husband and his hot young girlfriend. I tell her I'll be in my "new car"—which, of course, is the taxi I drive for my new job. I loved the piece, and did a good job.

The word was that I was too young; the producers had described Elaine as a thirty-three-year-old Italian New Yorker. But Joel went to bat for me, saying I definitely was a one-of-the-guys cabdriver type, but someone with enough femininity to work in an art gallery, which Elaine also did. He felt I gave off just the right energy for the project.

The casting dragged on, but I was soon so caught up in the family dramas playing out in Chicago that I simply couldn't focus on work, or my situation with Lloyd. Looking back, it was a godsend that I had almost no jobs the whole first half of 1978, because my real job was to be there for my ailing mother.

9
And I Love Her

~

My mom had gone back again into the hospital for a few days late in March. She simply wouldn't get better. She was in great pain, ran a persistent fever, and was in a dark mood.

On April 3, Christal, who was the most heartwrenchingly involved of all of us in my mother's daily battles, called with bad news.

"I think you should come home," she said. "But Mommy wants you to wait a couple of days to get her hair done before you do."

"Absolutely not," I said, upset. That was classic Mommy vanity. Hair was the least of her problems, but my mom was still an amazingly strong-willed woman with a threshold for pain that was superhuman. I have no doubt that when she was first wheeled into an intensive care unit at a local rehab hospital, looking good for us was foremost on her mind.

I had to borrow money again from Johnny in order to fly home, and he was, as always, extraordinarily generous.

I was shocked. She already had bedsores. If my mother had known what was going on around her, she'd have waved her hand in the air and announced, "This place is for the publics, get me out of here." She had no business even being there. This was a rehab unit, and they were trying to get her into whirlpools and putting her in a room with five other patients. The staff was obnoxious and seemed way out of their league with her treatment. Her motor control was off, and it was all the staff could do to get her to use forks. They thought she was a cranky old patient with an attitude problem. My mom was only fifty-eight; she didn't have attitude problems, she had grave *physical* problems.

I could not believe this frail, incapacitated woman was my mother. Her condition had seriously deteriorated. She had been teaching dancing right up until Christmas. How do you go from dancing to this in three months? I also felt pangs of guilt. Where had I been those three months? How could I have been so oblivious? How could this have gotten so far out of control?

Apparently, her arthritis had eaten its way into the upper vertebrae of her spine, which were essentially disintegrating and shifting out of position. She was virtually paralyzed from the neck down; she was getting almost no circulation in her leg. An infection on her toe, which had started in November, had still not cleared up. Her whole body, always so youthfully toned and limber, was rapidly aging and atrophying.

I was devastated—and outraged. I tried to assert myself and get control of the situation. They hadn't even done a myelogram—an injection of dye into the spinal column to get a clearer picture than a standard X ray gives—because she wouldn't sign a release. I was struck by this hospital's medical and administrative incompetence. No one seemed in charge, and she was going downhill by the hour.

Two days after arriving I called the administrative head of Columbus Hospital, where most of my family's medical crises had unfolded. I demanded they take her in.

Within twenty-four hours she was moved to their superintensive care ward, where you couldn't walk the halls without surgical scrubs, mask, and cap. This was serious.

There, two tiny holes were drilled into her skull to rig her up to a halolike contraption around her head. This halo was bolted into place by inchlong spikes inserted into the two holes and hooked up to weights and cables to support her head. This relieved pressure off the spinal column.

She was also on what we called the "hamster wheel." They would flip her upside down so gravity would also ease pressure on her arthritic vertebral joints by gently lifting the neck joints out of the spinal column.

In our desperate search for optimistic signs, we believed there was more circulation, more muscular control, nerve stimulation, and strength in her limbs now. Maybe she was rallying. Then this crusty gold fluid would collect in her mouth. We had to help her drain it, since her arms were immobilized.

I stayed in Chicago ten days instead of a weekend, and returned to L.A. close to midnight Sunday, the 16th of April. I tried to focus on my upcoming second *Taxi* audition, scheduled for the following morning, but I was haunted by a grotesque, Frankenstein-like vision of my mother wired and bolted in place.

I wasn't home long before I got even worse news. Christal reached me by phone at nine A.M. Monday morning. It was eleven in Chicago and she was at the hospital. "You know how her leg got swollen when they hooked her up," she said, "and how we thought that was a good sign that circulation was improving?" I knew things were getting worse. My heart raced.

"Well," she went on, "that infection in her toe's really gotten bad with gangrene and they're going to have to operate and she's going to lose her leg."

I listened, disbelieving, waiting to see if there was anything else. "They say it's like this: If she doesn't have the leg amputated she'll definitely die. She might die anyway, but if she has surgery, she has a chance to survive. What do you think?"

"I'm on the next plane."

"They have to do the surgery this morning."

"I'm on my way," I said.

There was no time for second-guessing or second opinions. The doctors came to Christal and Lorin in the hospital with a release to sign, and that was it. We were all scared to death of losing her, and if this was going to save her life, then we had to accept that fate. My mom wasn't even sixty. We hoped she could live for at least twenty more years, though we knew she would never teach again. Her legs had been her life, but now her left leg had brought her to the brink of death. It seemed an unbearably cruel, unjust fate for her to suffer.

In my family, even in our darkest hours, we found treasures of humor and poignancy. Lorin tells the wonderful story of how, after signing the paperwork, he was walking next to my mom as they wheeled her into the operating room. Despite being under heavy pre-op sedation, she was still conscious and trying to let him know something. "One thing . . . I . . . always loved about you," she gasped in a rough, slurring voice. She paused, just as they got to the swinging OR doors. Lorin was afraid she wouldn't complete her message. He leaned in closer to her. "Yeah, yeah? One thing you always loved about me *what?*" Lorin asked.

"—that . . . you were . . . a fetcher."

That's what it sounded like, but it made absolutely no sense. "A what?" Lorin asked quickly, as time was running out.

"A catcher," she said.

"Could you spell that, Mom? I really want to know what you're saying," Lorin insisted. There were just seconds to go.

Then BOOM! The doors blew open, the gurney rolled through, and as they wheeled my mother off, Lorin could hear her spelling "C-O-U-C-H-E-R."

Lorin was stranded, dumbfounded, as the doors swung back on him. *A coucher?* he wondered. He looked around and asked some interns, "Did anybody hear what she said? What did she say? Did anybody hear what she *said?* A fetcher? A coucher? A catcher? What did she MEAN?"

Lorin's worst fear, of course, was that my mother would take the answer to this riddle to her grave. "What's a coucher?" he quizzed everyone that day.

"Maybe she thought you liked to watch TV the most," someone teased.

Until Christal's call, the *Taxi* audition had seemed important. Now, my priorities were in place. I was just sorry I had bothered to go back to L.A. at all; but I felt I had to keep my life moving forward. It was what my mother would have wanted me to do.

Though Lloyd and I were barely speaking, I said: "You're coming to Chicago with me. I really need for you to be with me now." I felt so alone, so helpless and afraid. On the flight to Chicago, for the first and only time in my life, I took a five-milligram Valium to calm myself down. Lloyd and I sat in silence most of the way as I tried in vain to nod out.

While my mom was losing her leg and Lorin was losing his mind trying to divine what my mother loved most about him, my flight was pure agony—four hours at 37,000 feet of not knowing if my mother was going to be alive or dead when I stepped off that plane.

Christal met us at the gate and we drove straight to the hospital. My mother's leg was amputated just above the knee, but she was alive. She was sleeping, hooked up to all sorts of machines and monitors and tubes. One tube led from inside her lungs to a large water-cooler-type jug tucked beneath the bed. Into this sparklet's-type bottle drained a pinkish-orange fluid that looked like Hawaiian Punch. It was one of the most ghastly sights I've ever seen.

When she came around, she regained her lucidity, but never knew she lost her leg. Or at least never let on that she knew. No one ever mentioned it, and with the phantom-limb sensations, the odd position she was in, and all the technical paraphernalia around her, she never knew. All she said, incredibly enough, was that she resented being put under by anaesthesia and that she wanted a Tylenol for some pain she was having. That's all she said about it.

We all took shifts with my mom at the hospital. Lorin, who had not stopped wondering whether he was a catcher or a coucher, went to the source two days later: "Mom," he asked, "remember the other day when you were going into surgery you said that I was something like a catcher, or butcher, or something?"

"No, no, a *toucher*. T-O-U-C-H . . ."

"Wait, say it again."

"A toucher. You like to touch people."

He was so relieved. Now, he could go on with his life, living up to her answer.

I virtually lived at the hospital, because I was the only family member not working in town. I'd sing to her and rub Oil of Olay on her arms to keep them soft. We took backgammon breaks in the waiting area. Two of us always spent the night with her. We were all on emergency overdrive, giving everything we had to bring her around.

(To this day, I cry when I smell Oil of Olay and can barely stand to be in a room where backgammon's being played.)

Career issues seemed a million miles away, but news filtered back. *Paper Chase* was picked up and the heat was on to nail me down for the role, since I had market-tested quite high for "likability." CBS put the pressure on. Because the contract had been honored, I was free to say no—or negotiate. They offered me a mind-boggling $10,000 a week, at a time when I was practically on a food stamp program with Johnny.

With another *Taxi* audition just days away, in the last week of April, I held out. My mother was in stable condition and I was happy for a respite back home. Our feeling then was, as Daddy always said, "This too shall pass." Somehow, even with losing her leg, she would adjust, come through. Life would move on for us. Because our mother had always been so strong, we were still hopeful.

I flew back just long enough to do a good reading for *Taxi*. My mind and heart were hardly riveted on the words in front of me, but now there was more of a script and I had a better overall sense of Elaine. I knew I wanted this part more than the other one.

By this time I was getting used to the wearying commute. Soon I was back in Chicago for my mother's bedside vigil.

Once there, there was no avoiding the truth: My mother was fighting a losing battle. We struggled to keep positive energy flowing, but more and more we tried to make peace with what seemed inevitable. We were on an emotional roller coaster. At a family meeting in the house, we would talk about how she'd pull through, and how easy it would be to rig the house specially for her to get around, how life would again go back to normal. Then it would seem as if the amputation had resulted in little improvement, and even brought her to a point of no return.

It was spiritually draining for all of us. Lorin even recalls a moment when he thought she was so hopeless, and in such pain and so out of it, that he wished for her to die soon. It was exactly the kind of slow-motion agony people had in mind when, in the wake of my father's instantaneous, painless death, they had said things like, "You know, it's a blessing he went like that," or, "Better like this than some awful, drawn-out ordeal."

I had never understood those remarks until now, and I was beginning to see their point.

In her room, we all sat around her bed and chattered through the night to keep awake. We had to wear rubber gloves and masks to reduce the risk to her of a potentially fatal infection. When my mom was awake and more present, she took us through an almost delirious, and at times heartbreaking, stream-of-consciousness game of "Categories": Who was the easiest baby to deliver? The hardest? The fattest? The first to drink out of a glass?

My mother once asked me to rub her foot—the one that wasn't there anymore. She probably never accepted that her leg was gone. She was on her back mostly, sometimes lucid, but tired. One vital sign that never weakened: My mother, while going in and out of consciousness, would begin calling out dance steps, counting to eight over and over again, like, "Jazz square, one-two-three-and-four; five-six-seven-and-eight." It was surreal.

Curiously, Johnny had told me how his mother, at the end, had called out stage directions, since she had been a director. Ellen March's mom called out canasta or bridge bids. The eerie, unyielding, final cries of passion in waning lives.

It was not, mercifully, destined to last much longer.

I had flown to L.A. for the weekend to prepare for an audition for a TV movie on Monday, May 11. I didn't get the part, but afterward, I went to lunch with the actor I tested with. At lunch, I phoned Christal at the hospital for an update.

"It looks really bad," she said. "You better come back."

By the time I got to Chicago, my mother was still conscious and coherent, but her vital signs were bad. She had gone into septic shock, which is a massive bacterial infection of the blood. It is almost always irreversible and usually signals the beginning of the final forty-eight hours of a patient's life.

I became obsessed with the incessant beeping of her pulse monitor by the bed. By this time, my mom seemed mostly unaware of what was going on.

On Saturday, the 13th of May, the night before Mother's Day, a dozen family members gathered in her room, hugging, holding hands, and sobbing. The doctor had told us she might not make it through the night. My mother lay on her back, peaceful, still, and silent. The only sign of life was her beeping pulse monitor. We touched her, patted her, got up and switched positions, and took turns clutching her hands, all of us telling her over and over, "We love you, Mommy; we love you, Mommy."

Finally, with all of us around the bed—I was seated right at her side—watching her, her pulse slowed, then ceased, and the room was suddenly given over to the crushing stillness and finality of flatlining.

It was over. We hugged some more, and sobbed. Moments later, the phone rang in the room, and I quickly grabbed it. It was Uncle, my mother's brother Dan from his home in Mundelein, Illinois.

"Did she just die?" he asked, in an astonishing flash of telepathic energy I will never forget. Yes, I said, she was gone.

The lady in pain had been taken out of her misery.

Growing up in the Catholic Church, we learned how in death the body and soul are reunited. This was not something I ever actually believed.

But I did derive some comfort in knowing that Mommy and Daddy were now together again somewhere in heaven, smiling down upon us—dancing away on the wings of Eternity.

10
Life with the Fast Elaine

~

If handling money separated my parents in life, it also distinguished them in death. My father left us a financial tangle of unpaid bills. My mom, at her death, had tied up everything with such meticulousness that every bill was paid, down to the expenses for her headstone and funeral.

But there was one outstanding I.O.U. that we, in our grieving, did need to collect on: the debt of ingratitude shown my mother by our church in the last year of her life.

We knew that the priest intent on saying the funeral Mass was Father Shotkowski. He had meant to discourage only sixth-, seventh-, and eighth-graders from signing up for dance classes the previous autumn, but the impressionable younger kids, from kindergarten on, had also stayed away. That hurtful blow had wounded my mom and helped send her into a catastrophic tailspin months before her death. Though the church knew my mom's funeral would set some kind of attendance record—or at least a parking record—it didn't seem right that Father Shitface should officiate.

Christal and I made an appointment to see him.

"There are things we want," I said firmly, "or else we'll have the funeral someplace else." That got his attention.

We wanted her favorite Beatles song, "And I Love Her," to be sung. We wanted a collective letter we had all written to Mommy, which Melody would edit, to be read. "Fine," he said. We wanted a female pallbearer—Lynnette, Lorin's girlfriend (and now wife). Fine.

Then I got down to business. "Who's saying the Mass?"

"Well, I thought I would," he said, as if it were a given.

"Oh, that's, umm, the other thing," I said, getting nervous and choked up. "We don't want you to say the Mass."

He looked stricken. "Why not? What do you mean?"

"Do you really want me to tell you the truth?" He nodded. I took in a deep breath and gave Christal a sideways glance. We knew this would be one of the most emotional confrontations in either of our lives.

Growing up Catholic, one thing was sacred: You never told off a priest. But I had been away from the Church, I had been on Broadway, been in therapy, been in L.A. I had earned enough perspective to see him for the suppressed, uncaring jerk he had been.

"Well," I started, "we feel that in some way you behaved in an intolerant manner and are linked to the stress that caused my mother's arthritis to get worse at the end."

He didn't know what hit him. By now, tears were streaming down Christal's and my faces. My heart was racing with that "snorting snot" fury where you can barely catch your breath.

"Are you saying that I am somehow responsible for her stress, or . . . even for her death?" he asked. He was stupefied.

"I guess I am, Father. It broke her spirit."

I reminded him how attendance had drastically fallen off after his announcement that St. John Berchman's no longer endorsed, or was affiliated with, the studio. Most kids took that to mean that the church no longer approved of dance classes, so they stayed away in droves. Having lost her husband, having watched her once-teeming nest empty over the years, her little dance students were all she had left. I poured it on. "I really don't think it would be right for you to even show up at the Mass."

He was upset; our message had hit home. I couldn't believe what I'd said. But I was so pumped up it didn't smack to me of sacrilege. Father assigned the Mass to another priest, a tall, meek-looking blond guy with a wimpy voice who would definitely be over his head. Great choice. He was hardly what we had in mind.

After my mother died, JoAnn's ex-husband Bob, Melody's old boyfriend Chuck, and my trusty old boyfriend Steve had left their current mates and come to live with us at our house for four emotion-filled days. Melody asked each of us to write a letter to

Mommy, which Melody then edited into one letter. The letter said all the things we wanted said about our mother. I dropped it off with the priest who was officiating.

It was another standing-room-only Henner funeral at church the day my mom was buried. After teaching dance in the neighborhood for twenty years, this was her entire world. Christal's Jewish boyfriend, Mark, walked to the casket and sang the Beatles song in a beautiful a cappella voice that sounded like a bellowing cantor at a bar mitzvah.

When Father went around for the "Peace be with you" hand-shakes, I pulled him toward me and whispered urgently: "Where's that letter I gave you?"

"I left it on my desk. I thought I would read it out at the gravesite."

As exec-producer of the funeral, I was furious. "Well, not everybody's coming," I said, "plus the acoustics aren't the same." I was being such a bitch. And it wasn't even a priest who knew us well. *This* was sacrilege.

I ran from my pew to the rectory and pounded furiously on Father Shotkowski's office door. My anger was boiling over.

"What's going on?" Father asked once I stepped in.

"Where's his desk, where's that speech? He said he left the letter at his desk."

"He didn't read it?" Father asked. Now we were both all over the rectory hunting down our letter. Father grabbed it off the other priest's desk. As he handed it over, it dawned on me.

"Father," I said, "would you read it?"

"Do you *want* me to read it?" he asked, bewildered.

"Yeah," I said, eyeing him warily. *It'll be good theater,* I was thinking. With everything that had gone before, I knew he'd do a great job with his rich, resonant voice.

As Father Shotkowski strode into the church, all heads turned to him and whispered. It was like a surprise witness showing up in a Hollywood courtroom thriller. My family looked at me, knowing something big was about to go down.

Father took to the pulpit, then read the letter, a loving, heart-breaking tribute. He had a fire-and-brimstone voice that delivered all of the emotional drama of the letter.

Then, on his own, he made it all up to us: He put the letter down and gave a spellbinding speech about how he had been so wrong, and acknowledged how his mistake had broken my mother's heart.

It was a moving public apology to my mother. He almost showed some real class.

When he ended, there wasn't a dry eye in the house. It was a truly astonishing turn of events. It meant everything to us to make peace with our priest, and to be able to say good-bye to Mommy with his blessings—and with him having ours.

We were so drained we couldn't even deal with going home. There was nothing prepared, even though plenty of neighbors were coming back to be with us. A bunch of us made a run to Chick's hot dog stand right down the street, and brought back armloads of stuff. It was fitting enough: Chick's was a favorite of my mother's, so we felt she was still right there with us.

If God had been looking out for a way to help me cope with my grief, He revealed it to me back in L.A. I flew home a day or two after the funeral for my third and last audition for *Taxi*. Whether it was ultraconfidence or utter detachment rooted in a profound sadness, I don't know. But I reached down and found the strength to walk into the audition like I owned it.

"You guys better make up your minds and cast this thing," I joked to everyone, "because between making Elaine look like both a cabbie and an art dealer I'm running out of outfits."

By then, Jim Brooks and his renowned team of writer-producers were putting together "teams" to read scenes. This was no pilot going on here, this was for real. Brooks, on the strength of his phenomenal successes with *The Mary Tyler Moore Show, Rhoda,* and *Phyllis,* got from ABC an almost unheard-of sight-unseen, thirteen-episode on-air commitment. He and the other executive producers, Stan Daniels, Dave Davis, and Ed Weinberger, put together a stable of writer-producers, including Glen and Les Charles, who along with *Taxi* director Jim Burrows went on to create *Cheers.*

Taxi had *hit* written all over it.

It had originally been inspired by a September 1975 *New York* magazine article by Mark Jacobson about the wildly offbeat characters driving for a lower Manhattan cab fleet. One twenty-nine-year-old woman driver, much like Elaine Nardo, had three art degrees and was driving a cab to pay the bills while trying to become a part of the SoHo art crowd. (My own *Taxi* back story was that I had gotten seduced and knocked up by a guy named Vince Nardo and I was raising a thirteen-year-old daughter alone.) Grant

Tinker, Mary Tyler Moore's husband at the time and head of MTM Productions, had optioned the piece for an incredibly modest $500—but never went forward. After the option ran out, the rights ended up with Brooks.

I read with Barry Newman, a guy I later came to like but who had once tried to pick me up at a West Side health club two years earlier. His macho "hey-baby" come-on had turned me off. He was going up for the part Judd Hirsch would ultimately get. Maybe it was fate that we had our own little back story: I made mincemeat out of him at the reading.

A day or two later, I got the job. Jim Brooks later told me, "When we saw how you handled Barry in that scene, we knew we loved you. You were in."

The show had everything going for it—great cast, brilliant creative team, perfect time slot: nine-thirty Tuesday evening, in a lineup that went *Happy Days, Laverne & Shirley, Three's Company, Taxi,* and *Starsky and Hutch.* The buzz was that Brooks had hooked himself another major prime-time hit.

I had no idea how much getting *Taxi* would change my life. But I felt a healthy, cleansing thing would be to visit my family and the neighborhood with a sense of beginning, rather than with the sense of finality and doom that had hung over us all through my mother's bedside vigil—to be together again as survivors, not sufferers.

Johnny's *Grease* opening was the perfect excuse. Major premieres were planned for Chicago and New York. Before I left, I also decided to get my own apartment in Johnny's building at 100 South Doheny.

Going home was a great idea. Johnny flew in and came to my niece Lizzy's eighth-grade graduation. When he showed up at our house, my entire neighborhood went out of control. The old "Meaniacs," the nasty people who hurled scalding water on us if we played under their windows, now sucked up to us big-time. They followed us wherever we turned, their pens and paper poised for autographs. The German couple that lived next door was suddenly speaking English. Kids just ran over, froze in their tracks, and stared. I had never seen our backyard like that in my life. *So this is what it's like to be famous,* I thought. And maybe, with *Taxi,* my time had come.

I psyched myself up for my new TV life as Elaine Nardo. After a restful July 4th weekend with Johnny at Lake Tahoe, I showed up for my first read-throughs and rehearsals for *Taxi*. I was a bit heavier than I wanted to be, but my energy level was no problem at all: I was nearly levitating off my chair from being in the presence of some of the most gifted talents in television.

Jim Brooks was Mr. Classic, the man behind many great works in both movies and TV, from *The Mary Tyler Moore Show* to exec-producing *The Simpsons,* to writing and directing brilliant films like *Terms of Endearment* and *Broadcast News.* His team was the best and the brightest in TV.

It would have been easy for me to feel out of my league in a cast that included Judd Hirsch and Danny DeVito. But I had been picked to play Elaine from hundreds of actresses, and that had been a boost. I felt secure with the sitcom genre, which was closer to theater than filmmaking. Also, I had had a year of improv training.

In fact, I had known cast member Randall Carver from the Harvey Lembeck improv class. It was an invaluable proving ground. You're given a setup—"You're at an airport pay phone"—and you immediately have to discover your character and an objective. You learn to use everything. You learn to pull stuff out of the air. You learn to handle everything, from being really bad to being really brilliant. When you're good, you're a genius; when you bomb, you can't believe you actually signed up for this kind of sadomasochistic ritual.

But the class of twenty or so was supportive rather than cutthroat. You break the ice and see you can handle it, and then you chomp at the bit for another skit. The all-in-this-together mood nurtured the notion that I had some real talent.

Of course, with classmates like John Ritter, who was already in *Three's Company,* and a wild, almost scary, newcomer named Robin Williams, you pushed yourself to be as good as you could be, just to keep up. I always wanted to be in setups with Robin, because his brilliance sort of rubbed off. It was clear Robin was a genius waiting to become a giant star. He didn't wait long.

The week we started *Taxi,* Robin started *Mork & Mindy* at a neighboring soundstage. In addition to Robin and Pam Dawber, there was Ronnie Howard, Henry Winkler, Penny Marshall, and Cindy Williams doing *Happy Days* and *Laverne & Shirley.* For a while, Michael Keaton and Jim Belushi were in *Working Stiffs.* Later on, it was Tom Hanks in *Bosom Buddies.* The Paramount lot was the ultimate TV comedy campus in the late seventies and early eighties, a phenomenally creative spawning ground, and I got an enormous rush every morning just driving into the lot, knowing I was part of all that manic energy in the air.

As I sat there in those first weeks before shooting, I felt an instant comfort on the set. I loved these guys, and soon felt I belonged.

It was nice to have worked with Jeff Conaway years earlier in *Grease.* I had seen Danny's haunting and poignant work as Martini in *One Flew Over the Cuckoo's Nest.* I had seen Judd in the TV series *The Law* and the more successful *Delvecchio;* more recently, I had seen his wonderful work in *Chapter Two* on the stage. Judd was an amazingly intense, powerful talent.

I had seen Andy Kaufman do a very weird act at the Improv in New York, in which he came out in a tux and read a section from *The Great Gatsby* in such a flat, deliberately irritating voice that he got pelted with dinner rolls. The audience was crawling out of its skin. Then, just when you wished you had packed a small firearm, he stood, ripped off a strip of shiny black duct tape along the side seam of his tuxedo pants, exposing silver studs, and went into what was probably the world's best Elvis doing "Hound Dog." It was equal parts demented and inspired, and it pushed audiences' buttons.

By mid-1978 Andy's shtick had evolved. He would do an opening act as a hilariously obnoxious lounge singer named Tony Clifton, then come out looking totally different, as himself—without tipping off the audience that they were the same guy. You knew Andy was borderline—his stuff either worked brilliantly as cutting-edge performance art or it crashed and burned. There was an aura of tension and madness around him, which complemented the more typical "guy" energy of the rest of the cast. Andy/Tony were *both* signed on, given separate contracts and parking spaces. That's how weird Andy was—and how much Brooks wanted him for *Taxi.*

Tony Danza was adorable. From the moment we met, there was an obvious, almost blushing kind of chemistry between us that I knew had to go *somewhere.* His part had been created as a hapless Irish boxer named Phil Ryan; but a producer named Stuart Sheslow, casting boxers for a TV movie in the wake of *Rocky's* success, stumbled across Tony in the Gramercy Gym in Manhattan. Tony had been a pro middleweight for almost two years and had won six of his eight fights. Sheslow liked him for the picture, but the project got KO'd somewhere along the way. Then, when the producer became an ABC executive, he got Brooks to look at a screen test Tony had done. Once Tony came aboard, Irish Phil Ryan was floored by Italian middleweight Tony Banta.

My own character was going through changes of her own—as was I, once I grew to trust Jim Brooks's creative instincts. The first year I never felt comfortable as an actor, though I loved the guys like family. I was intimidated by Judd, and I didn't feel qualified to confront Brooks if I had questions about Elaine's speeches. I was a square peg in a round hole.

I remember that one line in an early scene with Judd—Elaine says to Alex, "You're maybe my best friend"—rang false. She was supposed to run to him and hug him, but they had just met. It felt inorganic. My discomfort with the direction, Brooks told me later, came from my not being "committed to her" yet. It was an important perception. Once it aired, I saw that the scene worked.

Another time, later on, I was supposed to haul off and sock a guy in the gut. Again, this just didn't work. It was irrational and something I would never do. Now, I could stand up and tell him so. "Just do it," he insisted. I was, like, "But Jim, I—"

"Do it for me, for my sake," he insisted. "Go against your instincts. See what happens."

I did, and it was possibly the funniest thing I ever did in my five years there. I was always grateful that Brooks, and our director, Jim Burrows, pushed me beyond my limits, and made me question my own instincts when they knew better. Ninety percent of the time a good actor's instincts are right. But sometimes you have to let go and flow with someone else's take.

That was a life lesson about trust when you're feeling a little out of control. Doing *Taxi* was five years of that kind of self-examination and growth for me, as both an artist and a woman.

Still, it took a while to grow into Elaine, in part because she was written as a thirty-three-year-old with a thirteen-year-old daughter. I was twenty-five. The feeling was that I looked too young to have a teenager, so they gave me kids of nine and seven, a boy and a girl. The boy they cast for me was the skinny kid from *Bloodbrothers*. He was thirteen, but he was so tiny he looked eight. Within two seasons, he had shot up to six feet, and had to be replaced. The transformation was startling. He was enormous. It looked like he had *eaten* the first actor.

From day one, the cast had a lusty, affectionate spirit that made me feel I had come home. Tony would walk in, back me against a wall or throw me down on a table, and kiss and grope me all over, as someone would yell out, "Is Tony in yet?" I could go up to these guys and say, "Nice booger you got goin' there." That kind of frisky energy drove life on the set.

At times, it occurred to me that we might be playing off—dissipating—some of our characters' energies before we'd get to the Friday tapings. It seemed sometimes as if we weren't putting across the same sexual texture and vibrancy in our characters that we enjoyed in our real-life interactions.

One thing I knew for sure: There was no way Elaine Nardo and Tony Banta could ever have had anything close to what Tony and I got going three weeks into the first season. We threw ourselves into a wild, vigorously sexy affair that both of us knew wasn't going anywhere. But even going nowhere, once you build that kind of frame around it, you can cover quite a lot of interesting territory.

I was ripe.

While I had been drifting into Johnny's sphere, perhaps out of habit and comfort, I knew I'd never go through that last door with him. Besides, given his global superstardom, our relationship was more commitment-proof than ever. Johnny was a media phenomenon; his life had unquestionably gotten more complicated. We took a two-week trip to Europe to open *Grease* in Paris, Deauville, and London. But it had become almost impossible to pick up and spontaneously go somewhere. He had people to answer to, and security was always an issue. So it was just what it was; any other expectations would have been a cheat.

"The thing" with Johnny always felt most romantic and permanent at those precise moments when it had the least chance of becoming either. I love being madly in love, when you constantly say "I love you" and "You make me love you" to the person, and nothing else seems to exist. I love having that total, crazy-for-you immersion. That's what being in love is like for me. It had taken three years to accept that I would never have that with Lloyd. Now, as many times as I had told myself, "I want this with Johnny," I knew I wasn't ever going to have it with him. He and I were simply incapable of that kind of love for each other.

Enter Tony. Tony was all over the place with girls, but he was technically free. He and I were the two youngest cast members, so we were like the two puppies scampering off together. He was totally lovable, with his intense, "neighborhood" street edge, that gorgeous body with a little tuft of hair on the small of his back, and his great sense of humor. He was a real sweetheart.

If I knew Tony and I were crazy about each other, with lots of sniffing around between us, I also knew there was no way he was destined to be my life's partner. It was the kind of built-in limitation that makes everything possible.

Plus, we so trusted the extraordinary affection between us that we could agree it would be an adventure—no more, no less. It was the frame we put on the painting—freeing us to use up all our colors, to cover every inch of canvas, and to wear out all our brushes.

So we agreed that whatever it was, however it went, it would end as soon as the first episode aired on September 12. We totally got each other, and wanted it. Besides, who was I kidding: There was no way I could work with seventy-seven guys and not end up having an affair with *someone*.

Tony and I went out for dinner one night, and then went out the next night, went back to his house, and just kind of cleared off the kitchen table. It was right out of *The Postman Always Rings Twice*. I stayed that night, and we were off and running.

Tony was about as wild as they got, and I had the rug burns to show for it. Hallways, airplanes—you name it, we did it. We often went for fifteen-rounders. We just zeroed in on each other's sexuality in a big, cheek-biting kind of way. Part of the rush was that I wasn't sneaking around on somebody. I was in control of my time and emotions, with no one to account to and no one reporting in. I was living in my own place after three years, starting a whole new life for myself and responsible to no one but me. I could call Tony and have him at my house in a second, and vice versa, after work or on weekends. And Tony didn't owe anyone any explanations, either.

The timing was perfect. Six months before or after and we might never have gotten together. But it was a freeing, satisfying, guiltless affair—and it filled a sweet little pocket of time for each of us. Neither of us ever got weird afterward and it never got in the way of working together. If anything, the affair brought us closer together and made lifelong friendship—if not partnership—a reality for us. I was on a roll, and Tony was the perfect guy to roll with.

There was no hiding what was going on. After taping the third episode, we all went out for dinner at Joe Allen's. It was a wild night, with twenty-seven of us from all the Paramount shows.

Everyone showed off his or her claims to fame: Penny Marshall opened a bottle with her teeth; I put my fist in my mouth. Then I walked over to Danny DeVito and sat on his lap with my arms around him. I knew he had figured it out about Tony and me—and would have something to say about it.

"YOU TWO!" he said, with a devilish, Louie DePalma grin. "You couldn't even wait *three weeks!*"

Danny got that right. And we were just getting started.

11
The Incredible
Shrinking Woman II

If, in the wake of my mother's death, my time had come to capitalize on my biggest career break with *Taxi*, it was also the perfect time to make the connection between food and mental and physical health. After her death I radically changed the way I ate and took care of my body. I came to feel that both my parents might still be alive today had they known what I and millions of others know today about nutrition and exercise. I vowed to make every sacrifice necessary to cleanse my body and rid it of anything that could cause or contribute to heart or circulatory disease and issues surrounding weight, immunodeficiency, arthritis, and energy. I was desperate to find a way to eat and enjoy food without fearing I was killing myself at the same time.

I threw myself into my education with a focused, obsessive zeal. I lived near an incredible bookstore called the Bodhi Tree that specialized in esoteric and spiritual subjects. I read several hundred books and articles on dieting; body chemistry; the yin-yang of nutrition; and the links between diet and cancer, heart disease, arthritis, stress, and hypertension. I studied up on vegetarianism; macrobiotics; the way "extreme foods" cause extreme moods (the basis of macrobiotics); metabolism; food combining; the nightshade (potato, eggplant, peppers, tomato) group's links to arthritis; dietary supplements; vitamins; minerals; herbal cures . . . the works. I began gradually, and over time underwent a radical transformation. I had been hooked all my life on dairy and meat products—I loved bloody-rare roast beef—loaded with animal fats. Sodas fizzled with caffeine, sugar, and chemicals. Sugar is, basically, kiddie cocaine, masquerading as jawbreakers, Cocoa Puffs, ice cream, soda, Lucky Charms, you name it. Fried foods slowed you down and clogged your arteries with saturated fats; sauces did it with heavy cream and butter.

Unfortunately, under the stress of working on *Taxi,* I was still smoking.

Meat was the first to go—my vegetarian "birthday" was August 15, 1979, and I have never had meat since. Not once. I totally flushed dairy out of my life, but you can find great nondairy soy-based cheeses to replace it.

Changing your eating habits is a long process of experimentation, of trial and error. You go through a healing crisis—when your body rids itself of toxins. Sometimes you experience violent headaches, profound lethargy, bad skin. Under the care of my first nutritionist, whose emphasis was on supplements, my healing crisis came when all the zinc from my body was removed and I felt the bottom drop out. I could barely move, I was so zonked. I needed a new diet guru.

In 1979, I heard of a Vietnamese nutritionist named Dr. Thich An Than who specialized in macrobiotics. I learned of his work through a friend whose wife had twenty tumors that all cleared up after going on Dr. An Than's macro diet. At the time, he was actually thrown in jail for his cures, and I helped bail him out. He was just a decade ahead of the rest of us. Today, he's a member of the President's Council on Physical Fitness and Sports. Dr. An Than made me kick dairy—a major breakthrough. Basically, he explained, cheese dehydrates, forms mucus, clogs everything, and is loaded with milk fat. (Really makes you want to reach for that wedge of Brie, doesn't it?) Cheese and dairy products require so much energy to break down and digest that you practically need personal days off from work to get through it. Hey, 50 million Frenchmen can't all be wrong, one can argue; but 50 million screaming babies with milk-induced tummy aches can't all be right, either. Their tiny tummies are trying to digest the indigestible. And problems digesting dairy can also be linked to bedwetting in children.

I trusted Dr. An Than and ditched dairy. I gave up the two gallons a day of Tab I drank and all the chemicals that slosh down with it. Sugar, sweets, and salt were tough to give up, because they're addicting, and they're what we're raised on.

Part of this process is reading labels and purging—the cupboards, pantry, and fridge, of all the toxins. Part of it is exercising and burning fat. The idea is to find the harmony and balance and control—the yin-yang of nutrition—that gets, and keeps, you where you want to be. For me, as for most women, it's been a battle, but the one most worth winning.

My look has changed so drastically it's ridiculous. There were times in my career when I'd be desperate to cancel days on account of fatness, and would go ballistic rummaging through my closets for something nice to wear. Now, when I go on location, my contracts stipulate that healthy (i.e., "macrobiotic") food must be supplied. I do that because I have learned, for instance, that to manage stress and maintain energy, I should load up on seaweed and miso soup. I was never bulimic or anorexic, but I went nuts fighting for self-control. Still, there were memorable lapses. In Italy once in the early days of my transformation, I plowed through some fabulous gelato—creamy Italian ice cream. My body went into a condition I can only describe as grand mal dairy. I wanted to kill my friend Flavio. I heaved through the night with my head in the toilet bowl, becoming dehydrated and weak. But I was at another milestone as a recovering junkaholic: my Ice Cream Birthday. I convinced myself that my true mission in life was to become a celebrity so I could save the world from dairy.

If I haven't, it's not been for lack of trying.

But my body and therefore my life changed forever on December 2, 1987, when I decided to break a sweat every day for ten minutes a day. That, along with food combining, gave me the body I always wanted to have. I never had to worry about my weight again. Free at last!

12

Nardo Loses
Her Marbles

❧

Not long after the debut episode of *Taxi, TV Guide* sent a reporter for an "on the set" article. At the end of the week, I asked the reporter what the guys had told him about me. He said I'd have to wait for the piece to come out. Then he added, "I will tell you this: You did get one marriage proposal passed along to me from one of them."

"Who, Tony?" I shrugged. "Probably Tony." He and I had recently ended our wonderful three-month affair.

"Uh-uh. I have a marriage proposal for you from Judd."

"Judd? *Judd?*" I was stunned. "Judd doesn't even talk to me. What, are you kidding?"

"I'm not sure, but I think this guy's in love with you."

I hadn't been able to warm up to Judd, though I had a crush on him because of that tormented Jewish intellectual edge that I love. But Judd was serious, he was a grown-up, the father of a growing son. Not to mention the fact that Judd was an established star—nor that I had been going the distance with Tony off the set practically since I'd gotten there. Judd just seemed out of range.

Until now. The next day I went up to him and said, "I accept."

He gave me that furrowed Judd glower. "Accept what?"

"I accept your marriage proposal." He looked away, embarrassed. "I can't believe you said that to that reporter," I said. "You never even *talk* to me."

"You never notice how I look at you?" he asked.

Hardly. I was intimidated by Judd's prowess, his intensity, and his rather volatile personality. Now I was embarrassed. This was beginning to sound like one of the Alex's girlfriend episodes.

From then on I was *extremely* aware of how Judd looked at me, and I found myself becoming more attracted to him. There was a growing—subtler and more profound—awareness of each other all the time. I got past my fear and, as we spent more time talking, driving around together, going for drinks—without anyone else knowing—I saw a softer side to Judd, and realized that there was something going on.

Finally, in early November, he came over to play tennis and go out for dinner with me. After dinner, Judd came in and went upstairs to get his stuff. He got a lot more than his stuff. He never left. It just seemed the most natural thing in the world for us to do. I spent the entire next weekend at his house, I met his darling son Alex, and we were on our way.

Over Thanksgiving, we met in New York after I visited Chicago. When you live in L.A.'s endless summer, New York in that cold, crisp, late-autumn holiday time can be very romantic. We had a terrific time. One night we met Jim Brooks for dinner. "Well," he said to us, "you've either doomed the show or improved it."

The more pressing question was whether or not Judd's intensity would doom or improve our *affair*. Judd was always on the edge, seemingly capable of blowing his stack at any time. He could have scary knock-down-drag-out fights, and I had the distinct impression he didn't break up with women well.

One clue: While at dinner at a restaurant in L.A., he took a phone call at the table, hung up, and said: "Come on, let's go. We're leaving."

"Why? Our food hasn't even come. What's the matter?"

As he hurried us from the table, he said, "Some girl I used to date is outside across the street and she's threatening to cause trouble. Let's sneak out the back way."

Just an *impression*.

But precisely because of his age, his depth, his nurturing side, his brooding intelligence, I could make the case in my head—and heart—that maybe Judd was the grown-up man I had been looking for, that the others had been boys and fun and games next to this.

After our weekend in New York, we went up to his cozy, secluded cabin near Woodstock, in upstate New York. Then we went to

Ventana, California, and stayed in a three-story home deep in the woods with a two-story ceiling in the living room, a huge fireplace, bookshelves and a sliding ladder, and a hot tub on the deck. A perfectly relaxing spot for us to cook, eat, make love, walk along the trails—a deliciously intimate time for us to discover each other. I had landed in quite the sitcom ensemble.

I was beginning to understand how Judd could trigger such powerful emotions in his adoring women and transform them into terrorists. Judd was one of the wildest, most passionate lovers I ever had.

Judd shocked me. He had an unbelievable sexual drive and stamina that made sense once you truly got the man's emotional fierceness. And Judd was a selfless lover who didn't make you do all the work. He definitely showed up and stayed for the whole picnic, no doubt about it, and I couldn't help but love that about him.

Back in the real world after our whirlwind getaway, I'd begun to feel a bit scared by Judd's temper. I'd seen it blow at work a few times. There was a room where we used to hang out on the set, and Judd practically destroyed it one night because something was upsetting him. He just got nuts and tore the place up. Judd was an artist who burned with an intense, roiling energy that drove his acting genius, but that energy wasn't easy to be around when it erupted.

Over Christmas, Judd came east with me again, first to meet my family, then to go to New York. On New Year's Eve, we went to a party. As soon as we walked in, some woman saw him and started smacking Judd and screaming, "You fucking asshole, you!"

There were other ugly encounters wherever we went. New York and L.A. seemed wired with the psychic land mines of Judd's former love interests.

I didn't quite yet see myself biting off the pin and hurling a grenade into his car or anything; I did see myself falling madly in love with him. But it also occurred to me that there was an aura of danger around him, that there were things I couldn't and didn't want to know about his past, that there was a real potential for getting hurt. Judd had started to display an obsessive jealous streak, even though I had cleaned my slate to devote all my time and energy to him. And he did have that short, argumentative fuse. Moreover, we did have a hit series to do together. . . .

As the first season's shooting wrapped, I figured it would be best for both of us—and the show—to cool off and pull back. Happily,

I got no argument from Judd and, as with all *my* love interests, we were able to move on to a wonderfully supportive, caring friendship afterward—and, obviously, to continue working together on a fantastic series. (Judd is now happily married to Bonni, the sister of Sharon Feldstein, one of my closest friends and business associates, and we're in touch all the time. His wife recently had a baby; our children were born a month apart.)

By then, nothing Judd and I could do together was likely to either doom or improve the show: *Taxi* had built its audience and critical admirers gradually through the first season, ending up as a Top Ten series for the season. The characters grew more complex, the stories were great, and, as an ensemble, we were starting to hit a groove.

What we had created was, I believe, remarkable. The *New York Times* critic called us a "first-rate repertory company"; moreover, the show made off, as our second fall season got under way the following September, with the Emmy for Outstanding Comedy Series. (Amazingly, the show would go on to win that Emmy its first three seasons.) One episode, Judd's wonderful "Blind Date," was nominated for Outstanding Comedy Writing, as were Judd and Danny, for Best Comedy Lead Actor and Best Supporting Actor, respectively. We had hit a grand slam.

I received a personal reward, if not an industry award. One of my lifelong fantasies became a reality when I was a guest on *The Tonight Show* in February of 1979. I was so pumped it was scary. Unfortunately, Sally Field had come out the night before and sprayed whipped cream—a gift from Burt Reynolds, and which she had concealed in her purse—all over Johnny Carson. When I showed up, it was like airport security. The word was Johnny was very upset over this unscripted gag, and in pre-interviews they warned me not to try to do anything smart. (They also tell you to make sure all your cute little anecdotes have a beginning, middle, and end. This wasn't Uncle and me pretending.)

I went out and gave Johnny a surprise anyway, unscripted and beyond my control. I was so nervous about making a good impression that by the time I walked onstage, my nipples were hard and practically poking through the sheer silk blouse I wore.

Johnny did not fail to notice.

"Oh," he said, "it must be cold backstage," nodding to my chest. I couldn't believe it. This was all I needed to ruin my big chance to shine with Johnny. I turned beet-red, clammed up, and froze. I struggled to gather my wits, but every time I opened my mouth I was afraid I was repeating myself and I wondered if I was at the beginning, middle, or end of my story. I was not in present time. For no reason at all, I began speaking with a phony British accent. I was totally disoriented, and terrible.

The *Tonight* staff called my publicist the next day to apologize. Johnny, they said, had reviewed the show, and had asked, "How many shows have we done like that?" He too had felt skittish, off his game. They asked me back as soon as possible—booking me with guest hosts George Carlin, Bill Cosby, and David Letterman before matching me with the King of Late Night again.

Going back for the second season of *Taxi* was fantastic. I knew the routine, the cast and staff were like family to me, and there were no more intra-cast love affairs to complicate things. The set had a wild, high-energy atmosphere, much like the one I had grown up in.

Tony and Judd bonded by sparring; Tony and I channeled our hormones into rolling around together and groping, or working out together at the studio gym. (I was the first woman ever allowed in there, believe it or not.) Guys were stealing security golf carts and crashing them all over the place.

Judd could be a wildman. He is six feet tall and a much more strapping brute in person because he hunches over a lot on TV. A couple of times he actually hoisted me over his head like an Olympic powerlifter.

Danny was a doll, and absolutely adorable—and, for my money, the cast member with the most PF of all. He reeked of it. He's got that twinkle, that spark. He just looks like he *likes* it—and he's already *down there.*

Danny cracked us all up once when my niece Suzanne visited the set. She was a precocious and stunning preteen, and Danny took one look and said, "Here's a dime, call me when you're eighteen. In fact, I'll pay for your college education."

Danny and I loved to give each other lewd, lip-smacking looks, as he'd playfully growl, "Ooooh, Henner, you know, if I wasn't with Rhea [Perlman, Danny's sweetheart, who played Zena on the show and later became Danny's wife]." Elaine was supposed to hate Louie, who gave her the creeps. But I found him so adorable and delightful that everything he did made me lose it. So it wasn't easy being Nardo to his Louie.

I have always found Danny incredibly sexy. Having classically handsome looks hardly assures strong PF. It's attitude, it's charisma, and Danny had it over just about everybody. I loved the episode when Danny says to Zena, who supplied candy bars for the machines at the garage, "Come on, you can come over tonight and we'll play slave girl and the emperor." That was pure Danny.

After *Indecent Proposal* came out, everyone was saying things like, "Of course I'd do it for a million dollars—Robert Redford? Come *on.*" I was the opposite—Redford couldn't pay me enough; Danny wouldn't have to pay me. I find Danny so much sexier than a Robert Redford. No comparison. Redford has his appeal, no question. But he isn't one of my two major types: the brainy Jewish neurotic, and the ethnic, neighborhood street type. Both have a sexy, soulful aura. I've never been one to go the Waspy, white-bread route.

Plus, Danny so obviously loves women; you see it in his eyes. He has a stunningly beautiful face and his body is adorable. If he did not have a powerful sexual presence, he would not be the major superstar he is today. I loved working with him.

Then there was Latka. No one added more of an edge of insanity to the set chemistry than Andy Kaufman. His Tony Clifton shtick got him off to a bizarre start with us. When offered a contract, Andy told Brooks & Co., who were on to his alter ego act: "I don't want a full thirteen-week contract. I'll do seven out of thirteen weeks, but I want my opening act Tony Clifton to do three."

"Tony Clifton's an unproven commodity," was the answer. "We'll let him do one episode, with an option for two more."

Fine, Andy said.

I found Andy's Latka Gravas brilliant. Andy was a real professional—when he was there. I didn't mind when he asked Brooks if when Latka had just a line or two in an episode, he could just come in for the Tuesday run-throughs and show up for taping on Friday. Brooks said okay, and this rankled a few cast members. But it wasn't like Andy's aura on the set was so effervescent that his absence created a spiritual vacuum. He was very hard to get to know and, once in character as Latka, there was no breaking Andy out of it: He stayed Latka.

In October, Ed Weinberger told us that our guest star would be a guy named Tony Clifton—and then tried to prepare us. "Okay, listen," he conceded, "it's Andy, but . . . it . . . *isn't* Andy. He has this character that he does—what can I tell you?" Ed shrugged. "Look, just play along. Nobody's supposed to say anything. Do the best you can with it."

Monday morning, Andy/Tony walked in for the morning read-through around the big table. He was unrecognizable, with stomach padding, a fake nose, a wig, makeup, and a cigarette. (Andy never smoked.) Unlike Andy, Tony had an obnoxious rap: "Hey, pretty lady, howya doin'? You're quite a looker there, aren't you now. Say, where's the director—anybody got a script for me? Hey, come on, boys, where's my ashtray?"

His slimy shtick was hysterical. And we were going, right, okay, Andy's in character, he's smoking and we're okay with it.

The problem was, as Andy's alter ego, Tony Clifton was a terrible actor who couldn't get his lines right. This was our warm and fuzzy holiday season offering, titled "Full House for Christmas." Andy/Tony was playing Louie DePalma's brother Nicky, a Vegas poker champ whom Louie hasn't seen in six years. He starts killing everyone at Sunshine Cab in poker and completely forgets about visiting his and Louie's mom. Louie then sets up a winner-take-all match with Judd's Alex, the garage champ: the garage receipts if Nicky wins, a Vegas vacation for Mom on Nicky if he loses. Alex wins.

It was insane to stake a Christmas show's success on such an awful performance. Andy's bad-actor act may have been perfect, but it hardly made Danny look good. He had to play his scenes off Tony Clifton, who was a bad actor, and that was risky.

It got worse. Tony didn't like his small, crummy dressing room. The next day he showed up in his own Winnebago with two bimbos in thick makeup and short miniskirts whom we assumed were hookers. He handed out gifts—toy mechanical dogs that went "ARF! ARF!" when you pushed a button. It was completely subversive—the whole set had collectively lost it and was colluding with Andy.

The Tuesday run-through was painful. By now, Danny saw that his big show was in jeopardy. Jeff wanted to rip Andy's/Tony's head off, and stormed off the set after tossing one of the Scottish terriers into a wall. Judd's fuse was burning down. Well, we figured, that's a wrap. Let's see what Wednesday brings.

Jim Burrows gathered us around when we arrived and announced: "We fired Tony. Actually, Ed called Andy and told him we were firing Tony. Andy wouldn't break the news to Tony. He said we had to fire Tony in person today. So be prepared for anything. In the meantime, we have a new actor [Richard Foronji] for Nicky."

Wednesday afternoon, as the soundstage bleachers started filling up with an unexpected audience of Andy's friends, we heard Clifton's voice from off in the distance, "Where's the director? I need to speak to the director. What is going *on* here?" And he started carrying on, with a bimbo hanging on to each arm. "You think you guys are the only ones with contracts? Nobody fires me. Bring on the *broads*. Let's get on with the *rehearsal.*"

It was total insanity. Ed went to him and said, "Tony, this isn't going to work out. I'm sorry."

"Sorry?" he exploded. "I'll sue your fuckin' *ass*. Are you kidding me?"

Finally, Judd, never one to pass up a psychodrama, took charge and confronted him as only he could, with his frightening scowl. "He wants a challenge," Judd muttered to me. "Go for it," I said.

"You think you're the only one with a contract here, huh?" Judd said, going chest to chest with Tony. They were seconds from a bloody brawl when a Paramount security guard got called in and separated them, dragging off the flailing Tony—who was forever banned from the lot—as he screamed, "Get my lawyer on the phone, call my agent. I'm going to be bigger than ANY of you!"

Whether it was a surreal piece of performance art or a carefully disciplined multiple personality disorder, Andy/Tony pulled it off with scary brilliance. The following Monday Andy/Andy showed up for work as if nothing had happened. No one said anything. That was that. It was just the most bizarre thing.

A few days later, Andy came to my dressing room and said something weird like, "I know what happened here with Tony and that you got pretty upset. But don't you see the beauty in the guy? I mean, there's something really beautiful and pure about him, don't you think?"

Was this Andy's crazy way of reaching out for some kind of affirmation or approval? It was as if some little boy in him was saying, Please don't be mad at me, because I really like you.

I really liked him, too.

He did have his cult. One time Andy developed a humongous boil on the back of his neck that was the size of a tennis ball. It was so disgusting you couldn't stop looking at it. The open-sore part of it was the size of a golf ball. It was so freakish that he announced to the audience during our Friday taping that they could touch it for a dollar.

Pay a dollar, touch Andy's boil. Most of the audience lined up. There was no middle ground with him.

Sadly, incredibly, Andy died of cancer in May 1984, about a year after *Taxi* went off the air. He was an absolute original, a thoroughly fascinating, unfathomable, complex, uncompromised, tortured artist who marched through his short, strange life to a very different drummer.

With such a rich chemistry within the ensemble, doing the show was the most creatively pleasurable time of my professional life. There wasn't a day when I couldn't wait to get to the set in the morning. Sitcoms blend the immediacy, dynamics, and live-audience spontaneity of theater, film, and *The Tonight Show*. What's great is that live audiences love it when you screw up. They feel they're in on a joke. Plus, you make the show's gag reel.

The hardest part was keeping a straight face. An episode from our second year was classic. Reverend Jim, played by Christopher Lloyd, takes his cabbie test. If you watch carefully, you see that during parts of a particular sequence I'm digging a pencil into my palm so I won't blow it on camera. I thought I was going to get lead poisoning when the tip of the pencil broke off into my hands.

There are other scenes where Tony and I had to kick each other under the card table for our next line because we'd get so into playing cards that we'd almost forget the show.

Then there was the great episode where Louie builds his Armageddon bomb shelter, and invites none of the guys to see it, only Elaine. So he promises her, in his hand-rubbing, mischievous way: "I've got a place for you, and just so I'll know it's you, Nardo, this is the password." At that moment, he whispers something in my ear, I pull back, scream *"Louie!"* and slap him.

Danny loved being a bad boy, and was such a brilliant improv comic that he could never leave well enough alone. So every time he whispered something, it was an even more filthy thing that would invariably crack me up. The more hysterically vulgar he got, the more takes we had to shoot.

Danny hated it when, because of repetition over the course of a week, you stopped laughing at his scripted gags. So he was always

29.

30.

31.

32.

33.

34. During *Evening Shade*

35. Johnny's pre–*Urban Cowboy* look, at Studio One in L.A.

36. I was named honorary cabbie of the year in New York City because of my *Taxi* role.

37. With my *Taxi* buddies. Clockwise, from upper left: Andy Kaufman, Chris Lloyd, Carol Kane, Judd Hirsch, Danny DeVito, me, and Tony Danza

38. Danny DeVito in "Louie Goes Too Far." He almost did.

39. Boogie-oogie-oogying with Tony Danza at Studio 54

40. A few days after *Grease* became the longest-running Broadway show, the producers sent 286 roses to the *Taxi* set, one for each actor who had appeared in *Grease*. It had been my idea to fly them all to New York for a celebration, and Pan Am agreed.

41. With Freddie Forrest in Cancun

EXTRA
The New Orleans Times
DESPERADO WEDS SHOWGIRL

42. This headline says it all.

43. During the shooting of *The Man Who Loved Women,* Burt Reynolds and I hit it off from day one. Our humor was contagious; our chemistry was obvious.

44. My favorite photo from *Johnny Dangerously.* Michael Keaton and I reminded me of my parents going out to dinner at a nightclub.

45. This photo from *Perfect* was taken from the credit sequence shot after I'd completed *Rustler's Rhapsody* and had lost fifteen pounds in Spain.

was totally cool, and worked because it didn't have the real ... of a Broadway number; instead, it looked like these guys ... Broadway. It took two days to choreograph, with the help of ...reat Pat Birch, and I was really proud of my work.

...y other favorite was "Shut It Down." A strike is called by the ...ers, because they feel their lives are being put at risk. It's not ... Latka's shoddy work as a mechanic, but also the company's ...dency to cut corners on parts and its refusal to replace broken-...wn cabs. Elaine ends up as shop steward, forced to negotiate ...ms with Louie. But Louie has cooked the books to make the ...mpany look responsible.

...Louie, under pressure to settle from the owner, agrees to ...gotiate a settlement with Elaine, on one condition: that she go on ...date with him. She agrees. But then they go over terms. She offers ... meet him for lunch, as long as it's at a crowded place, they're ...tting at separate tables, and no one sees them come or go. As we ...eal, Danny and I are walking in perfect sync with each other ...cross the garage floor; then we switch directions and go back. It ...was beautifully staged.

Now, he counters: He'll pick her up at her place, it's *dinner* at a *romantic* place, and, sometime in the course of the evening, "within earshot of at least ten people, you call me Stallion."

She agrees, but tells him, "Except Stallion."

"*Especially* Stallion," he insists. Elaine is furious that she has to lower herself to this, and demands that he never tell anyone about the date. It was a great scene.

Danny could put a look on his face at the word "stallion" that totally broke my focus and made me laugh. But by Wednesday, he saw that I had gotten used to his face when he said "stallion." Danny couldn't stand it. He came up with something new: He sort of lifted his head up like a horse when he said it now, and—forget it, it was one of the funniest bits of acting "business" I've ever seen anyone do. Once I adjusted to that, he added a horse-stomping foot, and we'd have to run through it three or four times in rehearsals to get it right. I was destroyed; no way could I ever pull off this scene without laughing.

Thursday night, I figured out how to do it: I went to sleep wearing the tightest, most uncomfortable boots I owned, just to give myself a vicious stomachache. I knew that one of the toes is neurologically connected to the pancreas. By the time I got to the shoot Friday, my

46. Among the pros of comedy—with Michael Caine, Carol Burnett, and Denholm Elliot in *Noises Off*

47. Burt and I dressed as the Tooth Fairy and Raggedy Ann for the Halloween episode of *Evening Shade*.

48. From left to right: Ann Wedgeworth, Linda Gehringer, Elizabeth Ashley, and I have fun trying on Linda's character Fontana's old strip outfits until the men find a way to lure us outside and lock us out—in a place called *Evening Shade*.

49. With Rob at our beautiful wedding in Carsoli, Italy

50. With my dear friend Flavio. *Viva la rivoluzione!*

51. My most famous (notorious?) talk-show appearance *ever*—with Sting on *The Tonight Show* with Jay Leno, May 1993

changing his lines and coming up with some ne~~~ It ~~
of the eyes, something to keep you off guard. He~~~ polis~~
This one we had to do twenty-five times. H~~~ doin~~
gonna spread your . . . ," or he would go on ~~~ the g~~
fucking continuum that got more disgusting as ~~~

Danny paid a price for his antics. I cracked hin~~~ driv~~
every take while trying unsuccessfully not to laug~~~ just~~
got so raw from smacking, they had to cover the s~~~ ten~~
more Pan-Cake.

Naturally, this scene ended up on some kind of b~~~ ter~~
and for two or three years, people would do all kinds~~~ co~~
me—from helping me tag baggage at airports to hailin~~~
New York—if I'd tell them what Louie whispered in ~~~

One of my favorite things about Danny was our s~~~ a~~
Louie the dispatcher calling out last names of people~~~ t~~
hired cabs and assigning them car numbers. Danny said~~~ s~~
him a dollar he'd say someone's name for you—a~~~
girlfriend, in-law, whatever. So everybody gave Danny ~~~
hear a name—except me. Tony recalls the bribe was~~~
wouldn't have mattered if it had been $1,000 when it cam~~~
Danny used to tease me that he wasn't after my dollars: "H~~~
he'd joke, "you want me to say the people you used to baby~~~
no problem, but that'll be another blow job on your tab."

My two all-time favorite episodes are "Shut It Down" I a~~~
which aired in January 1980, and another two-parter, "Fa~~~
Borough" I and II, which aired in May 1980.

In "Fantasy Borough," Herve Villechaize, of *Fantasy Isl*~~~
fame, leaves his glossies in Tony's cab. As Tony is trying to get th~~~
back to him, we all dream up fantasy scenarios for ourselve~~~
Elaine's fantasy actually seems taken from a page out of my ow~~~
Broadway musical days. On a dreary, rainy day, the guys ar~~~
playing cards and Elaine sits, bored in her raincoat.

Then, in a close-up of me, I softly start to sing "Lullaby of
Broadway." As Elaine's fantasy kicks in, I stand up and rip off the
raincoat to reveal a slinky, clingy dress. I get them all into it as the
song builds, with a huge orchestra sound, into a glitzy production
number. The climax has Elaine strutting down the stairs in Vegas
showgirl tuxedo and the guys in top hats and tails, dancing giddily
all around the garage. Even Latka gets in the act, bouncing across
the stage with a sparkler in each hand.

intestinal agony had forced me to focus on my pain, and allowed me to get through the Stallion scene.

Danny often got to show that Louie wasn't just an irascible buffoon. One episode proves how sensitive the *Taxi* writers were in texturing and modulating scenes for comedy and poignancy. Their collective genius for "feel" is what set our show apart from so many other funny, but two-dimensional, shows.

In "Louie Goes Too Far," Elaine goes to the washroom to change for a gallery opening after a shift. She discovers Louie has drilled a peephole and is spying on her—and pokes his eye through the hole. Louie's voyeurism makes her and the other women cabbies feel completely violated, and infuriates even the men at Sunshine.

When a National Organization for Women official investigates, Louie tries to hustle her—and winds up getting fired. This destroys him. He goes to Elaine's apartment to beg forgiveness—and grovel for his job back. It's all he's got in life. She hangs tough. "You don't even know what you did wrong," she chastises.

"No," he says. "You're not supposed to peek at girls?"

Elaine asks him, "Have you ever been violated?" She wants him to really feel what he has put her through.

Then, in a heart-wrenching, revealing scene, Danny/Louie delivers a wonderfully written speech about how, as a portly, very short grown man, he is often humiliated by having to shop at boys' departments, where kids stare at him and upset mothers yank their kids away as if he were a pitiful sideshow freak. The worst moments are always when he tries on a corduroy suit—and it makes a sound as his thick legs rub together.

Like most of the audience, I had tears streaming down my face.

Louie finally breaks down and sobs. "Is that the way I made you feel when I peeked?" he asks her. Yes, I say, it is. "Ohhh, Nardo," he says, "I'm so sorry." We hug and I give him a forgiving hug. It's a breakthrough scene in which Louie's repressed vulnerability, insecurities, and bitterness pour out.

It would have been out of character for Brooks to end the episode on such a heavy note. So, as we embrace, Louie plants his hand right on Elaine's butt—and the show ends perfectly with a freeze-frame of the grope that pulls you right back in, smiling.

Through the seasons, the line between character and actor got fuzzy. Our ensemble, as in any long-running hit show, was truly extraordinary. You realize that there are no other actors more perfectly suited for these characters. That's not only about acting; the *Taxi* formula of casting, writing, acting, and directing worked wonders, year in, year out.

Having been "miscast" (I was almost a decade younger than Elaine was originally written), I had to grow into the part. Early on, I felt I was playing my older sister JoAnn. Then, in the presence of true masters of the genre, I saw my craft get honed and advance by quantum leaps. I lucked out.

My one regret is that we saw Elaine's two kids in only three episodes and never focused on issues of single parenting that might have given her a whole other dimension. It was, like, what kind of mother is this who's always hanging out with the guys? She'd have been better off as a single woman and given other problems to focus on.

Sometimes I had the feeling that Elaine was crafted out of material the writer-producers never got to try out on Mary Richards, Rhoda, or Phyllis. They were more into writing for the guys, which made me sometimes feel shortchanged, and into writing Elaine as they wanted to see the woman or women in their lives. How else to explain that she would pass up going to bed with a charismatic, sensitive hunk played by Tom Selleck, but sleep with far geekier characters played by Jeffrey Tambor and Wally Shawn? Didn't compute.

One writer wrote Elaine as a feisty princess type with a twisted sense of humor. Another wrote her soft and loving and understanding. Still a third had her a dishrag sob sister with little to say. I had the feeling no one really had a handle on her because who I was was so different from the original Elaine concept, and because she was a mother with kids you never saw.

That tripped up even these fantastic writers. Elaine was their late seventies–early eighties female "voice," and so, in the absence of specific, well-sketched dilemmas and resolutions, Elaine risked becoming a generic for all Womankind. It took me longer than the guys to hit my stride, and my best season, without question, didn't come until *Taxi*'s fourth year, 1981–82, when they started writing with the way I talk and move in mind.

Those years were so good that I was disappointed when I did not get a Golden Globe for the second season, particularly for the episode titled "Nardo Loses Her Marbles," and did not even get an

Emmy nomination for that fourth season. (I got nominated for five Golden Globes, but never got an Emmy nomination.)

But most of the time, awards didn't faze me much. The glitter had worn off after attending the Academy Awards for the first time. I fell back on that old Johnny line when we were doing that hamper production number in *Over Here*—"I hope the PTA likes our show." Would it have been nice to win an Emmy then? Absolutely. But it never seemed that vitally important. It seemed political as much as anything else, so I never put that much energy on it. But if ever I deserved one, it was for the 1981–82 season.

The pace was frenetic, but Brooks ran a disciplined, well-oiled sitcom machine, powered by his gifted touch with character, story, and pacing.

There was the Monday read-through—usually a new script averaged thirty-eight to forty-two pages. If your stuff didn't work for your character, you flagged it and it was gone. Or if a scene didn't work in the overall scheme, it was gone. The goal was never to indulge the cast, but to achieve a tighter, cleaner, better episode. It was check-your-egos-at-the-door time.

Judd, Danny, and Chris Lloyd had unerring radar in locating the truth of their scenes. They knew their own—and their characters' —rhythms and mechanisms so intimately that even a word or inflection out of place required a change. They were perfectionists —not prima donnas—and their work inspired, and instructed, all of us.

We did standing run-throughs on Tuesdays, and any rewrites were completed by six A.M. Wednesday morning. Then we'd walk in to a fresh script, shaped, staged, and edited for precisely twenty-two to twenty-three minutes of shooting. Every word, every move, every second, counted once the cameras rolled.

By Thursday, we were doing camera blocking—determining exact placement and framing for the four cameras—and would run through each scene four times for rhythm and movement.

Friday was showtime. After we'd finish our dress rehearsal, the audience would show up at seven P.M. and we'd tape the show. Then we'd get the new script to read over the weekend, and it was on to the next episode Monday morning.

Having done theater, road company work, and films, I felt as if I had come home to the rhythms, format, and relationships of a sitcom.

A recurring theme in my career has been the attempt—probably

unconscious—to replicate my own powerful family ties in work
environments. I've had the good fortune to work on two series that
offered bonding, nurturing environments.

Of course, there's another thing—and my father sure would have
loved this: You get paid a lot of money for doing something you
love, and you work only seven months of the year.

With things falling so perfectly into place, it would have been
hard not to believe that everything was connected to everything.
The timing was simply too perfect for the connections to be
occurring at random—as I was about to discover all over again
toward the end of the second season of *Taxi*.

13
Fame

~~~~~

By the end of 1979, Johnny and I were in one of our holding patterns. Our two-week jaunt to Europe the year before had been an elegant, first-class romp: a suite at the Plaza-Athénée Hotel; long, romantic, predawn walks along the deserted Champs-Élysées to avoid his overeager fans; the Deauville film festival; a Royal Box in London for a command performance of *Evita*. And all of it on Paramount's tab, because Johnny was there to open *Grease*.

But there was a dark side to Johnny's global fame. I hated the London tabloid press and paparazzi, and at one point I thought we were going to get stomped and stampeded when fans circled his limo and started pounding on it.

And there was celebrity itself. By the time we got back—going through New Orleans to watch Muhammad Ali demolish Leon Spinks and have dinner with The Greatest himself—I was already missing my *Taxi* guys. I was starting to tire of getting sucked into the jet wash of exhaust behind Johnny's star-making engine, commanded by his imperious manager, Bob Lemond. It's not so much that the core of Johnny changed; it didn't. But now I was involved with an entourage, not a man. I felt swept along in an immense tidal wave.

Bob's problem was that when Johnny became a star, *he* became a star. Now, he was my manager, too, and telling me to *always hold something back,* to *never give 100 percent,* to *not do Johnny Carson.* "This is just a television show," he'd sneer, referring to *Taxi.* "Hold something back for the movies."

That's about as useful as telling a top-seeded tennis player during the pro tour, "Pace yourself; save your best shots for Wimbledon." For 15 percent off the top, he gave me the worst advice I ever got. I had business meetings with him at his home while he would be getting manicures and pedicures.

What made Johnny a star, besides his extraordinary talent, was his unpolished, rough edges and his spontaneity. Now, every move was calculated and orchestrated for its impact.

But no missteps were tolerated. Bob told us how to pose in Paris for photo opportunities. Johnny trusted him and, to be fair, many stars would have killed to get on his roster. After all, not long afterward, Johnny, the same kid who had once so giddily blown his $181 residual check with me on a night on the town, would get a check for $876,000—just for his piece of the *sound track* of *Saturday Night Fever.*

Still, I felt a kind of career constipation around Johnny that was the antithesis of the looseness and accessibility that made him Johnny. A part of Johnny *was* Tony Manero—he was one of the people. Now it was no talk shows, don't schmooze *down* in public with certain people, pull back, create mystique, let a buzz swirl around your persona. I found it all mostly nauseating.

The buzz in the summer and fall of 1979 was swirling in Houston, where Johnny was filming *Urban Cowboy.* I visited him, and we had a great time together. He stayed in character, which was fine with me. I just threw myself into that fifties cowboy mentality where boys will be cowboys and girls will be girls. It clicked between us. Maybe it was all that work on that mechanical bull at Gilley's—he was very sexy to be around.

In December we went to Las Vegas together and caught the new movie *The Rose,* Bette Midler's feature film debut loosely based on the life of Janis Joplin.

Midway through the film, I whispered to Johnny, "Who *is* that guy?" referring to the lanky, rugged actor playing Bette's love interest.

"Oh, that's Frederic Forrest," Johnny whispered. "I think he auditioned for *Urban Cowboy.*"

"Hmm. Never seen him before."

Figures prominently.

I sat through the rest of the film going, *Whoa, is this guy cute! I would not mind working with him at all.*

After a Christmas visit to Chicago, Johnny and I went to his ranch north of Santa Barbara, then planned to go up to Mammoth for a ski trip. But I told him our friend Ellen March was moving back to New York and I wanted to spend that Thursday in L.A. with her before we left. Johnny agreed to pick me up in L.A. before heading northeast to Mammoth.

That Thursday, I also had some business to attend to in town—an afternoon interview with director Wim Wenders and casting director Fred Roos. They were casting *Hammett,* a film to be produced by Francis Ford Coppola's Zoetrope Studios, based on the life of Dashiell Hammett, the famed thirties mystery writer. I was going up for the part of the librarian who lives downstairs from Hammett and gets involved with him.

I came out of there convinced they hated me. I did all the talking. They said nothing. They had a magazine picture of me on the wall and they had recently seen me on *The Tonight Show.* That seemed to be the extent of their interest in me.

Ellen and I went out for sushi and I got loaded on two sakes. Then we got a bottle of champagne and a big bag of raw cashews—my favorite pig-out food.

The next day, Friday, I was getting ready to leave for the ski trip when I got a call from my agent. Just then, Johnny drove up, came in, and started loading my skis and stuff into his car.

I couldn't believe what my agent was telling me.

"They want you to screen-test for *Hammett,*" she said, explaining that the spring shoot would be timed perfectly with my *Taxi* hiatus.

"Are you kidding?" I asked. I was incredulous. "I didn't think they liked me at all."

"Well, they want you to test—and right away. You have to do it today. Francis wants to go right into production. Look, it's up to you. But they'll deliver sides immediately if you can do it."

"Well," I sighed. Johnny gave me a let's-get-the-show-on-the-road look. I shrugged helplessly.

"Anyway, you'd be doing the screen test opposite a real fine actor."

"What do you mean?"

"Frederic Forrest is going to be there. He's Hammett."

"Frederic Forrest is going to be there?" He hadn't been at the interview. For some reason, this gave me a jolt.

"Yeah. Why? Is that a problem? Do you know him?"

"Well, no, I mean, *sure*. I know who he is. Frederic Forrest." No big deal.

I couldn't believe this. My tweakometer was smoking. It was kind of scary. I had seen him in *The Rose* only days earlier. "I'm supposed to *meet* him?"

"Uh-huh. They love you for the part. They want to see you two on film together. Tomorrow." There was no way I wasn't going to go for it.

"Where do I go? What time? What do I have to do?"

Johnny stopped dead in his tracks. "Are you kidding me?"

"Look," I said, "just take my skis up there. I'll do the screen test, drive up, and meet you there tomorrow night."

Sure, fine, no problem.

I wouldn't see those skis again for almost three years.

14
Freddie, My Love

⁓

Frederic Forrest is a spellbinding actor with an extraordinary gift for immersing himself in his roles. He never looks the same way twice. If I had seen his Dashiell Hammett on the street, I never would have associated him with his Huston Dyer from *The Rose.* The two weren't even from the same gene pool.

When Freddie imagined that one of his characters had never experienced traveling at more than 35 miles an hour, he instructed his location driver never to exceed 35 miles an hour—just to stay true to his character, even though he knew he would be keeping an entire set waiting for him. When he did a *Mrs. Columbo* episode, he decided his character would be a cross-dresser, so he wore lacy women's underwear. In *One from the Heart,* because Teri Garr tells him he looks "like an egg," Freddie put on twenty-five pounds so he would know how it felt to be shaped like an egg.

This method worked beautifully in filmmaking. Directors have always admired Freddie's uncompromising, passionate commitment to "the work." But directing a chameleon isn't the same as marrying one.

My problem with Freddie was that I fell in love with Dashiell Hammett, the intriguing, dashing mystery writer, but married Hank, his lovable loser junkyard-owner character from *One from the Heart.* And I didn't like Hank.

I fell madly in love with a beautiful, charismatically offbeat, sexually electric lover whose demons were under control; I married a man whose paranoid rages under the influence of alcohol set those devils loose on our marriage. It was scary. Freddie was a brilliant, tormented, adorable, generous, tenderhearted original.

And, I often thought, the biggest mistake of my life.

I was one of six actresses testing for *Hammett* that day, and things were running late. It was the end of the screen tests and people were loose. When I first saw him he smiled, but my smile back let him know I was onto the fact that another girl there was flirting with him. He showed me he liked that—so there was already a connection, a sexual tension, even before the test.

In my scene, my librarian character, Emma, helps Hammett with research, and he takes my glasses off. It turns into a taking-off-the-glasses-shaking-down-the-hair turn-on moment. I had been to hair and makeup and was in period wardrobe, so this was the real thing.

What was not scripted was the kiss. He and director Wim Wenders knew it was coming, but I didn't. They had added this kiss with the first actress and had forgotten to inform me. I felt shocked, but rolled with it. Then I came up with a surprise myself: I wouldn't stop kissing Freddie. And Freddie wouldn't stop, so, within seconds, we were making out right on camera and Wim was yelling, "Cut! Okay, you can cut. Hey, you two. *Cut!* Okay?"

I was immediately swept up in the moment—and by my powerful attraction. It was pure, visceral, and spontaneous. We had hardly spoken, other than my telling him how much I had liked his work in *The Rose*. Now I had a second opinion about Freddie: He was an incredible kisser.

In between takes, I had to fix my smeared lipstick, so I ran into the ladies' room and stared at myself in the mirror, put my hand over my pounding heart, and worked hard at not hyperventilating: "Now, come on, get it together. Go on out there; you're a professional." I rolled out my credits to myself—University of Chicago, plays, shows, *Grease*—to regain some self-control.

I straightened my skirt, pulled myself together, and walked out for another go, like, Okay, guys, ahh, yeah, are we ready to try again? I was trying to act very sophisticated and above it all! How Noël Cowardish of me!

This time Freddie and I looked at each other and chuckled, knowing the kiss was coming. And this time we got into it, using the safety of the fakery to communicate what we were really feeling. Not to mention sniffs, sighs, and some very discreet tongue

action. Instead of the surprised passion of the first take, now we
had some authentic heat building up.

Moments after we wrapped for the day, I looked for Freddie,
only to be told he was gone. I'd hoped at least he'd have said
good-bye. I was due home for my ski trip with Johnny.

But when I walked out to my car and opened the door, I heard
"Marilu?"

I turned and nonchalantly went, "Oh, hi. I thought you left. I
wanted to thank you so much for the screen test."

Very cool, very professional.

He sized me up, and awkwardly said, "So, uhh . . . you're
welcome. So are you married or living with someone or what?"

This came out of nowhere. "Well, uhh, no. Actually."

"You want to get a drink or something?"

"Sure," I answered, "but I have to go home first to make some
calls. Where do you want me to meet you?"

"I just moved into the Magic Hotel. We could get together
there." To me the Magic sounded like the Bel Air, the Regency. I
pictured a chic, well-appointed lounge with worldly travelers.

I called Johnny and bailed out on skiing. "I'll see you guys when
you get back." I got a bottle of wine on the way to the Magic. I
drove along Hollywood Boulevard and turned onto Franklin.

The Magic was a flophouse for actors in town for a gig—down
and dirty with a lot of colorful characters.

The second I walked in, Freddie's personality seemed totally
changed—he was crabby now, aloof, uncomfortable that I was
there.

I broke out the wine to break the ice.

"Oh, I don't drink," he shrugged. "I stopped drinking five
months ago. I'm an alcoholic."

"Oh, I'm sorry."

I poured some wine for myself, Freddie lit up a joint, and we sat
in silence as I asked myself what the hell I was doing there. An
icebreaker might not have made a dent in the mood.

On the wall above Freddie was the kind of bad painting you
always find in seedy hotels. This one was a lighthouse scene.

"So," I sighed, "how was the Cape that summer?" That cracked
him up. We laughed. "You're uncomfortable I'm here, aren't you?"
I said.

"Well, you know," he said, "I look at you and you're another pretty girl and I'm askin' myself, Freddie, can't you just let one pass you by? Pretty soon, I'll want to kiss you, and then I'm gonna want to sleep with you and then you're not gonna let me sleep with you and it's gonna be better that you don't and then I'm gonna feel closer to you than ever and pretty soon we're going to be dating and then we are going to sleep together and the next thing you know I'm going to be married to you."

After this soliloquy slid out of his mouth, I said, "Well, I'd better leave now before one of us gets pregnant."

I didn't. I spent the night with Freddie—kissing clothed, on the couch—until the sun rose over the junkies, the homeless, and the Pretty Woman hookers around Hollywood. By then, I was absolutely madly in love crazy about Freddie.

He wasn't a classic Hollywood bad boy in the Bruce Willis, Tony Danza, Alec Baldwin mold. Freddie was a different animal, more of a cowboy, a Western desperado. Freddie walked into walls, but was masterful on a horse. He always carried with him a small bottle of Tex-Mex smoke flavoring that he sprinkled over everything— scrambled eggs, steak, it didn't matter. He was a male type I had never found appealing, but Freddie's blend of sweetness and craziness got through that.

He was from Waxahachie, Texas, and thought he had grown up poor, even though he said his family's Forrest Florist was a very successful six-figure business. That was my first clue as to how distorted Freddie's sense of numbers and money was. In that, and many other ways, he was as far away from me as you could get. And I couldn't have been more fascinated by him, by everything that came out of his mouth.

Our next time together, we again spent the night at the Magic, and I still kept all my clothes on. Then, on Saturday night, we had dinner at a tacky Italian joint near the hotel that looked like the kind of place Dino, Sinatra, and the Rat Pack hung out at. Dinner went beautifully, but for dessert we returned to the Magic for a night of such combustible chemistry and scrape-me-off-the-ceiling sex that I thought: I'm going to marry this guy and spend the rest of my life with him.

Freddie's career was finally beginning to take off. A decade earlier he had been brilliant in Francis Coppola's *The Conversation*. His range was phenomenal through a slew of character roles in film and on TV. He played the title role in the TV movie *Larry*, a heartbreaking story of a guy who was put away after being misdiagnosed as mentally retarded, but who would wake up in the night and teach himself to read under the covers with a flashlight. He played Lee Harvey Oswald in a TV miniseries called *Four Days in Dallas* about Oswald and Ruby. He looked so much like Oswald in the film that, during one of our big fights, I yelled: "I was supposed to end up with someone like John F. Kennedy, and instead I ended up with Lee Harvey Oswald."

He was exceptional in *The Rose,* and was great in Coppola's *Apocalypse Now,* which like *The Rose* had come out in 1979. Francis was signing him to a million-dollar deal to join his Zoetrope Studios ensemble. It seemed like a bold, risky experiment that challenged the major studio system, and when I got together with Freddie, he was a darling of the critics and one of Hollywood's most dedicated, unbeholden artists, with the potential to become a major player.

A week after our first night together, I got the part in *Hammett.* It was a no-brainer: Francis, the exec-producer, Wim, and their casting people decided I had the best screen chemistry with Freddie.

It was an exquisitely romantic time for us, knowing we would make a movie up north together. I finished my *Taxi* season in late January and prepared to join Freddie in San Francisco. By then, we had turned the corner and were definitely a couple.

But in early February, as soon as we were together in San Francisco, weird things started to happen. Freddie's devotion to creating a character knew no limits. We stayed in a modest hotel, but the production company had rented out one of Hammett's actual apartments at 891 Post, just so Freddie could move in, sleep where Hammett had slept, wake up to his view in the morning, and soak up his being. If Freddie could have paid Hammett's utilities, he'd have demanded it in the budget. Freddie wanted it furnished exactly as Hammett had had it. In fact, the crew learned that someone in town claimed to own a radio that once belonged to the writer, and Freddie *had* to have it. Not that any scenes were going to be shot at 891 Post. No way. They had a soundstage for that. This was all for Freddie's research.

Freddie didn't even want me at the apartment much because, since Hammett lived there alone, I might have interfered with Freddie's process. But he invited me over to see it. We went to the address and headed upstairs. We shared a truly glorious moment in the early evening, making love on a bed with Hammett's view of the most romantic city in America.

After we finished making love, Freddie went into the bathroom. I was gathering up our clothes, feeling totally satisfied and in love. I got my jeans, flopped on the bed naked, and got ready to slip them on when I heard a suspicious noise out on the fire escape.

The wind was blowing and the translucent curtain contained the shadow of a Peeping Tom crouched outside the window.

"Freddie," I whispered, "there's someone on the fire escape."

Then, the curtain rustled in the wind, and I saw the creep who had been staring at us. I freaked and pulled a pillow in front of myself. Freddie wrapped a towel around himself and exited the bathroom, shouting, "Get out of here, you, go away."

The guy was like a deer caught in the headlights. Then he twisted around and got away.

That was enough research for me. We never went back. We joined the rest of the company at a Sheraton—which, while perhaps not what Hammett would have done, at least made us feel safe.

Until we tried to go to sleep. Lying in bed, we heard some commotion and a man's voice outside the door yelling what sounded like, "Harder, harder." I assumed it was just two party-hardy Bay Area guys.

Then, we heard more scrambling, doors slamming, and the very distinct shouts of "FIRE, FIRE!" Now we were about to go up in smoke. We darted out of bed and threw our robes on, and in a few minutes the hotel's entire guest roster had assembled on the pavement below as the local fire department rolled up to check out the situation.

From there, it was on to the Holiday Inn in Chinatown. Freddie got a large suite. Our first night there, we heard a body smash up against the door. We looked at each other and ran to the peephole. I saw a blond trash-type girl in baby doll pajamas being dragged by her hair, fighting and resisting a burly guy with a tank T-shirt. "Daddy," she screamed, "don't, Daddy, no, don't make me fuck you, Daddy."

After all this, it was easy to forget about, say, earthquakes.

The next day Freddie's wallet got stolen.

I didn't know that I was in store for some wildness of our own—off camera.

* * *

One of the pleasures of making the movie for me was making a nice connection with Francis Coppola, seeing how he worked up close. We shot a visually stunning scene in a ferryboat out in the Bay. But I had always had awful luck with makeup guys, and this one was no exception. I have become a makeup bitch over the years, because your look is your livelihood.

Francis asked the actors to join him in watching the dailies. He didn't like my look any more than I did. "Now why does she look like this onscreen," he called out, "when she looks like this in person? She looks so great right here. I don't want her to look like this for the rest of the movie." Then he looked at me and said, "I wanted a female to look great in at least one of my movies. You're the first of my Bombshell Club."

They let me call in my makeup guy from *Taxi*. Typically, it didn't end up mattering. The ferryboat scene didn't work anyhow and, rather than reshoot at great expense, the scene was cut.

Our last night in San Francisco, Francis invited us for dinner at his breathtaking vineyard and Victorian mansion in the Napa Valley. Some exotic foreign car was sent to pick us up.

At dinner, Francis pulled Freddie over and said something that would have a profound impact on him and on us. "You know, Fred," he said, "I've been looking at dailies and, I don't know, there's just something missing—don't know what it is. Just a feeling. Then I had the idea that what it was was the booze. I think the booze is missing. Here."

And with that, he poured Freddie a drink, explaining, "You know, just swish it around in your mouth, get that feeling again. You know, Hammett, he drank, had this whole whiskey thing about him."

Freddie had obviously had a whiskey thing about him too, which is how he ended up an alcoholic in recovery. You don't ask a recovering alcoholic to "just swish it around."

Freddie drank, got rip-roaring drunk at Francis's, and passed out. I didn't put it together yet.

Meanwhile, Francis and I were sitting up together until two in the morning as he tape-recorded an interview with me about *Hammett* and about life. We had a truly extraordinary evening.

Then Francis had his driver get us back to town. Somewhere between Napa and San Francisco, Freddie got so sick we had to pull off the road so he could throw up.

Then it hit me: Francis was a genius, an authority figure whose approval Freddie craved. For Francis to exploit Freddie's mania-cally specific method acting by goading him into drinking again was questionable, if not downright reckless. I had told Freddie, "Francis admires and loves you so much. You are his favorite star. He's made you the kingpin of his acting pool here." Freddie had come a long way—he had worked so hard to clean himself out for so long—and now, as I watched him retching and lurching all over the place on the roadside, my heart sank for him. He would have done anything for father figure Francis to push his artistic inven-tion to its peak. Now, it looked like he had gone too far, and I wondered if he could pull himself back.

I had not grown up with the problems of alcoholics. If someone had ever told me that I was going to get involved with a drinker, I'd never have believed it. I understood very little about alcoholism. When Freddie had assured me he was no longer drinking, my reaction was, "Fine, no problem."

Now, we had a problem.

Freddie dreaded flying, so the next day we took a train down to L.A. It was the longest eight hours of my life. Drinking or hung over, Freddie could be mean, abusive, crabby, and accusatory. He'd suddenly blurt out, in his jealous paranoia, "Now I know what took you so long there last week, I saw how you were looking at that guy." Dr. Jekyll had pulled a Mr. Hyde.

He was relentless during our train trip. It made no sense. My skin was crawling, and I couldn't wait to get away from him. I decided I never wanted to see him again. I was sick with disappointment.

Tommy picked me up at the station and Freddie and I went our separate ways. I went back to my place at 100 South Doheny. I couldn't believe it: Two weeks ago I was the happiest I had ever been with a guy; now I was alone. My vision of Freddie and me in love forever had vanished. And we still had a movie to finish.

An hour later the phone rang. "I miss you," he said.

"You've been a total creep to me," I shot back.

"Creeps miss," he said softly.

Oh shit, I thought; Mr. Hyde has a heart.

"Can I come over?" he asked.

I hesitated, but gave in to the sincerity. How could I not love a guy who says "Creeps miss"?

* * *

The good Freddie was a delight, an incredibly sexy, fun-loving, caring, sensitive, brilliant, sensual, generous, darling human being. Freddie, to his credit, never drank while shooting, and we had some wonderful times working together.

Under the influence, he could turn crazy and scary-nasty in a second. Then I would never want to see him again. But sober, he could win me over anytime. We got away, for instance, for a wonderfully intimate, romantic weekend in San Luis Obispo up Route 1. We stayed at the Moro Bay Inn, and spent much of our time in one of the world's great hot tubs, built into a redwood deck overlooking the ocean. The key was that Freddie stayed sober all weekend long.

We continued shooting in and around L.A. and had a fantastic time. Freddie's acting was wonderful, and I liked my own work very much, despite a run of bad-hair days. Like makeup, hair was capable of driving me wild. I not only had to have thirties-period hair, an old-fashioned marcel wave; I had a hairdresser who used period methods to produce it. She had been trained in the old MGM system and used such an outmoded technique that I had to be there at four-thirty A.M. It was painful. Today they use a crimper that takes a few minutes.

Everything else was taking so long it hardly mattered. We knew the rough cut was overlong. Wim was revising and reshooting in five, ten, fifteen takes. Moreover, in filmmaking, when you insert dialogue or a shot somewhere, everything else has to be rejiggered around it for continuity and sense. But I kept telling myself, It's okay, you're part of the hip Zoetrope avant-garde vision.

Then, in the first week of April, Freddie called from the set to tell me that Francis had pulled the plug on *Hammett*. With the film falling apart, his financing had shut down.

When in doubt, travel. Freddie and I promptly headed for a two-week trip to Cancún. He had gifts and love notes for me on the plane, and a note for me when I woke up at the Camino Real Hotel. The trip was off to a loving and romantic start. Sober, Freddie was frisky and affectionate and had no trouble communicating how much he loved me.

If nothing else, we were great together in bed, and our lovemaking was something we could always count on, even in the heat of a fight, to rekindle the core of love between us. Cancún was our first real vacation together, and it seemed our love affair could travel well.

And then the rains came—torrents that didn't let up for two full days. The place was clammy, flooded, and miserable. The plumbing shut down everywhere; the toilet wouldn't flush. You couldn't bathe or drink water. We decided to drive to the far end of town for a decent dinner at a restaurant. We sat down and Freddie impulsively started knocking back tequilas.

I was much more interested in the bathroom than in anything they had on the menu. I was dying to pee, but there was a huge line for the ladies' room. I waited for nearly a half hour.

When I got back to the table, our food had arrived, and so had the demons in Freddie's head. He got totally insane toward me—cold, distant, hostile.

I kept asking him what the problem was. All he'd say was, "You know, I get it, I know exactly what's going on here."

"Freddie, this is the best food we've had in—"

"Fuck you, fuck the food, we're outta here."

I was a long way from 100 South Doheny, so I had to slug it out with him. He tortured me with taunts and insults for an hour and a half before I finally pried out of him the irrational scenario his devils had created in his mind.

Freddie had noticed that the restaurant owner, who was also tending bar, had left the bar briefly to look in on the garden area near the bathrooms. In his paranoid madness, Freddie figured that the reason I had been away from the table for so long was that I was giving the bartender a blow job. That's what he said. He was certain of it. He never explained, in his fevered flight from reason, just how or where the bartender and I had *had* our red-hot little moment together. The bathrooms were jammed. The tables were crowded. None of that logic ever came up in his brain.

"I go to pee in the first decent toilet in two days and this is what I have to put up with?" I shot back. "There's no way I can have a life with you."

What I didn't get was how Freddie could go two weeks without a drink. He wasn't someone who woke up thinking about booze. He could have a beer and walk away. But when he would drink to excess, he went stark-raving nuts. Yet, in three months, that had only happened twice. It seemed to me that he had had it under control.

I was dead wrong. Freddie, in his pathological insecurity, was more terrified of freeing his devils than feeding them. As an actor, he had convinced himself that they were somehow integral to his creative process. He thought they drove him to inspiration; I saw them leading him to desperation.

My savior act was beginning to take on a subtle streak of masochism that was getting old.

When I told him I was leaving the next morning, he grew remorseful, begged me to stay, and revealed a pitiful edge of self-loathing. "I'm not good enough for you, am I?" he said. "You're too good for me. You're my little Nipper, you know, and I think I can handle this, but I can't." ("Nipper" was Freddie's affectionate nickname for me.)

I left a week early, but Freddie stayed on. I went to Chicago and New York to get him out of my system. When we talked by phone, he told me how much he missed me. He told me how he expressed it, too: He had gotten wasted again, and ended up with some island girl a cabdriver had scouted up for him—and with some antibiotics to take care of the souvenir sores.

Like an idiot, I took Freddie back. He was depressed over *Hammett,* but he would come around, get over it, pull himself together, he said. "I'll never do that again," he promised.

When I brought Freddie to Chicago to meet my family, it went beautifully. Lorin and his girlfriend Lynnette made us a wonderful gift—a cleverly personalized game of Monopoly in which you landed on all of our credits. Where Park Place and Boardwalk once stood, now you landed on *Missouri Breaks* (Freddie's movie with Marlon Brando), *Taxi,* and *Apocalypse Now.* One card from Community Chest referred to the story Freddie had told them of meeting his idol Brando on the set.

Freddie had fawned all over Brando, told him how he had always been a great admirer and how it was great to be getting to work with him. Brando gave Freddie a savage look and sighed, "My heart bleeds," then walked away. So the card read: "Your idol Marlon Brando brushes you off with 'My heart bleeds': Go back three spaces."

It was a fabulous, funny gift.

After this great trip together, the chameleon I couldn't survive another day with in Cancún was once again looking like the man I could spend the rest of my life with. He had completely given himself over to my family and, in the process, had won me over once and for all. Now we could even joke whenever I'd excuse myself to the ladies' room. I'd ask if he wanted to come along, and he'd grin sheepishly. "Nahhh," he'd say with boyish embarrassment. "It's okay, stop it, just go on."

Lorin and Lynnette were captivated. On another trip to New York and Chicago, they got Freddie to help them make a videotape that adoringly spoofed his famous clandestine lunch-hour stroll with Cindy Williams from *The Conversation*. Lynnette played Cindy and Lorin taped them the way Gene Hackman, the surveillance specialist, had recorded Freddie and Cindy as they'd moved through the crowded park in the movie. It was terrific. Freddie was such a consummate player he just threw himself into it. They did it all around Washington Square in Greenwich Village.

Then it was on to Chicago, where we shared a thrilling and romantic moment on the observation deck of the John Hancock Building, at a restaurant on the ninety-fifth floor called, appropriately, 95. It was a warm, balmy June night. We were embracing and kissing and madly in love. He gave me a gorgeous watch inscribed with MLH LOVE, FFF and the date we met. I kissed Freddie and whispered, "You know, why don't we just forget about the drinks and go back and make love. I just really want to make love to you."

We headed for the elevator in silence and started down with a bunch of other people in the elevator car. Suddenly, Freddie seemed aloof, and didn't even want to be touched in front of these strangers. We got to the street and when I tried to kiss him, he held me away and glowered suspiciously.

"Boy, you really are something," he said.

"What?" I couldn't *believe* this.

"Don't play dumb with me."

"Freddie, what are you talking—"

"You'll never learn, will ya? That's it, I'm leaving. You're some piece of work."

It took an hour of screaming, packing, going berserk. This was Freddie's story: We had ridden the elevator up with a handsome guy I hadn't even noticed because I was so focused on being with Freddie. The guy and I, he claimed, had made some sort of eye contact, so that all the things I had said to Freddie were actually meant for this mystery man, at whom I had been staring all through dinner. In Freddie's mind, the sexual urge I was expressing for Freddie was set off when I spotted the stranger leaving. That's when

he St. Anne Hotel for under $20,000. Freddie and I got
us suite at the St. Louis, a neighboring hotel.

t before we left L.A., Freddie and I had dinner at the
Inn and then invented a window-shopping game of
through Beverly Hills to see what we had in common.
smakers wouldn't have given us great odds based on the
lts: Freddie, who was considerably older, was pure, 100
r. Southwest who had a thing for Navajo rugs, smoking
moked Lightning on his eggs. His mother, the youngest
kids, was born when her father was sixty-five; he could
the Civil War. I was Miss Mediterranean–Art Deco, I
to my therapist once a week, no matter where I was in
, and my parents had been hip, urbane in their way, and

and I were a Generation Gap waiting to happen.
, I chose to focus on the few matches we clicked on,
filing ludicrous mismatches under "Opposites Attract."
esday I went to Chicago to get my Jean Harlow–style
dress, with a stunning, delicate turn-of-the-century lace
hursday, we flew to New Orleans. The first night in town
s a huge shower at which I received silly gifts. My favorite
stomized Wild West gazette headline that read, DESPERADO
WGIRL, from my sister Christal. She knew the score.
ids of honor were Christal and Ellen March; JoAnn was
g like the mother of the bride. Tommy, Lorin, Lynnette,
friend Barbara Shackel got off their plane to make a
on in Houston and started their party just a bit early,
their connecting flight. They made it just in time for the
shower.
quite an eclectic crew: Tony Danza, Harry Dean Stanton,
German masseuse), ever-sexy Doris and husband Pat, my
Dr. Thich An Than. Even Uncle, living up to his flashcard
amily's eccentric genius, burst in, sweating, fifteen minutes
the ceremony, bearing a carrot cake, my favorite from
od. He gave me away and went away, just like that.
eld the ceremony Sunday in Lillian and Jack Smith's
rd and partied at the Prince Conti. I did a wild dance with
anza, caught my lace top in his ring, and watched the whole
nravel as I twirled. No one slept and we partied almost till
It was a real blowout.
et people's boasts about sex on their wedding nights; I talk

I dragged Freddie into the elevator, so I could ride down with the mystery man.

I had no idea what man he was even talking about!

He was in a rage. It was now so long after the incident that I couldn't even know for sure if there had been a handsome man in the elevator with us. After not drinking to excess in New York for a week, he was now absolutely insane on booze.

The pattern repeated again—the going our separate ways, the tearful forgivenesses, the reconciliations.

By mid-July, I was back on my *Taxi* schedule, which was good for us. It built in time away from each other and we were back on pretty solid ground.

Then all hell broke loose in the industry when a devastating strike was called by the Screen Actors Guild. Life as all actors knew it shut down.

"Let's get married," he said.

"We can't. We're not ready."

"No, let's get married."

"Let's live together."

"No, I've lived with four women and it never worked out. We get married or nothing."

"Well, then, it's nothing."

It was nothing for a couple of weeks as I spent a week in Chicago over Labor Day and then Freddie went to the wedding of a friend, Dean Tavoularis, the production designer, at Francis's in Napa Valley. He was also beginning rehearsals for *One from the Heart*.

I was still in Chicago when he phoned me. "You know, I'm miserable. I cried at the wedding today, then I was driving back in the rain to the hotel and I said to myself, 'I've got to marry her.' Will you marry me?"

I thought for a few seconds and figured, What the hell.

When he was sober, he was sincere and lovable. The *want to want* was very strong in Freddie. He wanted to like the idea of being with one woman, of being faithful, of having a home, even of starting a family. These were his goals—and they were my goals as well.

Whether the achievement of these goals would have any bearing on Freddie's reality remained to be seen. If he could see it as a role, and if he could write himself a good script as husband-father-partner, then he could act it out with the same passion he brought to his work before the cameras. And as his romantic lead, in some recess of my heart, I knew that, with proper direction, script supervision, and line-producing (I'd control the budget), it had the potential of becoming the roles of our lifetimes. One thing was sure: Freddie had a great heart and solid values. I didn't want to lose him.

"Why don't we talk about this. Why don't you meet me in my apartment tomorrow at six o'clock," I said. I was due to leave Chicago the next day.

Freddie, who had been married years earlier, felt marriage would coax more of a commitment from him. I felt he had major issues with drinking; paranoid, jealous rage; the way he handled money; and the way he handled me. I wanted gradual moves—and living together was a big enough jump for now.

I got home to L.A., he came over to South Doheny, and, from Monday evening through Wednesday morning, we talked it all out, over and over, deciding. And we finally got to the point where there was nothing left to be said.

"Okay," I said. "Let's get married."

"Well, I want to be able to plan it. I'll get rehearsal—"

"Look," I said, cutting him off before he could think about it. "You know what? I'll do the planning. You just show up. That's all you have to do. Show up."

I had just agreed to spend the rest of my life with this crazy, sexy lunatic. I didn't think that was asking too much.

I had no idea.

15

The Desp
and the Sh

"To WHOM?" Johnny squealed over
his grammar, was right on the money.

I called all my old boyfriends to brea
were on good-friends mode again after
over nothing that summer that brought
month freeze. My call broke the ice, but
He knew I had done the movie with Fre
were involved, let alone getting married.

Lloyd got very upset over dinner and t
My *Taxi* guys were thrilled for me when
When I called Dr. Sharon to break the ne
You should wait, she warned. I told her
anyhow.

We decided to get married in New Orlea
place we both knew and loved. This way,
centers" (L.A., New York, Chicago, Texas
sented and the burden of travel would be s

We flew them in—sixty-six friends and
were offered the use of a gorgeous house that
and stepmother of Susan Smith, my agent
insisted the wedding had to take place o
twenty-fifth anniversary of James Dean's dea
it seemed, I went along. Why be a rebel, eve

Susan's stepmother, Lillian Smith, was a
who pulled the weekend together brilliantly

about sleep on my wedding nights. I've taken a poll: Most women save themselves for the Morning After rather than the Night Of; they're too pooped. At four in the morning, we finally fell off to sleep, but Tommy thoughtfully phoned to find out where the après-party party was happening.

Not with us, even though Freddie and I couldn't get back to sleep. My new husband started flipping out, going, "What did we just do?" It was pretty funny. I sat up and stuffed my face with carrot cake.

We finally made love as man and wife on Monday. It felt totally different to me—more spiritually intense, emotionally intimate. There's a feeling not so much of possession as of belonging, of being united by shared, lifelong goals.

The truth is, we only *thought* we had made love as man and wife. We weren't married—technically. We were missing some license or certificate. I thought Lillian, who had arranged for our judge, had taken care of it. The judge thought we had taken care of it. Freddie thought I had taken care of it.

Freddie, having grudgingly settled for a September 28 wedding, couldn't have been happier. On Tuesday, the twenty-fifth anniversary of Dean's fatal car crash (Monday, Freddie slept off the excitement of New Orleans's mint juleps), we finalized the paperwork and went looking for our judge.

The judge had gone fishing. It was three-thirty. James Dean was going to be dead forever, but we only had an hour and a half to make this date official. We rushed to catch a ferry across the Mississippi to Gretna Green, a small town where a lot of outlaws used to get married. We walked in on the justice of the peace.

"Do you have any witnesses?" he asked. I whirled around and spotted a janitor and cleaning lady in the hallway.

This was so hamper.

I went out and abducted them. "Would you sign something for us?" I asked. Though mildly dumbfounded, they cooperated. This was right up Freddie's alley.

We had had lazy, lounging-in-bed sex when we had only assumed we were husband and wife. Now that it was documented, we reached a peak that night—religious-experience sex, very intimate, relaxed, and sweet.

After lingering in New Orleans for the rest of the week, we took off on our two-week honeymoon trek across America. We rented a car to Waxahachie, then drove Freddie's Wagoneer.

The honeymoon was wild and telling. We had some close, tender moments and some unbelievably vicious fights. And we had reminders that we were, essentially, still strangers. Driving across America, you hit long stretches between radio stations. So I said, "Let's sing songs together."

"Great."

"How about some Beatles songs," I suggested.

"I don't know any Beatles songs," said my groom, the one who would ask, after John Lennon was shot a couple of months later: "John Lennon—which Beatle was that?"

Freddie was into early Bob Dylan, but when Dylan was singing about "a hard rain" in the early-sixties folk era, I was singing about "the rain in Spain," working through my Julie Andrews vibrato. We must have knocked off 100 miles of open road just trying to come up with one song in common. Fortunately, I was steeped in American standards, so we hit one: "It Had to Be You." A fitting enough title, anyway.

Fighting with Freddie was like fighting in a foreign movie without subtitles: When we miscommunicated, we missed big-time, and how little we truly had in common would rush to the surface. Worse, we always fought in and stormed out of the best restaurants. I was like, Why couldn't you have picked this fight last night in that crummy truck stop? Why do I have to leave this incredible pasta?

I made up for it when we got to stay. We both ate our way all across America. The itinerary was pure Freddie: Dallas to L.A. via Durango, Colorado, and Las Vegas. We stayed in motels—the seedier the better for Freddie. Some were obscure flophouses with "texture and character," meaning filth and rusty tap water. I had the impression Freddie was living out some thirties Dust Bowl dream of moving west. Whatever girlhood fantasies I had clung to about my wedding and honeymoon—perfect skin, perfect hair, perfect body/makeup/outfits/weather—were blown. They were simply irrelevant in Freddie's world. I had spent so much time planning and so little time on myself that there was no time for my thighs to peak, no time for perfection. And no need. I didn't care. We were together. We would make it work.

I had entered marriage with the bleeding-hands determination I had had when I cut my fingers carrying groceries as a kid. Now, instead of singing to myself to deaden the pain, the mind-setting mantra was: "I'll make this work, no matter what; I'll make this work, no matter what."

While up in the Rockies, I learned from my agent that the strike was ending. Reality struck. We had a bad fight after Freddie had been drinking. He was in a foul, surly mood all that Saturday. We barely got out of bed on a glorious autumn day.

Then it hit me: I was due back on the set, and on a structured schedule I had hardly been on since Freddie had come into my life. My heart started to pound in the dark as we lay in bed. My face flushed, and I kept thinking: Oh, my God, *Taxi* is my real life! What is this? What have I done? I'm married! How will I relate to the guys? I've made the biggest mistake of my life.

When I went back to *Taxi* I was fat and uncomfortable in my own body. I married at 138 and ended my honeymoon at about 145. Thank God, in our first episode, Elaine only had one entrance, one exit, and wore a coat over a blazer. I was relieved, but immediately started trimming down.

Freddie and I went house-hunting in the fall. By December, we decided on the tenth home we saw. Freddie loved it so much he told our broker, "Give 'em what they want, and then offer 'em another twenty-five thousand extra. I love this place; this is our house."

Our broker rolled her eyes. "This isn't how you do business in real estate." She didn't know she was talking to a guy who had been known to give $10,000 to a down-and-out casino loser in Vegas to restart his life. Someone who piled his expensive new Armani clothes in boxes with the tags still on and shipped them to a Native American reservation.

Armani, Apache—it was all the same to Freddie.

We saw the house at night while drinking champagne, with soft music playing and great lighting. I began to wonder, "Shouldn't we see this place in daylight, without music and champagne and dim lights?"

"Nahhh," Freddie would say, "this is my place and if you're my wife, then you're gonna live here with me."

"Well, what about the retaining wall?"

Freddie couldn't be bothered with details like a crumbling retaining wall at the edge of the property.

But I could. Even the owners acknowledged it needed shoring up, to the tune of ten grand—the amount held in escrow so the owners could repair it, as agreed, after the winter's rain. Even Dr. Sharon flagged this, again urging me not to go forward with a contingency like that.

Again, I plunged in. Despite its drawbacks, the house sat on top of a spectacular piece of property way up on Mulholland with a breathtaking 180-degree panorama of the San Fernando Valley. It had some great potential—a pool, lots of latticework, bougainvillea and ivy growing all over. There was something exhilarating and quintessentially L.A. about it.

Naturally, I went back alone, and, sure enough, in daylight we were talking about a run-down, funky little fixer-upper with a Valley view. I voiced my qualms. Freddie was unfazed, intractable. "We're gonna get it."

And for $450,000, we got it. The night we closed, in February 1981, Freddie and I drove to Torreyson Drive to admire our new home. Once inside, Freddie suddenly seized on a flaw he had somehow missed in his prior visits.

"It's not Spanish." He sounded stupefied, crestfallen.

"Yeah, I know, Freddie." I folded my arms and rolled my eyes.

"This isn't the house we saw. We bought a Spanish house."

"What are you talking about?"

"Don't you remember? There was the bookcase, the sliding thing, there was that whole— Oh, and remember the fireplace, we walked in and, I mean, this is L.A., you're supposed to have a Spanish house. This isn't my house. Whose house is this anyway? I can't live in this house."

"Freddie, calm down, will you?"

It was another half-year before we moved in. Until the end of spring, 1981, Freddie was tied up with *One from the Heart*. I didn't want to move in alone, and we had construction inside and out, and the retaining wall to deal with. Freddie was also making sure he had his "safe room" designed and built. It was his bullet-proof bunker, Freddie's Armageddon Room, where, in an earthquake or during a nuclear war, he knew he could find an open, dedicated phone line. For what, I had no idea. To make reservations? To call his agent?

As it turned out, the $10,000 retaining wall fund came up short—by about $165,000. We had basically bought a half-million-dollar toboggan that could at any time go mudsliding down into some other zip code in the canyons. Without a new wall, the pool could have gone anytime. They had to sink new concrete fifty feet into the ground.

Enough work was done up there to build a hydroelectric power plant for a developing nation.

It got worse. Freddie became so excited at the sight of bulldozers on the land that he wanted a new two-lane driveway with a white line painted down the middle. He hated the way cars had to pull out one at a time at people's homes. Once Freddie decided to realize what I guess was his lifelong valet-parking dream come true, $175,000 turned into $250,000.

We began calling our new home Terror, as in Tara. Naturally, when we went after the prior owner, she was nowhere to be found—missing without a trace. Two years later we learned through our private investigator that she had fled, in what must have been the real estate industry equivalent of a witness relocation program. She took the money and ran—to a cosmetic surgeon. She not only changed her name, she had her face totally redone. Because of the complex way she had moved the proceeds of the sale through her bank, we could never have gotten money out of her.

It wasn't as if Freddie and I were facing all this turmoil as a tightly united front. If we had ever had a shot at working everything out before buying Terror, we surely never did after. Now, I had the two biggest mistakes of my life—Freddie and the money pit. The retaining wall was the symbol of our desperate, costly attempts to keep up the facade of a fine, functional marriage between two people who loved each other very much—and in whom the want to want was so strong.

Late that summer, as we were about to move in, another chink in the wall blew open when I went off to New York to do a TV movie with John Schneider. It was called *Dream House*—not *too* ironic. The show was a cute romantic comedy in which I played an older woman in John's life. We went out on location to a New Jersey resort to shoot our romantic scenes. I adored John as a colleague and buddy, but there was absolutely nothing going on there. Our sets weren't closed, as usual, and resort guests were allowed to appear as extras. So the shoot was wide open to snoops.

Somehow, our dialogue lines were either recorded surreptitiously or simply Xeroxed from a pilfered script. Either way, someone apparently infiltrated the set and sold our dialogue to the

National Enquirer. From this fiction they fashioned an early August cover story alleging a torrid location romance between us. It was so preposterous; for cover art, they had taken a photo of John Travolta and me at a *Grease* premiere in Europe, replaced his head with John Schneider's, added hearts and flowers around our faces, and concocted a totally bullshit story.

A week after I returned from New York, we were about to go out to dinner when a Texas friend of Freddie's called to say, "Hey, that's some piece in the *Enquirer* about your wife."

Over dinner, Freddie went berserk, then dropped me off at South Doheny, where we were living while the Terror work continued. "I'm going to go get that *Enquirer,*" he said in a threatening tone. As I later pieced it together, he went to Hughes Supermarket and grabbed a copy.

"This is my fuckin' wife on the cover of this rag," he growled to a checkout girl. "Can you fuckin' believe this?" Believe it? This was a checkout girl with a heart of gold.

"What are you doing later tonight?" he asked.

Freddie apparently checked out at her place for a few days, calling me repeatedly and hanging up. Or else he would rail: "I hate you; I'm never comin' home; I hate John Schneider."

"Trust me, Freddie," I insisted. "The guy maybe had a little crush on me, but—"

Freddie then came home, got John's number, and started leaving messages on his machine, like "Fred called, Fred Forrest called. Frederic 'The Rose' Forrest called." I'd check in for messages and Freddie, parked at the phone for days on end, would answer, "Hello, John; that you, John?" He was crazed with jealousy.

John finally called in from a vacation in Hawaii to assure Freddie that the story was bogus. "She's great," he said, "but, Freddie, she is absolutely married to you."

The absurd episode died down, and Freddie and I decided to cool out for a week in Bermuda. Then we could come home to make a fresh start in our new home—just short of our first anniversary. My decorator friend Barbara offered to help move us in while we were away. Everything was back on track.

But our peacekeeping mission in the Caribbean broke down when Freddie decided that a confession was required before our fresh new start could begin. He broke down and told me that in those eleven months of marriage, he had had no fewer than seven encounters with different women. His M.O. revealed not only staggering energy, but an equal-opportunity liberalism in his selection process: an extra from *One from the Heart,* an aspiring screenwriter, a Hollywood hooker during a drunken binge, and of course his coupon-collecting cutie at Hughes Supermarket.

The good news was that the *Enquirer* ordeal now made sense. Because someone had gotten wind of Freddie's liaison with the writer, the tabloid assumed our marriage was on the rocks, and set out to prove it. Linking me to someone would do the trick. That, at least, was the not-so-twisted logic behind it.

I was in shock. Talk about Plan B. Plan A was a marriage to last forever, to a husband who would never cheat, and being a wife who'd never stand for adultery. Plan B was deciding to go snorkeling with an unfaithful husband and forgiving him, though I felt betrayed and devastated. Again, the mantra kicked in: "I'll make this work, no matter what."

It was now appallingly clear: Freddie's paranoid ravings were merely projections of his own capacity to betray me. The fact that we were apart for work much of the time accommodated him perfectly. That I hadn't picked up on it was alarming to me. His relentless accusatory barrages had succeeded in putting me constantly on the defensive.

It seemed Freddie had a staff of demon screenwriters living inside his head who churned out new episodes of *The Twilight Zone* everywhere we went. These demons weren't just hacks who'd have me hooking up with a tempting *Taxi* guy, or a safe, sexually proven ex-boyfriend. No. They scripted only wildly implausible, low-life scenes for me—with men and in circumstances I could never find sexy in a million years.

Where were my rewrites? Where were my cleverly plotted, erotic liaisons with handsome, seductive lovers? That would be far too conventional. Freddie's demons wrote for me scenes like the time he decided to invite some buddies over to watch football and I decided to call Barbara, and go to her place instead. The plot twist was that one of the guys showed up late. That was enough to kick in Freddie's beerfest fantasy: He later accused me of calling not Barbara, but the friend, and meeting him somewhere for a quickie before kickoff—thereby delaying his arrival.

Just my style.

Then there was the "Ski & Screw" fantasy. I took some friends skiing when I was still a novice. My first run took hours and traumatized me. I spent most of the time staring not up at the sun but down at my ski tips. I didn't even ski the second day.

Freddie's script would have read: WE PULL BACK TO REVEAL—NO SUNBURN.

Once Freddie saw my pale face next to the faces of my reddened, blistered friends and nieces, the screenwriting ghouls fleshed out for me an entire forty-eight-hour lovefest in the shade at Big Bear with some unnamed stranger. Freddie was so sure of this that he moved out for three days until he came back to earth.

Some days, he was just so nuts, so insecure, so pitiful; others, he was the most generous, loving, supportive, and adorable guy in the world. I never knew, once I stepped off the elevator on the tenth floor at Doheny and looked down the hallway, if I was about to walk in on Freddie or Linda Blair's head from *The Exorcist* spinning 360s.

Figures prominently.

After Bermuda, we finally moved into the Torreyson home, though I held on to Doheny as my own clean Safe Room when things got crazy or disorganized. That seemed all the more plausible a month later, when we got word that in two months, a full year and a half after the plug had been pulled on *Hammett,* we would finish the film. In three weeks, Wim Wenders was going to try to reshoot 70 percent of the film at Zoetrope in L.A. So I felt we should always keep a neutral corner, if for no other reason than to protect the work we would do together.

September 30 rolled around. It would be hard to forget a first anniversary like ours. After we had a huge fight, Freddie flew off to visit James Dean's gravesite in Fairmont, Indiana, and I checked into the Westwood Marquis to celebrate by myself. He brought me back some gifts to honor the occasion: a James Dean mug, T-shirt, and pennant.

Despite such grim terms of endearment, despite my increasingly clear misgivings, I still clung to hope. Given that commitment had once been an issue for me, I was proud to see that I had become such a fighter, that I had dug in. But I was paying an awful price, and with diminishing returns.

An anniversary like this one was hardly reassuring.

Nor was the episode a few weeks later, when Freddie, in one of his howling-at-the-moon states, decided to howl with a loaded gun pointed at his head up on Torreyson. He was truly drunk—blitzed out of his mind—when he reached me by phone at Doheny. I was so scared I got Dr. Sharon on the phone to get her to talk him down. In his rampaging, I feared he might inadvertently kill himself. Tommy, who was often my savior in those days, went over and talked enough sense into Freddie to chill out.

I spent most of that night and the entire next day sobbing. I was so upset I missed a half-day of work—the only time in five years I didn't make the *Taxi* set. Then, I had to do a guest appearance on *The Merv Griffin Show*. I was in such bad shape, it was like they were doing hair and makeup and ice on my face to reduce the swelling and inflammation around my eyes.

I was a total wreck.

For the *Hammett* shoot my character was totally changed, rewritten, and reshot. I was no longer Emma the uptight librarian, but now Kit, a very sexy downstairs neighbor. Brian Keith, who had worked on location before, was out now. In the film, he was eventually shown only from behind in the San Francisco scenes; he had been replaced by Peter Boyle for the reshoot. It was crazy.

For three *Taxi* episodes in a row taped in December, I didn't move from a chair. The reason: To accommodate my *Hammett* shoot, I was allowed to come in on Fridays at six P.M. and have my camera blocking and my few lines all ready. Brooks & Co. were amazingly nice.

In the movie, Freddie and I did an incredibly sexy scene that, much to my disappointment, was cut. He comes in downstairs and undresses me. I wore a beautiful period wardrobe and underwear. It was shot the day after Thanksgiving. We had shared a veggie burger for Thanksgiving so I'd look terrific in this scene. I figured that would be my reward for not stuffing myself. But I still felt inhibited by all the dramas Freddie and I were dragging around with us. I shut down a part of my actor's sexuality that one should always bring to a part. Freddie was such a different man from the one I had fallen in love with in San Francisco—and we were in such a different place. I know Freddie would hate to feel he had a dampening effect on me, because he was always so generous and professional as an actor; but it was unavoidable. I didn't give everything I should have, and it showed.

After New Year's, Freddie went to the premiere of *One from the Heart* in New York. I stayed home because of my *Taxi* schedule.

The film was savaged by critics. Freddie was mortified by the way he looked in the film, which bombed so badly it nearly destroyed Francis's brilliant career.

It also nearly destroyed Freddie. On his way home via Chicago, Freddie, who always hated flying, thought he was having a heart attack during the flight. Most likely he was having an anxiety attack. He was traveling with Harry Dean Stanton and Rebecca DeMornay, who was in the film and was seeing Harry Dean. As I understood it, he had been given oxygen in flight. They got Freddie off in Chicago and stayed with him. Rebecca called to tell me what had happened and to reassure me that he was all right. She said he would stay over in Chicago.

I went out to get a bite to eat, and when I returned I had a message from Freddie, who had clearly recovered his old form.

"Who the FUCK do you think you are. I almost fucking DIED on that plane; how *dare* you leave the phone and not be home. They had to give me fucking *oxygen!*"

When I tracked him down, he announced he wasn't coming home. "I hate you, I hate the marriage, I hate life, I hate everything—the business, the fucking movie." I tried in vain to calm him down. I later learned he had done a lot of cocaine the night before, and was crashing hard.

I reached JoAnn in Chicago and sent her to look after Freddie, but when she banged on the hotel room door at the airport, he called to yell into the phone: "Your sister is outside my *door!* You're like a goddamn fucking *octopus* is what you are. Your arms reach *everywhere;* everything connects to you; you find me anywhere I go. Well, I'm goin' somewhere you'll *never* find me."

Four days later, I had a flash of brilliance and found him. He had mentioned on our honeymoon a hotel in Denver where he had gone with his dad when he was ten, and where he had told me he would someday like to return for some peace of mind. I got the number and dialed.

"How *dare* you find me here," he yelled, continuing his last tirade without missing a beat. "I'm never *safe* from you," he screamed. Viciously, relentlessly, he attacked me until I simply could no longer stand it. Through my sobs, I tried to tell him what I felt: that I still loved him, that he should come home, that we could make things work out, that we'd get him on a health program and see about trying AA, that I knew it wasn't him, but the drugs and alcohol that were destroying our marriage—and his life. *We can make this work no matter what; we can make this work no matter what.*

I got off the phone, sobbing and shaking. But then the click happened. I just shut down. I got out of bed, staggered unsteadily into the bathroom, and threw up. I heaved and heaved until I hurt. I was violently ill. I got up and stared at myself in the mirror. I had a taping of *Taxi* that night, and what I saw was frightening. I had dark, puffy circles all around my eyes and vomit on my face.

Who am I doing this for? I asked myself. Not for me. This is so not the way I imagined my life. He is so not the person I imagined being my partner in life.

I am *not* going to make this work. I *cannot* make this work.

From that moment on, no matter what my head made me believe, my heart knew it was over.

As always, Freddie came back home—crying, penitent, "you're-all-I-got, I'm-never-drinking-again, you're-my-hope-my-life-my-light." I'd heard it all before. If I didn't swell with hope, I still felt love and compassion, and decided to hang in.

Finally, mercifully, Freddie made a courageous move to banish his demons. But not without one final harrowing descent into madness—and mayonnaise.

A few weeks later, in mid-March, I had a very busy week rehearsing to be host of *Fridays,* ABC's answer to *Saturday Night Live.* I was on hiatus from *Taxi* and had worked hard all week to do a great job. I was excited. Needing some rest before the long, taxing Friday of the live show, I turned in early.

Late that night, I was awakened when someone deposited Freddie on the doorstep—crazy as a loon, smeared head to toe in mayo, reeking of coleslaw, pickles, and booze. He had been drinking and ended up in a deli on Fairfax. There, he had either tried to turn himself into a club sandwich or had simply lost a very messy food fight.

That wasn't bad enough. When he came on to me and wanted to have sex, I emphatically refused to deal with him. I dialed, as always, 911-TOMMY.

"You've got to come over here and take Freddie off my hands," I begged my brother. "He's impossible. I have a show tomorrow. *Please!*"

Tommy saved me, but was horribly insulted by Freddie in his deranged state. Tommy loved and respected Freddie, and he was devastated to hear the rotten, hurtful things that Freddie said to him—things that Freddie later never remembered saying. The next day I apologized to my brother for having involved him. And I had one last message for my husband.

"Don't even *think* about coming home until you've been to AA. I refuse to have anything to do with you until you get help."

Finally, it hit home. The very next night, Freddie went to an AA meeting—probably the major turning point in his life. It was March 20, 1982—his AA "birthday"—and he has stayed sober ever since.

No one was more shocked by Freddie's decision to dry out than Freddie. He came home and we stayed together as he started his one-day-at-a-time recovery. His resolve was impressive. Then, after two weeks, he admitted: "There's just no way I can do this with you, Nipper. I have to get rid of these devils on my own."

And he left.

The first week in May, I was facing some troubles of my own. On what we would always remember as "Black Tuesday," May 4, Jim Brooks called to announce the shocking news that ABC had, after four great seasons, pulled the plug on *Taxi*. Within an hour, we were all in his office for what we called the wake. Jim and Company were already knocking back shots of Jose Cuervo Gold by ten A.M. Soon, we were all gathered around, getting pleasantly plastered and misty-eyed as we watched a video of highlights from the show. It was unfair, and it was incredibly sad.

Despite the show's string of Emmys, ABC had bumped *Taxi* twice to new time slots—including to a Wednesday-night grave-yard loaded with shows that would soon all get canceled. It never quite regained its footing after being switched from that great Tuesday lineup.

"I just spoke to Michael Fuchs over at HBO," Jim Brooks said, looking right at me, "and if HBO picks up the show, the first shot of the new season will be a close-up of your breasts, just to prove we're on cable."

"I'm in." I didn't give it a second's thought. The boozy wake traveled in a dozen limos—going from Jim's office to Tony's house, breaking off into other smaller observances at various people's houses, and lasting almost thirty-six hours.

Ten days later, Danny DeVito hosted NBC's *Saturday Night Live* and did a biting opening skit where he leaned down on a plunger and appeared to blow up the ABC building as they cut to a computer graphic of the demolition. It was hilarious. He said, "Because the show was so abruptly pulled, our cast never got to do its final bow, so here we are, the cast of *Taxi.*" We had flown in for this, and got a long standing ovation. Then we had another postwake wake, which went through the night and ended with breakfast for all of us in Danny's suite at the Berkshire House.

With such a volatile marriage, I had come to rely on the show as a source of financial and emotional grounding. Now, after four seasons, I didn't know what I was going to do. For the immediate present, I could at least focus on our trip to the Cannes Film Festival, where *Hammett* was entered into the competition. Freddie was then to go to Bangkok for a BBC miniseries, *Saigon.* With *Taxi* somewhere between purgatory and permanent hiatus, I planned to spend time with him there after a side trip together to Paris.

Hammett's premiere was a success, and we enjoyed a great Saturday evening with Wim and my fellow Chicagoan Roger Ebert. Cannes was quite a scene—the swarming film press and paparazzi following us everywhere, the gossip, the yachts, the stars, the wanna-bes. An explosion of intense, sexy, scene-making energy on the Riviera. We were put up like royalty at the opulent Grey D'Albion Hotel. Freddie was flying high, since the film seemed a front-runner for the coveted Palme d'Or for Best Film and he had a shot at Best Actor.

Meanwhile, I felt some weird tweaking going on. I ran into my old Broadway costar Treat Williams, who was on his way to Naples to make a movie. He told me to visit after the festival. Freddie's and my *attachée* was an incredible woman named Simone Benzakien, who was Egyptian by birth but who lived in Paris and Rome. She was headed for Rome after the festival and invited me to visit. And I was already thinking of visiting my masseuse friend Uta in Genoa.

Italy. *Figures prominently.*

On Sunday night we had a two-thumbs-up fish dinner with Roger and a few other people in the old section of Cannes along the wharf. On our way back, Freddie, out of the blue, said, "You know, something about you is really bothering me." Freddie hadn't had a drink in over two months. I asked what that could possibly be.

"You're not southern."

Here we go again. The house wasn't Spanish. I wasn't southern. "That's right, Freddie," I answered. "I'm not. We've been to my home. In Chicago. I'm a Polish-Greek girl from the Midwest, Freddie." He was now jealous that Roger Ebert and I came from Chicago—a chilling measure of just how far out there Freddie was. The booze gone, his devils were in their death throes.

In Cannes, I got some fabulous news. Brooks called on May 21 to let me know that NBC, its ratings in the toilet, would be picking up *Taxi* for the fall season.

"If everyone agrees to come back at their fourth-year salaries," Jim said, "they'll do it."

"Count me in," I said.

"Now, listen. We've decided that the first episode is that Latka and Simka, after getting married, try to match everyone with their dream person. We've decided that for you it'll be Wally Shawn. Now, Wally's over in Cannes, with *My Dinner with Andre*—so if you run into him, tell him to call me."

I never saw Wally in Cannes and completely forgot about it.

When *Hammett* didn't win any prizes or awards at Cannes, Freddie's mood went into a nosedive. By the time we took our rather precarious show on the road to Paris, a city I had swooned over with Johnny a few years earlier, we were miserable. Our tiny hotel room, cluttered with eight huge valises, a bed, and bureau, hardly helped, so we moved into the Intercontinental. Not to mention that Freddie was studying his script and psyching himself up for his character in *Saigon*—a guy who has just ended a relationship and was swearing off women and sex.

Naturally, Freddie refused to have sex with me.

This is perfect, I told myself, seething. I'm in Paris, and my lover's in character.

I spent most of my time strolling the city's spectacular boulevards alone, sobbing and shopping, shopping and sobbing—and wondering what the hell I was doing with my life. Freddie did step out of character just long enough to continue his search for the perfect pair of white shoes—he was up to seven pairs—and to have a screaming match with me somewhere scenic on the Left Bank. The fight started over the shoes—and quickly escalated to familiar terrain: the value of things, Freddie's inability to take care of himself, wasting money, being an adult.

Finally, I snapped: "That's it. I'm going to Italy. We need time to cool off. I'll meet you in Bangkok in two weeks."

My decision to go to Italy immediately felt so liberating, I should have marched out of Paris under the Arc de Triomphe. I refused to let myself feel defeated.

As I got off the plane to visit Uta in Genoa, though, I was bloated, pasty-white, depressed, and furrowed. We visited some friends of hers in Naples, where we slept on the floor for a week. Italy was an instant comfort zone. We then went down the Amalfi coast, where I heard people talking about a movie being shot in the region. It turned out it was Treat's movie, so Uta and I hooked up with him too.

This telepathic tweak turned into a total blast. He put me on the back of his Vespa scooter to get groceries and drove me along the awesome, winding coastline. I was happy to be with a familiar, trusted friend when I was feeling so low.

I called Simone Benzakien and arranged to visit her in Rome for a couple of days. "Come on the four A.M. train," she said. "That way I won't have to get up in the middle of the night to let you in; it'll be morning when you arrive."

The exotic notion occurred to me that these events were all leading somewhere predestined, that it was not simply coincidental that both Treat and Simone had invited me to visit them after Cannes, or that Uta would be in Italy as well, or that I would come across Treat's location, or, for that matter, that Freddie and I would go our separate ways at a street corner in Paris. If everything was connected to everything, as I had long believed, these events were all linked by the eerie energy of synchronicity.

It was as if it was now my *destiny* to discover and identify with Italy. I felt peculiarly at home the moment I set foot on Italian soil. True, the entire country of Italy struck me as slightly hamper. But I left open the possibility that something major was going on. For starters, I was discovering how much easier life is when you're not dealing with someone who's crazy and depressed all the time.

I stayed out late and boarded the four A.M. to Rome. From Rome, it would be on to Thailand. On the train was an adorable porter who kept passing my compartment and giving me the eye.

Finally, he stopped and asked me, in sexy broken English, "You go to slip?" It wasn't until he cocked his head sideways and rested his cheek on his clasped hands that I got it.

No, I said, shaking my head, no slip.

"Good. Then come weeth me."

This adorable young man's name was Flavio, and we stood in the corridor hallway and talked all night as the train rumbled along. Our eye contact was so intense it was frightening. An unlikely, instant spiritual connection seemed to be forming in the almost total absence of grammar and information.

We did manage to cover important ground. It turned out that like me, he was married. That was okay. This trip wasn't about seduction. It was about self-discovery. Also, as he said, "You *no mangia carne e formàggio*—no possible," which meant: "I can't believe you don't eat meat and cheese."

The train went into a long tunnel, and when we came out of the total darkness our eyes were locked and my heart was pounding with the knowledge that I would know this stranger for the rest of my life. I felt blessed.

Then the train was halted for three hours until sunrise—between stations in the middle of nowhere. It seemed some people had been demanding their station be changed to an express, not local, stop, and they had thrown themselves on the tracks in protest.

"Rivoluzione," Flavio said.

Si, si. *Rivoluzione.* My own.

As we got to Rome, he said: "You in my home, dinner, my wife, my mother, all people, many confusion, is wonderful."

Sure, sure, I said—who was I to say no to an offer like that? Flavio picked me up the next day and I visited his apartment outside Rome. Then we all went to the tiny mountain village of Carsoli, where the family had a house. I felt like a Greek Kunta Kinte, coming home to my mother's southern Mediterranean roots—that same lusty joie de vivre and one-for-all gusto. For two blissful weeks, I lived in a village with one phone and no TV, stomping wine grapes, digging in the mud for porcini mushrooms—a true paisana.

We got by with fractured French, English, and Italian, and much shouting and charading. We joked how instead of Esperanto—a mix of English, French, Italian, and German that never caught on as the international tongue—we were speaking Exasperanto. That

joke alone took about half a day to deliver. I fell in love with Flavio
and his wife Maria, with their family, their village.

Flying to Bangkok, I couldn't deny that crossing paths with
Flavio had had a profound impact. He exuded a simple, unassaila-
ble wisdom and love for life that was thoroughly magnetic. It was
useless to wonder what might have been had we not each been
married. By channeling that energy into a platonic "soulmate"
bond, I had seen the futility in holding on to my marriage. Italy had
reminded me, in painfully clear terms, of what my life was really
about—what I had grown up with, what I truly wanted and needed
from a marriage and a partnership.

After the Riviera, Paris, Rome, and the countryside, I didn't
appreciate Bangkok's open-sore look. I hated being there. I found it
filthy and disgusting—except for a tiny Thai woman who walked
on my back, twisted me around like a pretzel, and gave me the most
amazing shiatsu massage in my life.

The first day I visited Freddie's set—five weeks after Cannes—I
walked right into Wally Shawn. My energy field was tweaking
around the clock. Neither Jim nor I had any clue that he was in
Freddie's movie, or that he was going to be in Thailand. I told him
to call Jim, and he ended up, sure enough, as my nebbishy love
match Arnie Ross in episode #91, "The Schloogel Show."

In Bangkok, with Freddie losing himself in the fall of Saigon, I
was finding myself in the end of our marriage. He and I agreed it
was time to just let go and get a divorce. There was no drama or
craziness, just deep sadness and resignation, mixed with a nodding
admission of inevitability. We just hadn't known enough about
each other when we'd decided to get married.

But we agreed there was no law against going out in style, so we
blew it all out for one last weekend as lovers at the outrageously
posh Peninsula Hotel in Hong Kong. On a good day, there was
nothing wrong with our incredible sex life together. And here we
were, together in the Far East, so what the hell?

It was a poignant and bittersweet last hurrah. Without a doubt,
our room was the most fabulous hotel room I have ever stayed in.
Plus, it was a real trip watching Freddie make the switch from
converting twenty-two Thai bahts to the dollar to six Chinese yen
to the Hong Kong dollar. Only Freddie could bargain his way into

paying $2,500 for a custom-tailored $300 suit. That was all I needed to see to feel assured we were making the right move. That was Freddie, a man who, when offered a million dollars to make a movie, had to ask me how many zeros there were in a million. I don't know who Freddie's guardian angel was (probably James Dean), but he had the best in the business, because no one rode the edge like Freddie.

I was relieved to know that, without booze, he could now walk the edge with clarity and survive. In fact, he has turned his life completely around since then, and has continued to do great work in films like *Valley Girl* and *Falling Down*. When we've gotten together to say hi and catch up, it breaks my heart that he doesn't even remember most of the crazy times we went through. It's like it happened to someone else.

He went back to Bangkok to finish *Saigon* and I took a couple of days in Hong Kong by myself to clear my slate. For the first time in my life, I felt completely alone in the world, a strange blend of shaky, depressed, and elated. But I was emancipated. There was apprehension about what the divorce might cost me, spiritually and financially. But I was going home to a familiar and secure job, and I would be among friends through a process of redefinition. Whatever the future would bring, it was time to move on, and there was no turning back.

Yet, as I rode the Kowloon Ferry, it stung to feel so all alone in the world—and for the world to suddenly feel like such a vast and empty place. If Italy was exciting because it connected me to my Mediterranean roots and some vibrant new friends, now I felt farther from home than I had ever felt: *No one knows me here, no names to look up, no more coincidences, no more tweaks. If this boat goes down, they won't know where to start looking for me.*

Nothing felt connected to anything. The flip side of my new freedom was feeling adrift, unsure, a million miles from home.

I got off the ferry and rode the cable car up the mountain for a panoramic sweep of Hong Kong. I got inside the car, and eyed everyone around me. I looked at the conductor, whose gaze lingered curiously on me for an extra instant. Then he shot me a weird half-grin, and glanced back at what looked like a Watchman mini-TV screen, broadcasting something in Chinese.

I stepped forward for a furtive glance over his shoulder and it all fell into place with a potent jolt of close-up, flickering recognition: my face, and Elaine Nardo's words dubbed into Chinese.

There was, I had to admit, a reassuring, cosmic symmetry in all this: Just as Freddie had exploded into my universe with the big-bang mother of all tweaks, he was now leaving it with another one. And, with what looked like half of Asia spread out before me, I knew that the universe was, somehow, still very much intact.

This was an epiphany that sent my spirits soaring: You can travel to the far side of the planet, only to come home to the sight of your Chinese-spewing face in worldwide syndication. I cracked up and thought: *No matter how out there you feel you are in this world, you aren't ever totally alone.*

It was exactly the boost I needed before starting out on the long trip back into the new life awaiting me at home.

16
Johnny, Dangerously

~~~

"Hey! Henner, what have you been doing?" The reassuring sound of Johnny's voice made me glad I'd decided to get in touch. "Well, not skiing."

Johnny still had my skis. It was early November—almost three years since he'd packed them in his Jag and I'd gone off to the *Hammett* screen test. Who knows what might have been had I gone to Mammoth with Johnny that night instead of to the Magic with Freddie.

We made plans to get together the next day.

By then, Freddie and I had begun divorce proceedings. He had barraged me with beautifully deluded postcards and letters from Bangkok promising that everything was going to work out fine. I saw him for a rather pathetic anniversary dinner at the Biltmore. Now I had two demises to honor every September 30—James Dean's, and ours.

The divorce was emotionally amicable—and financially disastrous for me. We had split the cost of buying Terror down the middle, but Freddie decided to keep the house because he owed the IRS $500,000. Somehow, I had the nagging sense that I'd never see the hundreds of thousands he owed me.

Johnny and I snapped back into our old ways at a time when I needed grounding in the familiar. He was never to be the love of my life, but it was just what I needed after my walk on the wild side with Frederic "The Rose" Forrest.

I didn't look my best—not at 137 pounds I didn't. I was still experimenting with food combining in a shedding process that was bringing me back into myself. After shedding Freddie, being with Johnny felt a lot like going home.

Food had become an obsession. I was never bulimic or anorexic, but I became obsessed with trying to figure out the best way for me to eat.

Johnny had figured it out for himself. He'd never looked better. He had been training for *Staying Alive,* the sequel to *Saturday Night Fever,* to be directed by Sylvester Stallone. Johnny was dieting and exercising with ferocious discipline and his body was incredibly cut for the movie.

I was so impressed by Johnny's buffed new look that after the New Year I began working with his trainer, who helped give me focus, discipline, and a new set of goals.

After all the drama about coming over from ABC, and despite the welcome addition of Carol Kane to the cast, our *Taxi* season on NBC had been strange. Jimmy Burrows, a father figure to us who had directed most of our shows, had moved on to *Cheers.* Our new directors were all fine, but the ensemble found adjusting to their shifting styles jarring. Also, NBC broadcast no new episodes between mid-December and the end of January 1983, bumping us from Thursday to deadly Saturday in the process, and then to Wednesday when we resumed. That alone can kill audience loyalty. When the season shooting schedule wrapped in February, we didn't need any network press releases to tell us what we knew in our hearts: that our wild and wonderful *Taxi* ride was finally over.

Our huge wrap party became a festive, wistful celebration of all we had shared and accomplished, not only as an ensemble, but as dear friends. It had been a breakthrough time in our lives; now it was time to say good-bye and move on to the next phase. The party was a perfectly raucous send-off.

Fittingly enough, my dear friends Flavio and Maria were making their maiden voyage to America that week, and, once again, they were present to witness a major transition in my life.

Flavio, who made $100 a week, and Maria, who made $75 a week as a secretary, had started saving up for their trip when they had met me.

Their timing was *perfetto!* It's not as if "TV Sitcom Wrap Party Week" is listed in international tour guides. But that's what was happening—and we hit the beach running.

The first night they got to L.A. I was a guest on *The Tonight Show* and got the guest host, Bill Cosby, to introduce them from the audience. The next night was the *Cheers* wrap party, then the *Family Ties* wrap party. Then, they came to the taping of *Taxi*'s final episode on Friday and, of course, our wrap party the next night. That weekend was Johnny's birthday, so on Sunday he flew us all up to San Francisco in his private jet for dinner.

On Monday, when I began meetings for my new film with Burt Reynolds, *The Man Who Loved Women,* they tagged along and had lunch with Burt. Then Tony Danza took them to an L.A. Kings hockey game at The Forum. Their heads were spinning.

"Hey," Flavio said, his English improving slightly, "een Eetalee we no ima-jeen America ees so wonder-fool."

"Yeah," I said. "Trust me—it's not always like this."

My plans after *Taxi* were definite. My agents would likely be fielding pitches for sitcoms and movies of the week, but it seemed like a great time to throw myself into features. When producer-director Blake Edwards cast me in *The Man Who Loved Women* without even reading me, I was thrilled. Shooting started days after our *Taxi* finale, so I figured I had made a remarkably smooth and auspicious transition.

I loved working with Burt, and felt a strong, instinctual chemistry with him—both personally and professionally. His approach to show business was extraordinary. He and I ad-libbed 80 percent of our scenes in the movie, and I felt completely comfortable with him.

Burt had been seeing Loni Anderson, and even though they split up briefly during this time, I never saw it going in that direction between us anyway.

Blake and I also hit it off from day one. Blake was one of those people in Hollywood who you knew just instantly *got it.*

It turned into a self-affirming time for me. My workouts shaped me up. I lost weight, got toned, ate better. Johnny and I were on a great roll then, spending almost every weekend together, giving lavish parties at his place in Santa Barbara. And I now had two Hollywood heavyweights nurturing and pushing me to my best work, making me feel appreciated as an actress. It's great when, in the absence of swirling domestic or location dramas, you are encouraged to be wonderful—and you *are.* I loved doing that movie, and I'm proud of my work in it.

The setup for my character's scenes was simple enough: Stuck in traffic, Burt sees a pair of long legs walking across the street—he

Of course, after we wrapped in early May, they began test
reenings. Filmmaking by consensus. Inevitably, endings are
shot because test audiences have rejected the one you already
ot. After *Hammett,* I was turning into the Reshoot Queen.

The test cards showed audiences didn't like the movie's ending
th Burt's dying—which shouldn't have been too much of a
wner, since the movie *opened* with his funeral and was struc-
ed as one long flashback. They didn't buy that all nine of his
eving lovers would be so chummy, either. So Blake et al. decided
shoot a new ending—a raging, four-day bitchfest at the Julie
drews character's house. I had some of my funniest lines in this
stly ad-libbed sequence.

'hen, they came up with a real twist ending: They tested both
shes, dumped the four-day reshoot, and went with the original
t hadn't worked to begin with.

looray for Hollywood!

he movie could have been better paced, but I was happy with
scenes. So was Burt. While we were still shooting the movie, he
d me to perform in a production of Neil Simon's *They're
ing Our Song* at his dinner theater in Florida. I was flattered
honored. I felt Burt and I truly understood each other. He
ld come up to me after a take, crank up one eyebrow with his
us deadpan look, and mutter, "You know, you're really
."

e six weeks I spent at Burt's theater in Jupiter, Florida, was a
en time. Just being back in the theater atmosphere after five
s on a soundstage put me in a groove that helped me create
of my best work ever. At the time, the theater gave its visiting
a two-bedroom condo with a health club and car—the
arpet treatment.

rt's dedication was astounding. He scouted and auditioned
ns of kids from Florida schools and brought in the best to
ntice for a year or so. Either they were sponsored by parents
ir neighborhoods or Burt lined up funding to support their
They'd attend acting classes with Burt, Dom DeLuise,
es Nelson Reilly, or other visiting luminaries, then get
-on experience in lighting, wardrobe, makeup. By year's end
have worked every aspect of stage production and earned
ll-important Equity cards. Many of the kids later went on to
with us at *Evening Shade.*

never sees the face—and gets obsessed. He puts the le
with a license number and tracks her down. He make
meet her in a gas station. It's me, but not my legs, which
major plot point. I have to confess—and convince hi
legs belong to my cousin Cynthia. I do this by agreei
shower at his place—and then some. Siskel and Ebe
gas-station scene one of the ten greatest seduction
time.

And it led to my nude scene with Burt. Praise G
workouts! Though still a touch porky, I looked
woman—rounder, fuller, more voluptuous than too
nately, you can't ask directors to delay or reschedul
days around PMS, or, say, "because my thighs will
Thursday." You just hit your cue for nudity and
lighting and camera angles.

I did the scene buck naked, tits and all. It was shot
that was not especially flattering, but at least no one
me of having implants. You get Naired from top to
one obvious out-of-frame exception—because eve
body hair casts a shadow. Then they coat your skin
body makeup. They buffed me out to the point th
creamy pale and smooth as porcelain. I felt like a st
shipped to a museum.

I was the last of nine women who shot bedro
Burt. For two days, the other actresses—Kim
Andrews, Cynthia Sykes, etc.—were hopping in
bedroom set. By the time I slipped into and out of
under the covers with Burt (whom I never obs
naked—damn!), everyone was getting pretty u
breasted drill.

The location was a private home, so, unlike th
John Schneider shooting, there was no risk of a p
cleared the bedroom of all but the necessary cre
been shown completely nude with anyone in a fil
plot point to see my legs, so there was no fakin
Burt's right and bent my knee up and across his
couldn't see much. The shot is a camera pan up
scripted to move or slide around (thank G
inadvertently "get in touch" with Burt's nakedn
even get in touch with my own, because if I'd st
self-consciousness might have shown up onscr

Burt set a laid-back tone. Part of Burt, I've always felt, doesn't realize he's a major movie star. He does terrific films like *Sharky's Machine*, or *Starting Over*, he says, for his "career," and then grinds out the sillier action movies for the location or the money. He's never too hung up on career strategies and industry perceptions about him. He comes from a generation of players for whom the "trappings" of movie stardom worked to support the myth, not the other way around. In today's more manipulative, greedier film industry, where agents and publicists have more power than ever, the hype and myth seem to come first, in order to support the ego and the trappings. Now that I know what goes into making a movie, it's amazing to me that any good movies ever get made. Like me, Burt gets the joke of the "A-list" party circuit, and keeps his distance. He's most comfortable in jeans, sweaters, Western shirts, and his Florida college football jackets.

In Jupiter, I had the sense I was being groomed for some bigger role in Burt's world that was not yet being revealed to me. There were hints, however. Given the flirtation between us, it could have definitely gone in a different direction. But with the exception of one lovely balmy night of kissing that barely got to tongues, neither of us dared act on it in the close quarters of the theater.

Even today, we joke and go, "Oh, God, how come we never had that affair?" On the other hand, if we had pursued it—as great as it would have been—we might have jeopardized a working relationship that has proved durable and important to me.

The chemistry was clearly there, particularly by the time I went off to Tucson to do *Cannonball Run II*. For all I knew, Burt might have had a let's-pick-up-where-we-left-off attitude for our two months in the Arizona desert.

But we didn't. Captain Johnny flew me in and out of Tucson in his private jet so we could spend weekends together in Santa Barbara. Things were still unsettled with Burt and Loni. Burt being the true gentleman that he is, it became a dead, unexplored issue when he saw how together I was with Johnny.

Our healthy restraint at least entitled us to poke horny fun at ourselves when we began *Evening Shade*. "First season, I think we're allowed to kiss," we would joke. "Second season, tongues. Third season is groping; fourth, wilder groping. Penetration, yes—but only if we get picked up for a fifth season."

Figures prominently.

The *Cannonball* shoot was miserable and Arizona-hot. We had to do all our shooting between five A.M. and two-thirty P.M. because of 116-degree heat. Once I was in my itchy nun's habit, I understood why the sisters at Madonna High were so crabby all the time. They not only weren't getting any action; they were stuck in those hot, heavy wool habits.

Landing my next film role was a breeze: When Johnny took me to the *Staying Alive* premiere toward the end of my Tucson shoot, our picture made the front page of the *Los Angeles Times* Calendar section, and someone decided, "This is Lil, our actress opposite Michael Keaton for *Johnny Dangerously*."

Out of nowhere, I got my first leading role in a feature from a photo op. If only they had been able to make me look that good in the film.

You know a film is in trouble when the wrap party lasts until six-thirty in the morning and the female director shows up with a dog collar around her neck as you sit around and watch a gag reel (outtakes and bloopers) of the shoot. It's the kiss of death. It means you've been having too much fun making the film and that all that energy dissipated before it got put onscreen.

That was always my theory. Then it became my nightmare.

I loved working with the director, Amy Heckerling, and I think she got talked out of doing a lot of what she had in mind. It could have been a solid film, but it was a classic case of film by committee sabotaging a movie's chances.

For starters, I looked awful. Though my bodybuilding, aerobics, and food combining had streamlined my body, none of that energy translated to the screen. Here I was playing a supposedly sleek and glamorous twenties nightclub singer, but I had the beefy arms and muscled neck only a Polish wrestler could love.

I saw this project as a *huge* career break: Since *Taxi,* I had rebounded with Burt's theater gig and this, my third feature in four months. This was a major Fox project starring the very hot Michael Keaton, who was coming off the smash hit *Mr. Mom.* I figured I was on my way to movie stardom.

In my gratitude, however, I found myself abandoning my inner voice—my gut instincts—and trusting hair, makeup, and wardrobe people. "You'll look great in this color," they tell you, or, "This outfit works beautifully for you," and, "I love your makeup this way, don't you?" I went along.

Therapy gives you a sort of X-ray vision that commits you to seeing the other side of the story, whether it's your own or someone else's. And while I'm someone who gives good benefit of the doubt, that can also be a cop-out.

Your look is much larger than life onscreen and lives on forever in video infamy. I should have said, "This hat doesn't fit my head" or "This color is horrible for me."

It was an important lesson about what I call the Adult Trust-Me Pile: Someone assures you that they know more than you do. They say: "Would I want you to look bad? I've won Academy Awards. This is the big time. Trust me."

Kiss o' Death. *Trust me.*

It may be awkward to insist you have the right to express yourself and stick up for Number One, but it can be painful not to.

The picture was intended as a buoyant homage to the old Jimmy Cagney pictures we had grown up with, but somewhere along the way it turned into *Blazing Saddles Meets The Roaring Twenties*—a far broader, forced version of Amy's film. It's almost impossible to see a film's forest for its trees while you're working on it. You shoot out of sequence, you do multiple takes of every setup, the script is constantly being revised, and you have no idea what choices the editor and director will make in postproduction. Then you've got music, effects, marketing—and we had not been allowed to watch dailies. As actors, you're virtually shooting in the dark, hoping for the best.

But why complain about shooting in the dark with Michael Keaton, or being in a makeup trailer every morning with him and Griffin Dunne, one of the funniest people I have ever worked with. The set was our own little period playground.

Amy became my best friend during the filming and we all hung out on weekends. But the shoot really turned into a big party when Johnny started working on *Two of a Kind* with Olivia Newton-John on a soundstage next door.

I had the maddest, heart-poundingest schoolgirl crush on Michael, who, thank God for me, was married. Talk about PF! I found him extremely sexy. He has adorable, mischievous eyes and those Jimmy Cagney eyebrows, a look my father had. There is something delicious and devilish about Michael, and I had such a good time with him. He nicknamed me "Marilu-I-Can't-Finish-a-Sentence-Without-Laughing-Henner."

If he wasn't available, his character was, so I threw all my energy into Lil's being crazy about him. The film ends with an enormous

production number in which he dies in my arms. Then he gets up
and dances through the end credits. It was a cool, unusual concept
and should have worked. There was simply no way this film, with
all that fun, creative energy, could be anything but incredible and
brilliant.

Was there?

By now, Johnny and I were getting into a very comfortable,
almost ideal, groove. After *Johnny Dangerously* wrapped, I flew to
join him on the *Staying Alive* junket in Rome, where we hooked up
with Flavio and Maria. After Christmas and over New Year's, he
arranged another incredible family getaway to Martinique, where
he chartered a spectacular sailing ship for a weeklong Adventure in
Paradise cruise around the French West Indies. After a rough,
eighteen-hour sail out, it was pure pleasure—island-hopping off
the tourist path, diving off the side of the ship, tanning on deck or
on white-sand beaches, exploring the interior, and bunking in our
cozy, funky rooms.

My bonds to Johnny were unlike any either of us had ever had:
Our relationship had lasted well over a decade, had been through a
half-dozen incarnations, had survived my two-year marriage to
Freddie and several girlfriends of his; it had swung between a
bedrock brother-sister friendship and, on trips like the one to the
Caribbean, charged-up sexual passion.

Watching Johnny on his tightly organized trips made me think of
the remark someone made about how Pope John Paul XXIII "sure
knows how to Pope." Johnny sure knows how to "Star." He was
comfortable with being the center of attention, but he never lost
sight of his values. He was a selfless host, and loved sharing his
wealth with an energized and imaginative extravagance. But nothing ever changed the fact that Johnny has always had the world's
biggest heart.

My luck in films didn't change with the New Year. I got tangled
up in a classic Hollywood horror story. Blake Edwards, after *The
Man Who Loved Women,* said he would love to work with Johnny
and me sometime. I trusted and believed Blake, who, after the
wrap, had given me a gold, and ten scripts to look over.

I picked the one called *Kansas City Jazz,* which he wanted me to
consider doing with Johnny. In it, a private investigator has a
torrid affair with a socialite. I told Blake I loved the script, but saw

myself more as the hot, sassy secretary, Addie; the socialite seemed too stiff and boring. Fine, he said, he would rewrite and make Addie much bigger for me.

I loved the rewrite. Addie was now a colorful, feisty character. I showed the script to Johnny, but he wasn't into it. Blake gave the script to Burt. Burt loved it and immediately saw Clint Eastwood in the minor cop role earmarked for Charles Durning. But Burt told Blake it would have to be rewritten and expanded for Clint. Blake rewrote again, and now the three of them were in on it. The script had been lying around for twenty-five years, had been set in motion by my enthusiasm, and was now budgeted at $32 million. I was *dying* to do this movie.

It wasn't that simple. In November, I got a call from Blake that blew my mind. Blake told me that Clint liked the project so much he had insisted his girlfriend, Sondra Locke, play the socialite, Caroline, who ends up with Burt's P.I. (Addie ends up with Clint.) The problem was, Blake insisted on Kim Basinger for the socialite. Clint didn't like that, so he decided that no one who had ever worked with Burt or Blake or him could be in the movie. So Sondra *and* Kim were out. I found all this astounding.

Then the other shoe dropped: "And your part," Blake told me, "is now going to Marsha Mason."

I was crushed. I had to open my big mouth and ask for a bigger part. This *sucked.* I had had this movie resurrected for myself, and I wasn't even in it anymore! Over Christmas, 1983, Blake's *The Man Who Loved Women* bombed and Clint's new movie went through the roof. Ultimately, there was a major hassle involving Clint, Blake, and the studio, ending, of course, with the studio siding with red-hot Clint. They bought Blake out of the project, hired Richard Benjamin to direct, and called the film *City Heat.*

Now, Blake, in his very decent way, called and said, "I want you in my next picture." (A variation of the "Adult Trust-Me Pile.) He arranged to screen-test me for a terrific character in *Micki & Maude* with Dudley Moore. My faith in the system had been restored.

For five seconds.

The week of my screen test, Oscar nominations were announced, and Amy Irving got one for *Yentl.* The studio promptly sent down the commandment to offer my part to Amy—no test, no reading. Just an outright offer. I never even had my screen test.

* * *

At least things had been sailing smoothly with Johnny in the eighteen months since Freddie. We were flying all over the world together, and this was exactly where I wanted it. Our week in paradise had shown me that this fantastic life together could, in fact, go on forever. We weren't in each other's way. I didn't need to live with him and cramp his style. We had weeknights at my place, weekends in Santa Barbara. It was what both of us seemed to need at the time.

Or so it seemed.

One night, in January 1984, at the Westwood Marquis Hotel, he said, "I can't do this anymore."

"What are you talking about?"

"Everybody sees us as a couple, and I'm just not good at relationships. I can't make it work. It's just too hard for me."

My reaction was: Fine, now tell me something I don't know. It was a slap in the face, all right, but I felt as if I'd just flunked a test I never even knew I was taking. Was it ever really supposed to be something else? He had kept me in the dark and set me up for his bombshell as a way to remain in complete control. I was more angered than shocked.

But it was true. For years I had known that the bottom line for us was that we would never fall in love and commit to making it work. It just wasn't our destiny. Just when it had begun to feel like we were "supposed" to spend every weekend together, he'd pulled back.

When a guy has a pilot's license, his own copy of the OAG, and a private jet to go with it, is it so unusual for a girl to wonder about his desire to commit?

The curious thing was that Johnny's wanderlust was equal parts wander and lust. Routine, predictability, and expectation all turned him off. That last door at the end of the corridor was never going to open. Having resisted the temptation to see it differently when things were pretty much perfect—as they had been on the cruise—I had scaled down my expectations to suit Johnny's limits.

Of course, three weeks later, we were back together.

Then, that other *Johnny Dangerously* came back to haunt me. When I finally got to see the film in early 1984, I went into shock. Ninety percent of all the fun we had had was missing from the movie. It was a whole other film from the one we thought we were shooting. They had, of course, test-marketed the ending and learned that audiences hated that Michael died; so they screwed around with a new ending and made us reshoot a silly, slapstick ending that did not work at all. It was cool that he died, just as Cagney did in *The Roaring Twenties.* Now, it didn't work.

Plus, my hair and clothes made me crazy.

I hated everything about the movie, and I was flattened. This was a major blow. I went out with my brother Tommy afterward and got wasted on two bottles of champagne, four entrées, and a half-dozen desserts.

"We're going for *numb* tonight," I announced.

In early May I took a brief trip to New York. The night before I left I had a bizarre dream about Andy Kaufman. I couldn't get him out of my mind and quietly cried the whole way there. I had run into Andy in February in a health food restaurant and I was alarmed. I knew he had been diagnosed with cancer within months of our show's cancellation a year earlier; but now he was so gravely ill that he was all but unrecognizable. I couldn't help thinking that Andy was dying. He had asked me to a screening of a weird movie he had written, directed, and produced called *My Breakfast with Blassie,* a takeoff of *My Dinner with Andre,* starring wrestling bad-guy Freddie Blassie, one of Andy's heroes.

When I got back to L.A. a week later, I learned that Andy had died that day of lung cancer at the age of thirty-five. None of us could believe it when we got together for the memorial service at the Improv. We thought maybe it was a Tony Clifton–type prank. But it wasn't. I had to give a speech and I was so sad and so broken up with sobbing that I don't even remember what I said.

My grieving for Andy seemed to fuel the low, self-absorbing funk I had been fending off for weeks, maybe months. I couldn't snap myself out of it. After the glorious success of *Taxi,* my momentum in films seemed spent. I was treading. I went up for movies I didn't get. I made movies in which I hated my look. I liked my look and my work in movies that bombed. Johnny and I were having a ball going nowhere together. He wasn't committed, and I wasn't looking around. It was one disappointment after another.

And now, seeing Andy waste away and die so young threw me into a funk.

I felt as if the blinders I'd been wearing had dropped off, forcing me to see that my life wasn't turning out to be what I had envisioned. My sunny pink cloud overhead—my family's positive, assertive values, my determination to get out of Logan Square and make a fantastic life for myself, the faith in my own capacity to keep on moving forward—had suddenly darkened.

The Black Dome of Depression crashed down and engulfed me in the bleakest time of my life.

17
Figures
Prominently

~~~

I moped my way through the summer of '84. Sure, the Olympics had come to town; sure, I was shooting *Perfect* with Johnny, and I was signed to go right into a Western to be shot in Spain, *Rustler's Rhapsody* with Tom Berenger. Any picture in Europe, I figured, would put me close to my beloved Italy.

However, none of this made much of a dent on my depressed state.

Perfect brought it all into wretched focus. *Perfect* was Johnny's picture with Jamie Lee Curtis, in which he plays a *Rolling Stone* reporter doing a piece on the trendy eighties health-club-as-meat-market scene. It was based on a *Rolling Stone* article that journalist-screenwriter Aaron Latham had written. I played Sally, one of three unhappy single women featured in the film's B-story: The journalist "seduces" them into opening up to him, but his piece gets rewritten by a ruthless editor in a way that depicts their petty jealousies and melodramas in a harsh, unflattering way.

I had a terrific time working with Johnny, Aaron, and director Jim Bridges, but like Sally, I came to feel ripped off and exploited. Again, I hated the way I looked and walked through the shoot. It hardly helped that I was a long way from being in optimum shape on the set of a movie about women obsessed with their bodies.

There were such long delays between lighting and camera setups that I ate way too much. I was faking my way through my workouts. I had a weird, competitive vibe with one of the other actresses on the project, who actually had me removed from the aerobics class numbers. The cast was not what you'd call a tight family. I'd been spoiled by so many great and happy sets, and there was just something off here. Maybe that's why people told me they liked me in it, because we were playing sad characters and I was miserable much of the time.

When I finally did see it, I was devastated.

It was nice, though, to roll out of bed with Johnny at the Westwood Marquis and share a limo to the shoot. I adored Jim Bridges, who kept insisting I was "incredible" in dailies and that I was "a star waiting to happen." I kept waiting; it kept not happening. Not with *Perfect*.

Just before I finally wrapped, on August 23, I went out to see a friend perform in *Equus*. Toward the end of the reception afterward, I was met by a video crew for *Entertainment Tonight*. They needed a sound bite on the subject of rape victims. I thought it a strange question to ask after a show like *Equus*, and it was only then that I learned I had just attended a benefit for a group calling itself Victims for Victims.

"Uhh, no one should be a victim," I blurted out, or something to that effect. I felt like such an idiot.

Just then, a very handsome, dark-haired guy came straight up to me and introduced himself.

"Hi, I'm Robert Lieberman," he said. "I'm a big fan of yours. I directed the film *Table for Five* with Jon Voight."

It wasn't a movie I had seen, but this Robert Lieberman did have one of the two looks I've always gone for—beautiful, sparkly brownish green eyes, an intense, searching, intellectual look, the trimmed Jesus-rock-star beard.

"Oh, I loved that movie," I said, acting like I had seen it. He then acted like he had loved me in *Taxi*, but I could tell he hadn't ever watched. Soon we were standing there, bullshitting each other as the evening wound down.

"You know, Jon Voight and I work out at the same place," I volunteered cheerfully—as you by now know, I have always loved "connect-the-dots"–type coincidences like that.

"Oh, really? What's this workout place?"

"The people who trained John Travolta for *Staying Alive* opened a gym with him and they work with celebrities one-on-one. Actually, it's for anyone who wants to pay that kind of money."

"So what did you think of the play?" he asked.

"Oh, I know somebody in it. It was great."

Well, well, well. My, my, my. Small world.

We chatted on and on. Rob was one of the world's leading directors of television commercials. He had done something like 1,000 of them and won scads of Clios, which is like the Oscar of thirty-second films for ad agencies. It was his company that had put together the evening's production and benefit.

Rob's movie had come out the year before to strong critical praise but modest business. It was his first feature, about a divorced man played by Jon Voight who tries to get back into his children's lives by taking them on a Mediterranean cruise. When his ex-wife dies during the cruise, he has to confront her second husband, played by Richard Crenna, the hands-on, possessive surrogate dad who wants them back. As I learned when I finally *did* see it, it was a powerful, beautifully played tearjerker.

What I also did not learn until much later was that when Rob had seen a crowd of people around a "somebody" bathed in floodlights, he had peered over the cameraman's shoulder and seen "an angelic, incredible-looking glowing human being who took my breath away with her translucent skin, glowing red hair, an blue-green eyes."

Thanks, Rob.

He had been taking his date out to the car when he'd spotted n He pulled his business partner aside and said, "That's Ma Henner, and I've been wanting to meet her. This is my chance. now or never." He asked his business partner to watch his dat a few moments so he could make contact.

It turned out that Rob had seen me on *The Tonight Sh* March, when I'd talked about the closeness of my family, an had impressed him. He had sworn off dating actresses recently ending a turbulent four-year relationship with Bedelia. After seeing me on *The Tonight Show,* he decid make one last exception because of a feeling of kinship could only meet me.

Now, like a director losing his light, Rob knew his w opportunity was shutting fast, with a date waiting by parking stand. It had been almost twenty minutes. "So gym sounds great. How would I go about getting the num workout place if I wanted to start working out there?"

"Well, I'll give it to you." It occurred to me that callir Jon Voight might have worked too, so I realized someth going on here.

"And, so, umm, how would I go about getting *your* number if I
wanted to take you to dinner sometime?"

"I'll give it to you." I had no intention of going out with him at
the time. He came on too fast and direct, with a slick Vegas quality
that didn't go with the sensitive-director bit. So I gave him my safer
service number—an appropriate enough move at a rape-victims
benefit.

I didn't know it then, but this was as far from Rob's nature as he
could get. While seeming to "hustle" me, he was dying inside. He
later told me that when he wheeled around and walked away, he
was floating on air, amazed and thrilled that he had actually gotten
my number.

As he watched me walk out and get into a car with a hunky gay
male friend of mine, he told himself: "What chance have I got with
her if she's with this great-looking guy?" I couldn't blame him. My
gay actor friend was drop-dead gorgeous. We had met six months
earlier when I played the one female in a TV production of *Mr.
Roberts.* I walked onto a set crowded with forty guys in sailor
uniforms, took one look around, spotted his face, and said, "I want
him." It was love at first sight—until he told me he was gay. I
didn't care. He was going to become my close friend and will
always be in my life.

If Rob was intimidated, it didn't keep him from calling me the
very next day. I told him I was going off to Spain the next week for a
couple of months but that he should call me when I got back. He
apparently marked the date down; I didn't give it another thought.

I had a fantastic, life-changing, eight-week adventure in Spain
while making the spoofy Western with Tom Berenger, G. W.
Bailey, Sela Ward, and the director Hugh Wilson. We all played
slightly twisted clichés. I played a dance hall hostess, the hooker
with a heart of gold who never slept with anyone, but just got them
to talk.

The movie of my own life turned out to be every bit as absorbing
as the script we were shooting. We spent two weeks in Madrid and
then five in the wretched town of Almería. Still, I loved the late
evening light, the way Spaniards eat late and stay up all night. I
found the Spanish people elegant and beautiful—and far better
organized than the Italians.

There's always something going on romantically on locations,

especially exotic ones like Spain. But it's less than movie fans probably assume. G. W. and I became fast, fast friends. I was crazy about Tom and his girlfriend, Lisa, so we all hung out as pals. I did have a wild crush on our darkly gorgeous Spanish soundman, who barely spoke English, but I kept it quiet.

I made the most of my time alone and channeled my energies into a major health kick. I focused on dealing with my problem with pronation—the turned-out, tilted-hip dancer's misalignment in my walk. I had had trouble with impact aerobics and jogging because of it. My first week on location was mostly wardrobe fittings, so I decided to go on a private mission to turn my life—and body—around. (My trainer had given me corrective orthotics to insert inside my running shoes before I left.)

It was "no Spain, no gain" for me, as I whipped myself into amazing shape and finally got the sleek, toned, high-energy body I had always wanted. I was free to get into myself, to be alone, to focus on what I needed for me. I was disciplined about food combining, aerobics, and major "power-walking." I forced myself to break a sweat and move at between 5 and 5.5 miles an hour. In one week alone, I clocked 84 miles on my pedometer. I decided: *Make yourself look fabulous. If you're going to be depressed, at least be depressed and thin.* I lost 20 pounds in a month—I got down to 118—and I looked my all-time best. Working hard on my body and working overtime in therapy, I completely recovered from the "dome crashing" depression that had plagued me for months.

My body was so totally redesigned that by the end of the shoot my entire wardrobe had to be cinched in four inches at the waist. I was flying. I felt exhilarated from being, finally, thoroughly in control of and in touch with my body and my life.

Naturally, Flavio came and visited from Rome, winding up as an extra for a day. When the film wrapped in October, I flew off and visited him and Maria. It was a wonderful break and I came home to America on Halloween feeling rejuvenated and vigorously healthy. In fact, I still had to shoot the final credits for *Perfect* after I returned, and I looked like a different person from Sally.

Of course, applying my Kiss of Death theory from *Johnny Dangerously* to *Rustler's Rhapsody,* I knew it would bomb because we had such a blast making it, with those three-hour lunches and endless siestas. And bomb it did, a year later. It went from being a smart-ass parody of the Western to an homage to the Western, losing in postproduction all the spark and energy that had gone into making it.

In early November, a week after returning from Spain, I went to a screening at Universal and was running late for my weekly therapy phone session with Dr. Sharon back east. Instead of driving in heavy traffic over the hill from the Valley to South Doheny in Beverly Hills, I decided to go to my gym in nearby Toluca Lake and use a pay phone there.

As I breezed in, I immediately made eye contact with Rob Lieberman—pedaling away on a stationary bike. I almost died. He clearly hadn't lost any of *his* spark since August.

When I finished a half hour later, he came up to me. "Hey, look!" he said, as if stunned to see me. "I work out here now." He didn't miss a beat. "So how was Spain? How about that dinner?"

The word "incestuous" suddenly came to mind: Johnny owned the gym, and we were on our way to the Caribbean for Love Boat II; Jon Voight worked out here; now Rob was connected here too—we even had the same trainer now.

"You know something?" I said, putting him off again. "I'm actually on my way to Jamaica for a vacation. Why don't I call you when I get back." Rob remembers telling trainer John that I was just too wired, too hyper, that he couldn't deal with my energy.

Did *that* remark ever come back to haunt him!

Johnny and I made our second magical escape to paradise on a 93-foot boat, and I found myself truly falling in love with him, once and for all. This trip turned into the most romantic and intimate time we had ever shared—helped by the fact that I felt terrific and skinny and sexy.

But what was I thinking? Back on land, it was clear nothing had changed, that nothing would change. The New Year only reinforced what I already knew: Johnny's and my relationship was just what it was—which wasn't enough anymore.

What *had* changed was me. I wanted a commitment, a partner, a life with someone I was madly in love with.

The first half of the year was a letdown after the reign in Spain and the trips with Johnny. I felt we were finally winding it down. As adventurous as we were in the air and on the high seas, there was nowhere else for it to go in our hearts.

But there were some unusual connections going on with Rob
Lieberman; that situation seemed to be taking on a life of its own.
In January, he breezed into the gym and rushed over. "You're
never going to believe this," he said, "but I'm doing a commercial
shoot with your ex–brother-in-law, Bob Carney."

This was pretty odd. I hadn't even seen Bob in five years, and
now he and Rob were teamed up, as director and producer,
respectively, for a commercial. It got stranger: I learned that Rob
had worked with Bob twelve years earlier when he'd entered the
business, cutting commercials for him. That link, from so far out in
left field, seemed like one of those amazing connect-the-dots
moments suggesting a higher purpose.

"Why don't you come visit the set?" Rob asked.

"You're never going to believe *this*, but I'm leaving for Vegas to
do a TV movie called *Stark*. I'll talk to you—"

"—when you get back."

We had this routine down.

Bob Carney called the next day. "Oh, God, every day, this
director guy Rob Lieberman keeps asking me, 'Is your sister-in-law
coming to the set today?' "

I sighed and told Bob I thought Rob was just too intense. He
liked me too much, and was putting way too much energy on me,
when I was more into vamping. I couldn't handle that serious edge
of his.

In short, he had marriage material written all over him.

In March, after coming back from Vegas, I was working out
daily, paying $1,200 a month to work with trainers at the gym. One
day I was lying on the floor doing my ab and stretching routine next
to another celebrity client and his trainer. My trainer saw the three
of us in a row and said, "God, you have the three tightest stomachs.
I bet I can walk across them without it even hurting." I was
between the two guys, and said, "Okay, sure, go ahead."

He was right. It didn't hurt—until he tripped and fell on top of
me and cracked two ribs. *That* hurt. I could hear my ribs snap. I
was in agony and had to wear a brace to protect and heal them.
There was no way I could work out for three months, and I lost the
cut I had worked so hard for—and which had recently earned me a
place among *McCall's'* Ten Best Bodies.

But in the third week of May, a remarkable turn of events
changed everything. Johnny and I went to New York for the *Perfect*
press junket, and stayed at the UN Plaza Hotel in the East

Forties—not the most likely place for showbiz people. Rob, meanwhile, was down in Guadeloupe to shoot a commercial, accompanied by an actress—I guess she must have been another "exception" to his rule about *not* dating actresses—with great legs and strong family values.

He thought she was down there to be with him; she thought she was there to get a part in the commercial. Rob broke it to her that that was not going to happen, and she left the next day. As he told me later, "She was sexy, but in a really cold, plastic-surgery way. She probably thought she was fucking her way to the middle."

After a grueling two-week shoot, Rob got down in the dumps and wanted to vanish to the far side of the world, to someplace he'd never been. So he booked a trip to Brazil. But it would be like a twenty-four-hour series of flights, and May was Brazil's November, meaning he would be going from one cold beach to another.

At the last minute, Rob changed his mind and headed to New York instead. He had been nominated for nine Clios, and the awards night was that week. All his friends in advertising would be there and he could party with them and, most likely, collect a Clio or two. When he flew in, he decided to stay, of all places, at the UN Plaza.

The moment he checked in and went upstairs, his partner found him and said, "I just saw John Travolta in the lobby."

"Oh God, that means Marilu may be here." He asked around and learned the *Perfect* junket was going on.

Meanwhile, Johnny and I were having our own private drama up in our suite. We had come to the decision to split up. It was time for us, after almost fifteen years, to let go, say good-bye, and move on with our lives.

"If I can't make it work with you," he said solemnly, emphatically, "then I know I can't make it work with anybody. You're someone who deserves so much more than I'm giving you."

I could no longer deny the truth of what he was saying. I did deserve, and want, more. I had more or less ignored Johnny's previous attempt to end it, but this time I heard the finality in his voice. This was a major sadness, but I had to get real: I was ripe to settle down and make a life with someone. I was in my thirties, and he and I had been going at it longer than most people stay married. Emotionally, I was deeply invested in holding on to Johnny, but I knew this was it, the end of the road. It was an unbearable, if inevitable, loss.

I couldn't stop crying. We hugged, we sobbed, we went through an extremely painful, bittersweet, tearful farewell. Soon we had to go downstairs and ride off to a party with Yoko Ono, where we would meet the press and answer a million questions about a movie I had never enjoyed making or watching. We agreed not to mention the split.

As hard as I tried, I couldn't hide my anguish. My hairdresser, Mary Ann, who was working with us for the junket, came upstairs to get us.

"Mar," she muttered in the elevator, "there is the *cutest* guy in the lobby. Oh my God, he is so your type it's scary. You know that Jewish kind of guy you love." If she was trying to cheer me up and take my mind off Johnny, it didn't work.

I shrugged and mumbled something like "Oh, please," not wanting to betray that anything was amiss with Johnny. The elevator doors drew back and I heard Mary Ann whisper, "That's him."

I was staring straight at Rob's face.

"Oh, for God's sake," I told Mary Ann, "I know this guy."

Without thinking it strange—given how I had blown him off for so long—I ran over to Rob and gave him a big hug and a kiss. (Rob hadn't been sure I would even recognize him.) It just seemed so natural; he looked like someone really familiar, like somebody I knew well. And he looked incredible. He had lost about twenty pounds at the gym and was, as he would later point out, buffed.

Johnny came over and I introduced Rob as the director of *Table for Five*. Johnny loved the movie and was highly complimentary toward Rob. Then we were whisked off to a waiting limo. I knew Rob was blown away as he watched us.

The door closed and Johnny said, with a teasing jab of the finger, "That man looks guilty for every lustful thought he's ever had about you. He's *wild* about you."

Rob and his company threw a lavish party in his hotel suite, but they struck out 0 for 9 at the Clios. He was bummed.

The next day, he flew back to L.A. and promptly left a message on my machine to call him back. I didn't. I was in mourning over Johnny and felt nothing but deep sadness through the whole month of June. I walked around listening over and over to James Taylor's song "Her Town." I had lost one J. T. but was hanging on to another.

There was nothing for me to do about Rob, who seemed so sure of his feelings and intentions. I knew that if we got together and hit it off, he would definitely want to make it stick. So often it's hard to find a man so pro-commitment.

But I knew I couldn't handle his intensity so soon after Johnny. For me, it was the end of an era.

In July, I went to Toronto and did a *Broadway on Showtime* production of Jules Feiffer's *Grown Ups,* with Charles Grodin, Jean Stapleton, and Marty Balsam. The play is about the breakup of a marriage, and I really got into it. I did some of the best work I've ever done, for which I was later nominated for an Ace award.

In the middle of the month, I sat down and made a list of all the things I wanted for myself. I often did this, feeling that just writing them down and putting them out there in the universe helped tweak them and make them happen. This list was about wanting someone truly significant in my life. I had some requirements: sense of humor, great sex, PF, heart and soul. The usual.

What was unusual was that the day I made this list—July 16—was, I later learned, also Rob's birthday.

I began to come out of my funk in Toronto. I loved the city, the people, the project; it was a totally wonderful experience, and I had to be dragged away kicking and screaming.

August turned into my "Sweepstakes Period"—meeting, dating, getting fixed up, dining. And no action. When it came to relationships, I was drifting and confused. I didn't feel attached to anything.

For four months I had avoided calling Rob.

But he was at the gym on September 12 when his trainer said, "Marilu Henner was in the other day. She asked about you."

"She did?" Undaunted by four months of silence, he called and left a message.

I was in Chicago. I beeped in, heard his message, and returned the call from my sister's house. "I'll be back Tuesday and I'd love to have dinner with you," I said right off the bat.

It was thirteen months since we had met.

Rob said, "Forget about dinner; you're only gonna stand me up anyways. I know you figure me for a heavy-breather type. It's only been, what, thirteen months? You'll never show, so why bother? But I've got an idea for a date I think you'll be comfortable with."

I was listening.

"There'll be sixty-five thousand chaperons, witnesses, whatever, so I can't make a move on you. That should make you feel safe. I've got tickets to the Raiders football game Sunday the twenty-second. How'd you like to go?"

"I can't," I said. "I've got a shoot the next day for an *Alfred Hitchcock Presents* and I don't want to get sunburned because I have to match what I've already shot." If anyone could understand, it would be a director, but I knew I was stretching Rob's patience. "So why *don't* we have dinner?"

We made a date for Wednesday the 25th.

I did have the shoot, but the real reason I canceled Sunday was that I was going on a fifth date the night before with a doctor I had seen and grown to like. A reconstructive cosmetic surgeon, he worked on trauma cases, not the face-lift type. He worked with kids, and I thought he had a good heart. I left open the possibility that something might click over dinner and that I'd wind up spending the night at his house.

Saturday night, the MD turned into an obnoxious prick. Maybe it was that I was a celebrity—who knows? But he became so macho and full of himself and hostile that I said to him, "This is so not working out for me that I'm just going to leave now."

And I did just that.

I woke up Sunday morning and thought, What a *perfect* day for a football game!

I called Rob. "Is that ticket still available?"

He asked me to hold on while he figured it out. He actually had four tickets. After I'd declined, he planned to take his son, Lorne, who stayed weekends at Rob's house up in Ramirez Canyon; a client; and his houseboy, Michael, a Pepperdine University student who also looked after Lorne.

I'd assumed we'd be going alone.

Rob put his hand over the phone and said, "Michael, you're not going." Then, back to me, he said, "Yeah, I still have that ticket for you."

He came by and picked me up. I dressed like Mother Teresa, swathed in sun-protective layers. We stopped at my health food store. Rob grabbed an apple, but before the checkout girl could put it on the scale he said "Just a minute" and took a huge bite out of it. Then he put it back on the scale.

What an asshole, I thought, though it was actually pretty funny.

We got to the stadium and started walking to our seats when I realized I had forgotten to bring a cap. When I mentioned this, Rob said Lorne had some kind of French Foreign Legion hat in the car and sent him after it.

After Lorne left, Rob and I stood there in silence, looking into each other's eyes and smiling. It was the first moment we'd ever been alone together.

Out in the vast, sun-drenched parking lot, a flash of recognition zapped us—a fleeting look, a deep, reciprocal awareness. Just recalling it still gives us a shiver.

Because it was in that silent split second that we both understood with a kind of mesmerizing absoluteness that we would be together for the rest of our lives.

18

The Boy with the Moon and the Stars on His Head

~

I didn't need to do any Monday-morning quarterbacking to know how to play the situation with Rob. The only question was when we were going to run a deep pattern and score. After my thirteen-month delay of game, I was ready to play ball.

Still, lurking in the back of my mind was the memory of my big mistake with Freddie: We had gotten married way too soon.

A dozen white roses were delivered to me on the *Alfred Hitchcock* set, with a note that read, "My Dear Marilu, I wish you skin as white as these roses. My son has a crush on you and as the saying goes—like son, like father. I can't wait till Wednesday."

The closing was classic: *Your adorable, Rob.* Apparently this was an unconscious slip on his part. Instead of telling me I was adorable (i.e., *You're adorable, Rob*), he let me know he thought *he* was adorable—and used the second-person possessive to do so. In other words, he was not only adorable; he was all mine, too.

We went for sushi in the Valley on the 25th and spent the entire evening gabbing away and discovering each other at breakneck conversational speed.

Rob had grown up in Buffalo and gone to the University of Buffalo. He was articulate, reflective, and extremely funny, with the sardonic, edgy Jewish humor I love so much. We just clicked in every way. He wanted a relationship, and he didn't have the kind of "poseur" energy I loathed in so many Hollywood men. He didn't have an actor's ego, he was secure enough to not be a Mommy-wipe-me type, and he had been out with enough model-actress brats not to be hung up on vacuous poses or intimidated by "celebrity." He loved his mom, took good care of her, clearly cherished women, and was a strong, loving father to Lorne and Erin, who were then eleven and thirteen. If there was anything wrong with this picture, I didn't see it. And he was very sexy and romantic.

Rob even broke down and told me about the low point, and turning point, in his life—when he had suffered a nervous breakdown and been locked away and medicated for six weeks back in 1977.

I wasn't turned off or frightened by this extraordinary story. I was moved, and fascinated, that he had turned his life around and become so successful. Maybe it was because I had been through therapy and understood something about the yin and yang, the ups and downs, of people's lives and careers—or because I find it distressing that people squander so much psychic energy trying to be the idealized version of themselves. Here was this amazing, gifted guy willing to strip away the bullshit pretense and self-delusion that are so rampant, particularly in my business, and to reveal his pain and struggle along with the triumphs.

I often think of people walking through life as if they are holding up masks of themselves on sticks in front of their faces—the "face" they're putting out to the world. But then the mask needs another mask in front of it to put on a different act for some other reason, or some other reward, and soon you're so many masks deep, and so far removed from the human being behind them, that you find yourself working awfully hard to smash them. Rob seemed to have already cracked through most of his. He took a risk in opening up to me like that so soon, but it showed how much he prized honesty over some personal-ad fantasy checklist. I felt a sort of rush from his emotional courage.

If Rob, the crafty director, was pulling a "figures prominently" on me somewhere with all these dark revelations, I missed it, or chose not to focus on it. I was more than happy to suspend my disbelief.

Indeed, I was feeling so exhilarated that out of the blue I reached forward, grabbed his cheeks in my hands as he was speaking, leaned over the table, and kissed him. He didn't know what hit him.

In the parking lot, I told him about my idiot savant–type

1. Did your parents have any kids who lived? My brother Tommy and me. My mother had four other children just to compensate.

2. With my first boyfriend Steve Babler

3. With Johnny on our Caribbean cruise—my favorite trip we ever took together

4. With Freddie at our wedding in New Orleans

5. My *Taxi*
fantasy sequence

6. Me and my *Taxi* guys . . . uh . . . gals. I never thought
I'd get to work with the Andrews Sisters again!

7. With Judd

8. One of the rare pictures of the six Henner kids together. From left to right: JoAnn, Tommy, me, Lorin, Melody, and Christal

9. On location for *Rustler's Rhapsody*

10. I was named one of the "Ten Best Bodies" by *McCall's* magazine in 1988.

11. Just a little something I throw on to open the door

12. With Steve Martin in *L.A. Story*—my all-time favorite movie experience

13. The cast of *Carnal Knowledge* modeling our wrap gifts from Gregory Harrison

14. My wonderful family at my sister Christal's wedding in Chartres, France, in 1990. From left to right: Joe Rowley, my sister JoAnn, my sister-in-law Lynnette, my brother Lorin, my niece Lizzy, Christal, my brother-in-law Roy, my niece Suzanne, my brother Tommy, me, my nephew Adam, my husband Rob, and my sister Melody

15. Rob's and my Christmas present to my family in 1992—two weeks in Snowmass, Colorado. Some of the gang; first row, from left: Lizzy, me, Suzanne, and Christal. Second row, from left: Adam, ski instructor Sean Mullen, my stepson Lorne, Rob, our friend Ben Sellars, and Roy.

16. Two weeks before my finest production—on *The Tonight Show* with Jay Leno in April 1994

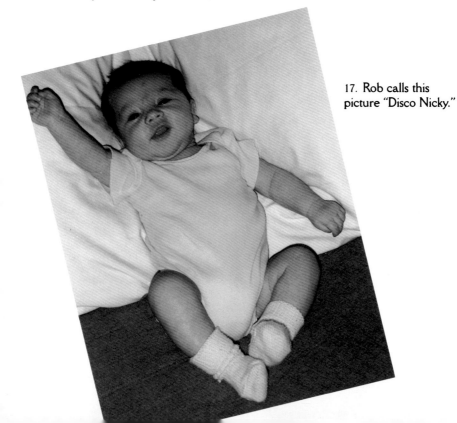

17. Rob calls this picture "Disco Nicky."

memory. Like most people when they first hear of it, he seemed skeptical. "Give me a date," I said eagerly.

"July 16, 1947," he said with a sneer. "The day I was born." Then it hit me that the day I had made my "What I Want" list in Toronto was his birthday.

"July 16, 1947," I repeated slowly, as I let my internal laser disk drives click into *search* mode and whir around until I locked it in.

"It was a Wednesday."

"Okay, just a second." He reached for his car phone and called his mother, Sally, who lived in the Valley. "Mom, listen," he said, "on what day of the week was I born?" He waited for her answer, and then he nodded with a self-satisfied smirk. "It was a Tuesday," he gloated.

As he continued to listen to his mother recalling the story, he shot me a look. "Now she says it was just after midnight, so it was a Wednesday." We both had a good laugh at that one.

The day after our sushi dinner Rob invited me to the MGM studios, where he was screening *Table for Five* for a new talent agency with whom he had just signed.

I was impressed. *This guy's a real player, he's got money, he's successful,* I thought. The only major thing I figured I would have to work on with him was his posture, which, if not a deal-breaker, did bug me. He hunched over way too much; it would have to go. Otherwise, the checklist was looking good.

It was sweet the way he held my hand through the whole movie, and then, as promised, he got me home at exactly ten-thirty. It was funny: He didn't even kiss me good night. Our only kiss had been the one over sushi.

"So what about tomorrow night?" he asked. Thursday.

"I might have plans." It was true. I did.

"I thought you could drive out to the beach and I'd cook dinner," he said.

I knew what that meant.

Maybe I don't have plans, I thought. I canceled dinner with Jonathan Krane, who was managing my film career, and his wife, Sally Kellerman, both friends. They totally got it, and understood.

"Are you sure you want to do this?" I asked him over the phone the next day.

"Oh, no, I'm really excited. I'll cook."

It took me an hour and a half to figure out what outfit to wear

knew I was going to spend the night. By now, I knew this was it. I wanted to look appealing and vulnerable and a little bit naughty.

Rob says I showed up looking like Little Bo Peep.

I went for clothes that didn't provide easy access—clothes that took time, made you think, made you work to get them off. My theory is that every woman has a fantasy about being undressed in layers by a man, to be peeled back like an artichoke. (Maybe guys like to be peeled like a banana, women like an artichoke.)

I like buttons, I like layers, I like lace-up boots. It was all so calculated. My room looked like a tornado had ripped through it. I tried every combination imaginable. Meanwhile, I lied and told him I was working late—buying a little more outfit-planning time at home. Finally, when I had it all worked out, I called to tell him I was on my way.

Under my outfit, of course, great first-night underwear: lacy bra and panties, camisole, a little pink top that buttoned up while allowing a peek at the camisole, white skirt, stockings, lace-up boots. As Rob said, long after the deed was done, "All you needed was a staff and the little lambs." It was a sweet, girlish, fresh, summery, naughty-virgin look. I never dressed like that again for Rob.

I drove up to Ramirez Canyon in Malibu, way up near Paradise Cove, but on the inland side. Barbra Streisand owns a huge chunk of that canyon. Rob was renting a gorgeous storybook home with a front gate, spectacular landscaping and flowers blooming everywhere, and rolling hills behind the house with a creek and a bridge arching over it. It was a California fantasy that took my breath away.

Rob came out looking earthy and sexy in a flowing white shirt, jeans, and bare feet. By now I believed that Rob was no desperado hustler. His slickmeister facade hid a nervous, insecure—but forthright and honest—core. I loved that about him.

"Can we just sit here a second?" I asked. I wanted to inhale the late-afternoon air and light, to freeze-frame this moment of exquisite anticipation before our first night together. The week had gone beautifully between us and we both sensed we were on the threshold of something momentous, as if the sole purpose of all the other relationships—their hardships and heartaches—had been to lead us to this moment.

Pressure? *Forget* about it!

Inside, I got the tour. The bedroom was beautiful—with French

doors leading out to a deck overlooking the rolling hills and the stream. The decor was tasteful California Malibu.

My first thought was to count rooms and sleeping quarters to see if my whole family could stay here. I was already deciding.

Out back, a waterfall flowing down the hillside fed into a small Jacuzzi that, in turn, flowed into a pool. Everything was built into the rocks. It didn't get much more romantic than this.

In the living room, the fireplace was going (for that bone-chilling 70-degree ocean breeze), the music was murmuring in the background, the lighting was soft and perfect. He *is* a director, after all—and knew all about wardrobe, set design, sound tracks, and, of course, cinematography. For a second, I thought of Steve McQueen and Faye Dunaway in *The Thomas Crown Affair*, and imagined some cognac and a brief game of chess before the big seduction.

Rob was also quite the little chef. He prepared a tasty dinner of sautéed orange roughy amandine, sesame stir-fried vegetables, a salad, and Dom Pérignon (this was before Cristal became our champagne of choice).

He poured and offered a first toast: "Here's hoping this is everything we hope it to be."

It was—and so much more. After dinner, as I got ready for The Incredible Seduction Scene, Rob gave me instead about four hours of show-and-tell: baby pictures, childhood pictures, family albums. He showed me every commercial he had ever shot, he showed a cast picture from when he did *The King and I* at the age of twelve. To be safe, I picked out the cutest kid in the shot, thinking it was him. Way off. Rob was the funny-looking one with big ears, braces, and a huge nose. I knew then that he too was from the blood-from-a-stone school of improving your looks.

It got worse. He broke out his guitar and did a medley of Cat Stevens numbers. I had driven up here to fall in love and tumble into bed with the man of my dreams; somehow I had ended up at a hootenanny, swaying patiently to "Ooooh, baby, baby, it's a wild world."

Rob was dying of nerves. Here we were, glowing in exquisite anticipation of seduction, but instead of Don Juan I got Don Ho. He later admitted he was never a sweep-'em-off-their-feet type. Having heard his Cat Stevens impersonation, that somehow didn't shock me. To his credit, what counted for him wasn't scoring, but comfort. He wasn't one to disingenuously confuse intimacy with fucking. His own "Sweepstakes Period" of casual sex had only left him feeling needier and emptier. He had guy friends who scored two, three times a week—but he hardly envied the transience of that lifestyle.

"I only want one woman," he said. "I don't know how you say 'Good morning' to multiple women on successive days." To Rob, directing his own life meant monogamy, which brought continuity. His story arc flowed better that way, and it paid off for him in stability, growth, emotional richness, and partnership.

Rob's parents, like mine, had been sweethearts all their lives; it was one of the first bonds we discovered in each other. (His father, sadly, died two years after we met. His mom, Sally, an incredible powerhouse and a real character, had lost her sight shortly before I met Rob. She still lives in the Valley, not far from where we now live.)

Rob grew up prizing attachment to women. He is not an abuser, a destroyer. He is capable of complete faithfulness, and he is even more of a nester than I am. Like so many Jewish guys whose mothers did a great job raising them, Rob is not only "in touch with" his feminine side, he is also wise and self-respecting enough to nurture and celebrate it. For instance, he is a fantastic cook. He even knows how to flip things, like omelettes. Where I grew up, that stuff tended to get squelched by a sort of macho neighborhood posturing.

It was never on Rob's agenda, having waited more than a year to see me, to simply "get laid" that night. For him, it had to be the real thing. So while there was an obvious lighthearted humor, warmth, and sweetness in the air, he didn't make any moves to bed me. He was endearingly tentative, doing everything in his gentle repertoire he could to "stave off," to use his words, our rush toward intimacy. He knew this was the real thing; a case of the jitters was forgivable.

But he came *this close* to blowing it with that guitar bit.

If Rob wasn't doing anything to lure me into the bedroom, neither was he sending me home. So, in the absence of any clear direction, I decided to hit my cue for passion. I went through the bedroom, into the large bathroom, and took off my clothes—layer by layer, eyelet by eyelet. I was a bit disappointed, but was determined to let nothing spoil the fun. I threw on one of his big T-shirts. "Let's just get into bed like we've done this every night," I said. In my head, I was thinking: I like this guy so much that if he pulls down his pants and has a cock, I'll teach him the rest.

I neatly laid out my clothes just the way I did at night as a

Catholic schoolgirl. If Rob could fall back on Cat Stevens, I could fall back on compulsive rituals to calm my nerves and maintain order.

And then, we were naked in bed, really kissing. It was the first time I could remember getting under the sheets with a man without having first accompanied him on any delicious make-out "picnic." I kind of regret that Rob and I never had a couple of evenings of four-hour kisses on the floor and that teasing, crazy-making buildup to, "Are we going to do it yet?" I've tortured him many times for that.

But if we missed our cues for the picnic, we both definitely showed up for the banquet—a wondrously tender, easygoing, natural, satisfyingly intimate experience. Rob made me feel beautiful, special, loved. As I drifted off to sleep, I knew that I could be with him forever. It felt as if we had been doing this for years—in the best sense.

I knew I had finally come home.

As early sunlight streamed into the bedroom and woke me—the bitch list had already grown from bad posture to no blackout shades—I wondered, just for an instant, if Rob might go into a few verses of "Morning Has Broken." He didn't; now that we were lovers, I figured, the Cat Stevens act had been retired.

Over the weekend, we had a wonderful Sunday together that cemented it. I hung out and read a script in his bedroom all afternoon as Rob cooked pasta, and we'd take little "love breaks" through the day. His kids came over and we all had dinner together. I loved watching Rob be a daddy to them, and, if I still had any doubts about how I felt, they were blown away by the next morning.

Our next date was at a Japanese restaurant. I said to Rob over sake, "Let's have one night together where we can say anything we want to each other." He said fine. I let it rip: "Will you marry me?" With little hesitation, he answered: "I'm going to."

The next weekend, I was joined by my brother Tommy and niece Suzanne for dinner at Rob's. As the front gate swung open and Suzanne, who was eighteen, got her first glimpse of the house and property, she blurted out, "Marry him."

I knew that fate was on our side when, after two weeks of dating, I managed, on a technicality, to get myself out of escrow on a new two-bedroom condo I had been ready to buy myself. I sensed Rob was someone I would end up living with—and if things indeed kept going in that direction, this place would be too small for *us*. By getting out of escrow on a place I loved, I was betting on my future. But it made sense: We were both good catches; each was what the other was looking for. Was it too good to be true, since we had been under each other's noses for so long?

Rob had been hearing so much about my family that a week later, we decided it was time to see if we could take our show on the road. He bought us tickets to Chicago and New York to visit my family. (Christal, Lorin, and Lynnette were in New York.)

In Chicago, JoAnn and Joe, Melody, and Melody's son Adam were gracious and sweet to Rob, though when they uncorked a bottle of Cristal Rosé they had been saving for a special occasion, it was totally flat. There wasn't a bubble in there. Welcome to the hamper Henner family.

Rob, who had shot countless toy commercials, easily won over Adam by bringing him a box of Legos. He plopped down on the floor and showed him how to build stuff. He knew exactly how to zero right in on kids' world of make-believe.

Rob and I discovered something we both enjoyed doing when we got back to L.A.—house-hunting. As much as we both loved his gorgeous place, it was a bit cramped, it was a rental, it was a long drive to anywhere either of us went socially or professionally, and there was no way to expand it. So he was resigned to giving it up.

The good news: He was already thinking in terms of "us."

I made my own adjustments to the us we were becoming: I cut way back on work for the first six months we were together. This struck me as more important than loading up credits on a resumé. I didn't want to be on the road or stressed out every day. I wanted to nurture *us* in a positive atmosphere.

I even did what I could to protect the new love of my life from my therapist. While in New York, I brought Rob in on a session— three weeks after our first date. I felt it was possible to overanalyze your motives and your moves and talk yourself out of, or into, anything.

"Don't blow this for me," I warned Dr. Sharon in front of Rob. "I need your help. I want this to work."

Our lives began to mesh with a workable rhythm—the weeks at South Doheny, weekends in Malibu. We shared a terrific Thanksgiving with our families at Rob's, and then decided it was time for the ultimate test: Europe. Italy had become such a core part of my soul—like my family, my therapist, and my closest friends—that I had to see how Rob fit in. We planned the trip for after Christmas.

Then, while we were at Fung Wong restaurant on December 6, I noticed that Rob was twitching, preoccupied, and being very weird. I excused myself to the ladies' room, and when I came back he was practically levitating off his seat. "I'm not really very good at this," he said, "so I'm only going to do it once. Here."

He reached down and, as he handed me a small box, said, "Will you marry me?"

I almost choked I was so taken aback, staring down at a gorgeous, two-carat, oval-shaped diamond in a gold-platinum Tiffany setting. My first thought: How can I marry him? We haven't been to Europe yet! We haven't lived together; we haven't even *decorated!*

I saw that he wanted a serious response. I looked him straight in the eye and spoke directly from my heart. This was no time to bullshit. "Umm, listen, I feel like I'm going to spend the rest of my life with you, okay? I just feel, maybe it's just too soon, we haven't spent enough time. I'm afraid our relationship will become all about getting married now, instead of getting to know each other. Instead of seeing how we travel and discover Europe together, the trip'll be about planning a wedding. It's too much pressure to put on a new relationship."

He paused and took it all in. "Okay. I just felt it would be really cool going into Christmas if we were engaged." He paused again, measuring his words. "Okay," he said. "I'm giving this ring to you just once. If you want to marry me, put it on. If you decide not to, give it back."

"Okay, that's fair." I put the ring on, but wore it on the ring finger of my right hand. To me that meant we weren't engaged; it also meant I loved wearing it.

I did get in a trip to Europe—before Christmas, and without my new faux-fiancé. Rob had to shoot a Kleenex commercial in Minnesota, so I took Christal. For four days, we were treated like royalty in London, where I appeared on the U.K.'s top talk show. We flew first class, stayed at the posh Savoy Hotel, had a twenty-four-hour limo, per diem pocket money, did Christmas shopping at Harrods. Amazing trip. Then it was on to Italy to give a talk at L'Aquila Film Festival near Carsoli, and, naturally, to visit my friends. L'Aquila was like having my own retrospective. It was wild. They showed clips from my movies—especially those with

American movie stars like Burt and Johnny—and I gave lectures about location work and the Hollywood scene.

It was quite the whirlwind season. I flew back to New York and met Rob for five days of romance at the Park Lane Hotel along Central Park South. We had definitely missed each other, and New York at Christmastime was an absolutely magical setting for our reunion, with the crisp December air mixed with roasting chestnuts, the sunsets bouncing off the glass skyscrapers, the festive department store windows, the Christmas lights strung through the bare trees along the avenues, the energy of jam-packed buses, streets, and bars.

From there we trained to Chicago with Christal, her boyfriend Marvin, and Lorin and Lynnette, who were just getting engaged. It was a fabulous Christmas together with my family. From Chicago, Rob and I flew to Rome, where he made a terrific connection with Flavio and Maria.

If it wasn't quite like going to the Vatican for the Pope's blessings, it did count for plenty. He—and *we*—had passed all the tests, and proven that this was, without a doubt, The One.

19
Hooray for Hollywood!

~

$\mathbf{A}$ lot of people gripe about the fact that there are no good roles for women over forty. As if the roles for women *under* forty have been so wonderful all these years. Yeah, right.

I've seen and read so many dumb parts for women under forty, under thirty, and in their twenties that hitting forty hardly seemed to be the point. Aging has never preoccupied me as a career issue. I not only didn't start looking and feeling my best until I was in my mid-thirties, which was when Rob and I began seeing each other—but I've experienced so many other strange scenarios for things not working out, especially in the four years before we got married, that the standard gripe about age seems almost irrelevant.

What is a drag for women is that, once you hit forty, staying on top isn't merely a question of *covering* your ass, as it is in corporate America, but of *tightening* it as well. That quest for physical perfection, crazy as it is, just comes with the territory.

I've never been a moaning mouthpiece for the suffering of women in Hollywood. As my mother would have said, "Forget it, Mar, that's for the public." Why perpetuate negative views of women while struggling to improve things within the system? Empowerment is about figuring out how to make the system work for you.

From the beginning, I went after my dream with my eyes open. Never for one day have I felt like a victim, though I have had my share of frustrations, my producers and agents from hell, my meetings of madness, and all the Hollywood horror stories that everyone else has had. But to claim disillusionment and victimization implies you expected something very different.

That was never me. I had a good reality check.

My one self-criticism is a Henner-family lazy streak. I sometimes wish I were more of a steamroller, more demanding and "in your face," and less of a conciliatory team player. In a town that seems to reward devious, often vicious, gamesmanship, maybe I've been too quick to understand other people's positions.

But then friends say, "Are you kidding? If you were any more 'in your face,' you'd have been shot by now."

Maybe it's in the yin and yang of things—and in the nature of long-term therapy—to see the validity of all sides before making judgments. My talent, tenacity, and drive have always pulled me through, but I do think at times I've wimped out and failed to serve my own best interests.

There were times when I felt that merely because I weighed 135 pounds and felt self-conscious, I wasn't entitled to complain about not getting the right treatment, or about hair and makeup and wardrobe. My mind game was that speaking up would only attract more attention because I'm ten pounds overweight. So I'd clam up.

One of the keys to survival in Hollywood is coping with disappointment, keeping perspective, letting go of anger in the midst of the madness, and moving on. No one's come through a long career without getting-shafted nightmares. I'm so grateful that I had my therapist, my family, healthy values and self-confidence, a sense of yin-yang balance, and, through the second half of the eighties, a great relationship with Rob to support and anchor me during a sometimes exasperating roller-coaster career ride.

My expectations were tempered not only by the challenges and fulfillment I'd enjoyed on stage before coming west, but by watching Johnny's spectacular ride through the seventies and eighties. That gave me an up-close sight line on the often disturbing star-making process. I saw some cold, ruthless people pulling the strings, dehumanizing and toying with people in the grand tradition of chewing 'em up and spitting 'em out.

Very little has shocked me. Seeing the ebb and flow of Johnny's career was a wake-up call. I saw him ride at the top with his two huge bubblegum musical blockbusters, then get devastated after doing *Moment by Moment* with Lily Tomlin, then soar to the top again with *Urban Cowboy*.

This is a notoriously fickle business. Everyone's looking up the mountain of power to see who can pull *them* up, not looking down to see who *they* can pull up. Sure, everyone's out for Number One, but whining and scapegoating are a waste of time and energy. To make it takes guts, not gripes, not sour grapes. Even when I felt my blinders getting ripped away after *Johnny Dangerously,* I kept moving, kept working so I wouldn't get deterred by all the bullshit.

As much as I crave order, I never saw my career as a clear, linear hike up just one kind of mountain. I used to marvel at a clique of New York actors who hung out in a Hell's Kitchen joint called Jimmy Ray's. They'd sit around all day sipping coffee, telling one another how they'd never do commercials, never be caught dead doing TV. No selling out for these purists. Only prestige gigs like the Public Theater, La Mama, and off Broadway. Of course, they were nursing coffee for six hours because they couldn't afford anything else. To me that elitism just seemed so foreign, so naive and counterproductive. I was more enterprising than that when I was seven years old and earning fifty cents an hour to baby-sit.

When I met Rob, I was looking for that next uphill hike—mostly in film. It wasn't like if I didn't land a blockbuster I was a failure. I loved working, and never cared whether it was TV, stage, or film. But it's amazing how complicated and tortured the quest can get in this business. So while I was enduring my share of typical letdowns and lunacies in the late eighties, I was also busy working my tail off, on TV movies like *Love with a Perfect Stranger, Grand Larceny,* and *Ladykillers,* in theater, and in developing projects for Rob's and my own company, Crystal Beach. I've never been out of a job for more than a few months.

With today's films costing an average of $30 million to make, even A-list actresses struggle to find substantial parts that are also bankable. And they have to fight to protect their work in the editing room. Meanwhile, studios want to green-light formulaic projects with global stars who can open a movie with a $15 million weekend.

That's why so many women form their own production companies—to seize a measure of control over the creative pipe-line. It's also why I know of so many women refugees from film trying like crazy to get a TV series. The good news is that TV is a far more effective power base for women than film—from Lucille Ball in the fifties to Goldie Hawn in the sixties, Mary Tyler Moore and Carol Burnett in the seventies, to Candice Bergen, Roseanne, Kathie Lee, and Oprah in the eighties and nineties. Not to mention the high-powered women writers, producers, and network journalists.

I'm lucky: I can always leave town, as I did in 1987, and work on Broadway. I was still looking for a sitcom when I got back to my roots with the female lead in Andrew Bergman's play *Social Security,* with Mike Nichols directing on Broadway. I stayed at Randal Kleiser's apartment, where *9½ Weeks* had been filmed. The move provided the perfect quick hit of big-city energy that I needed, the ideal antidote to Hollywooditis.

It was great for both Rob and me. By then we had lived together for a year. Rob was wonderfully supportive, commuting for weekends together through my three-month run, and spending as much time with me as he could in our rented apartment. We had a great time in New York, where I saw many old friends from the seventies' *Grease* and *Over Here* days.

But once back in L.A., as self-protective as I tried to be, I found myself caught up in some mind-boggling power games. It was nothing new to me. I've learned to work hard at handling this stuff. I let go of the bad energy and tell myself, It's a small business, you'll work with these people again. Or, It's the way the planets are lined up.

The point is: It's the *only* way to survive the business. You have to be prepared for anything.

Early in my career, I was up for two movies against Liza Minnelli. (One was *Arthur.*) It was down to the wire both times, and it's like someone runs into her at a party and she gets the job. I wanted very much to do *Big,* for example. I wanted *Jacob's Ladder, Broadcast News, Thelma & Louise.* I didn't get them. Life goes on. Why cling to anger and give yourself a disease? It isn't worth it. Even an obsessive-compulsive control nut like me has to accept limits. You can make yourself crazy in a business where studios spend $30-plus million to create a *Howard the Duck;* over $40 million to create *Ishtar;* or $100 million for a catastrophe like *Last Action Hero.* Why wrap yourself around that insanity? Let go, move forward, and focus on the work.

Even when people in power feel they owe you one to make up for a prior disappointment, they can let you down.

One such producer-director was Blake Edwards. When he called to tell me, "I have your next picture," I knew by then to run for cover. Kiss of Death time.

This time around it was me and Bruce Willis, he said. My character, he explained, "has red hair, big tits, great legs, great memory. It's a formality. It's yours; come in and meet Bruce."

I was doing theater in New York at the time, so after my Sunday matinee, I flew to L.A., woke up to meet Bruce for the formality on Monday, then red-eyed home in time for Tuesday night's show. In time to find out I didn't get the part. I was too "on the nose."

I wanted to kill. I was, like, "Blake, just make her a brunette with no tits, bad legs, and amnesia."

Ultimately I was relieved I didn't do the movie. *Sunset* didn't turn out quite the way Blake intended. They gave the part to Kathleen Quinlan, who wore a red wig, I suppose, so she would look more "on the nose."

But that didn't keep me from feeling as if I'd been kicked in the teeth—and by someone I felt I had a personal relationship with.

In 1988, I had a strong shot at the female lead in *Black Rain* opposite Michael Douglas. I was flown to New York for a big-deal three-scene screen test, with wardrobe, hair, the whole bit. The part was a Midwestern blonde who had gone to Japan, got caught up in the gangster element, ran a lavish brothel, and now had a slutty quality to her. It was down to Cathy Moriarty and me. One scene was an unbelievably hot seduction, one was a cat-and-mouse mind game, and one was where she helps save his ass from a band of thugs before they make love. Michael was a delight to work with and we did some great stuff together during the screen test.

But the timing wasn't great. Rob and I had long-standing plans to go to Europe immediately after the test. Rob said I should get an answer from the casting director before we left, so we would have the option of canceling, rather than just shortening, our plans.

Moments before getting on the plane, I got hold of the casting director: "Shit, I wish we didn't have to let you guys know," she said. "They want to see more, but if we have to let you know now, the answer is no."

I was devastated. I couldn't believe it hadn't worked out.

Then I learned what had really happened. The producer, Stanley Jaffe, one of the most powerful men in Hollywood, gave the order: "Get me a girl who's had a hit movie."

What are you going to do? The role went to Kate Capshaw, who had been in *Indiana Jones and the Temple of Doom,* and who would later become Mrs. Steven Spielberg. When I finally saw the film, I was over it, and realized it was no big deal. Kate's part had been greatly diminished. The scenes I tested for no longer existed. Her character now was more like window dressing in a few scenes.

Many times you have to remain grounded and realistic because the odds of landing a plum role are simply against you. As for *Thelma & Louise,* I wasn't stroked—courted and encouraged—by producers and casting agents, but even if I had been I'd have figured there was no way they weren't going to hire two Oscar-level stars for a big-budget film driven by such a hot concept (a female buddy film with all kinds of gender-reversed plot hooks).

But there *are* times when you get so stroked it's absurd; you almost know it can't work out. I was once being seduced aggressively for a leading role: I heard all about how I was *perfect,* how I was just her age, had exactly her look, exactly her ethnic, down-to-earth appeal, exactly her body type. It was one of those "Oh-my-God-I'm-looking-at-you-and-you're-her-she's-so-you" come-ons.

"The unfortunate thing is," I was cautioned, "the offer's already out to another actress. But if she passes on it, I'm going to slam-dunk you in there for this. You're perfect!"

"Uhh . . . who's the other actress?" I asked warily.

"Whoopi Goldberg."

What's scary is when someone on your own team trips you up. Though I was going up for all these feature film roles, I missed everything I had enjoyed on *Taxi,* and it had been nearly five years. It was time to nail down a series.

I made the rounds of all the studios and production companies and met with their television heads. Everyone had a great series for me; everyone wanted an exclusive deal. I didn't want to be tied down. I needed to cast as wide a net as possible.

Finally, *Sisters* (not related to the current series) came to me from Columbia, and I loved it. Though I was mulling over a switch of agencies, I told my agent, "I want it. This is my series." It was an hour-long drama about a radio talk-show therapist who's just had her first baby, but who also has a really hot, sexy marriage. Perfect.

My agent disagreed. "You shouldn't play a mother on TV," he said. "Mothers aren't sexy on TV." It was the same old rap: Your choices are to be a shrill, desperate single career woman, a saintly but sexless mommy, or a slut who wants to end world hunger. The three faces of network womanhood.

I didn't buy it. Get it, package it, I demanded. The TV divisions of the film studios—along with independent producers—create much of the potential "product" for TV, but they must then sell it to the major networks. Some, but not much, programming is generated in-house at the networks.

By the time this fabulous little project had its talent packaged and in place, it had grown so ridiculously expensive and top-heavy that no network would take it. "I can't believe this is happening," I said to my agent—but it was. It died a slow death in development.

While *Sisters* was going down the tubes, I happened to meet Jeff Berg, who was president of the giant agency ICM. We had a little chat at a screening. Next thing I know, I got a call from Berg's office. He wanted to meet with me.

When you're signed to one agency and you visit another, you feel like you're visiting an abortion clinic. There is nothing worse than sitting in the waiting room of an agency you don't belong to. You see an actor you recognize, you exchange furtive, awkward glances. You're terrified that some tabloid or gossip column snoop—or worse, someone else from your agency—will spot you and disclose your adulterous deed. I trembled, I shook, I wanted to wear a veil. Then they whisk you up a back stairs so none of the other agents get wind of your move.

The meeting with Jeff went great. We both said all the right things to each other, and a switch to ICM was, in my head, a done deal.

I called my then-agent with news of my switch. "Berserk" doesn't quite capture his reaction.

"You're *dead*," he fumed, with a brittle viciousness I had never heard in my life. "I will mourn your death the way I would mourn the death of a friend from AIDS!" My ego was out of control, he said. To purge me from memory, he sent back my latest Christmas gift, photographs, videotapes, everything.

But I was a much happier camper at ICM. Like the Transitional Man/Woman after a long relationship, it proved to be the ideal Transitional Agency—and, like a switch of agencies I would make in the early nineties, led to a tripling of my income.

But even there I went through a screwup a month later. I was being aggressively courted for a new TV series called *Channel 99*. Like *Taxi*, it had an A-plus creative team—executive producers Ron Howard and Brian Grazer, and writers Babaloo Mandel and Lowell Ganz, the comedy wizards behind *City Slickers, Night Shift,* and *Parenthood*. This looked like a winner—except it got stalled out by a devastating Writers Guild strike that all but shut down production at the major studios and production companies.

My agents had a strong offer in place. This was early 1988, so it would have debuted the same fall season as *Murphy Brown*. This show could have become my *Murphy*. The idea came from Brandon Tartikoff, then head of NBC television; it concerned a woman who'd once run a network but who had had a nervous breakdown and was now running a tiny, tacky UHF station in small-town Elmira, New York, surrounded by pathetic-funny characters. It had a great premise, and I figured it would all come together in the rewrites. I was on my way to New York to join Rob, who was shooting the pilot *Dream Street,* and told them I would think about it over the weekend.

Meanwhile, I was interested in another TV project, a series being developed from the feature film *Baby Boom,* which had starred Diane Keaton. I was crazy about the creative duo behind both movie and series, the husband-wife team of Nancy Meyers and Charles Shyer. I had met them a few years earlier when they were interested in John Travolta and me for their picture *Irreconcilable Differences.* They had written a fabulous script, but Johnny wasn't into moving forward on it, so they went with Shelley Long and Ryan O'Neal. That was a heartbreaker, but a friendly one, and they left me with a very promising and sincere "we'll-definitely-do-something-together-someday" feeling. I was excited to read *Baby Boom.* I went east to join Rob. I loved it and called my agents early in the morning. "I want *Baby Boom.* I love kids. I'm perfect for this. Get me this series. I'll fly back and meet with them."

My agents told me to cool my heels back east. "Chuck and Nancy don't see you in it," they told me. "You'd have to fly in and read for it and really convince them."

"Fine. I'll come in and—"

"But you can't come in and do *Baby Boom* unless you give up *Channel 99* first."

I was dumbfounded. Something here did not compute. I adored these people; they loved me. "I don't get this. Just put me in a room with Chuck and Nancy and, shit, I'll convince them. They really *said* that? I can't believe it."

"You'll have to give up *99* first."

I still didn't get it. "This is amazing." I thought a few moments and said, "Okay, I'll do *Channel 99.*"

Kate Jackson signed on for *Baby Boom.*

A few months later I ran into Nancy and Chuck at the opening of Danny DeVito's movie *War of the Roses.*

"We couldn't believe you didn't do *Baby Boom* for us," they said.

My jaw dropped open in shock.

"We did everything to get you. My God, we'd still be on the air, we'd all be millionaires if you had done it. You were perfect. We wrote this with you in mind. Didn't you read the script? You were in our dream cast."

I wanted to kill. "You can't be telling me what I'm hearing," I fumed. "You don't know how much I wanted that part."

I beat myself up big-time for not calling Chuck and Nancy myself and getting to the bottom of things. I rationalized that it wasn't meant to be. But this is that lazy, conciliatory, wimping-out side of me I hate; a case could have been made for steamrolling and bitching my way to the truth. But making people reject you directly can backfire. They resent it, and you risk burning a bridge. Besides, it's what agents get paid 10 percent to do—be the wearers of Armani suits and bearers of bad news.

I went home and did some digging. What I heard was outrageous, if hardly uncommon. My agency, ICM, already had what is called a "packaging fee" on *Baby Boom*—a lucrative bonus for delivering the main talent on a project, usually a star or two, director, writer, and/or producer. For *Baby Boom,* the agency had Shyer and Meyers. But on *99,* ICM still had to deliver *me* to get the packaging fee for *that* show. Hence, the pressure on me to bag *Baby Boom.* In my ignorance, I went with *99.*

The series never got picked up. A noble failure, a royal shaft.

Fortunately, for much of this time, my personal life was in great shape. I had a terrific summer in 1988. During the long Writers Guild strike, I did some theater in Williamstown, Massachusetts; and I did *Carnal Knowledge* for a few months in L.A., playing the part my all-time hero Ann-Margret had played in the film. It was the hardest thing I've ever done, and the most rewarding. I think it was the best work of my life.

But by early 1989, Rob and I were going through our first real rough patch. We had been together three and a half years, and were clearly in the midst of some sort of change: Either we were getting married or we were going our separate ways. We were fighting all the time.

But I don't bail; I salvage. When everything has been tried, then I end it. I wasn't at that point with Rob.

I pretty much sensed we would get married, so my feeling was: Marriage is for the rest of my life; give me three weeks completely to myself. I took a suite at the wonderfully funky Shangri-La Hotel on Ocean Boulevard in Santa Monica. It was more of a self-discovery retreat than a last-hurrah romp. I knew I was coming home—and I didn't have any affairs.

But I did have a fine time alone, on my own schedule, walking up and down the promenade high over the ocean, hanging out at the beach. It was a serene, centering time for me. The Shangri-La was the perfect hideaway. It took me out of our loop, took me a long inner distance from home, and helped get me back into myself so I could figure out what to do.

In the days that followed, we did a lot of talking and healing, and we came up with a plan: marriage within a year. That had been part of our problem—we'd been drifting in the absence of a commitment. Once we realized we were truly going to be together, I went back with him the second week in May.

Just days later, I went back into the world of features with *Chains of Gold,* a low-budget independent film I shot with John Travolta. My friend Jonathan Krane, who had been Blake Edwards's partner on *The Man Who Loved Women,* started a management company that was going into film production. He and I had become very close friends, so I was happy to work with him in one of his company's no-frills features, which was their focus.

Johnny Travolta, another Krane client, and I had stayed in touch since Rob had come into my life. He helped put the film together for Jonathan and me. We had never played opposite each other as leads on film. Friends of his wrote the film, and created the role for me.

The story is a drama set in the adolescent cocaine scene around Miami, where we spent a month shooting. Johnny plays a social worker who's trying to help a mother get her impressionable young son away from a drug-dealing gang of kids. I play an ex-girlfriend of Johnny's who's become a lawyer for the gang's head drug lord, and I help Johnny go underground to find the kid, played by Joey Lawrence, most recently the young heartthrob on *Blossom.*

It was an extraordinary—and frightening—experience to go down into the Miami neighborhoods and observe these eight-year-old Latino extras handling vials of "coke" (it was actually sugar). They seemed to know exactly what they were doing.

Rob proved to be the world's best sport—and support. He was

not only behaving like a devoted, loving, sexy mensch at home; he rewrote one of my big dramatic speeches—about how devastated I was when Johnny and I had broken up. It was a strong moment, thanks to Rob's classy writing.

He could have cared less that I had to do a love scene with my ex-lover. Rob's ego was, and still is, so in the right place about all that. All he wanted was to see me shine. He put zero energy on my Johnny back story. Rob showed an amazing degree of health and security about it—and, in so doing, about our relationship. My old boyfriends have never been a threat to him. He knows I've pretty much beaten them all to death—emotionally, that is.

Johnny and I got to ad-lib some great scenes as lovers getting a second shot. We lifted dialogue from our own history, and it helped make for a very good movie.

But that never guarantees success. Indeed, *Chains* definitely lived up to its modest goals. The movie not only had no frills; it had no *release*. Sadly, Jonathan, a profoundly decent, trusting soul, trusted some of the wrong people in the business and the company went bankrupt. The film never got distributed in theaters, but went, as the euphemism goes, "straight to cable."

The unkindest cut of all was that my body absolutely peaked in that film. I looked unbelievably sexy, but I never had the satisfaction of seeing myself on the big screen when I looked the best I ever looked.

Sometimes, you just can't get a break!

20
Viva la
Rivoluzione!

~

Δll things happen for a reason. Everything is connected to everything—even to the things you don't end up connected to.

I had been gung-ho to do a TV pilot at the end of 1989; but I pulled out when things seemed to get a little crazy in the early going. It was the old "artistic differences" bit, combined with some serious Hollywood insanity.

The show never aired, but if it had—and with me still on board—I'd never have worked with Steve Martin in *L.A. Story,* which has some of my best work on film; and I might not have been available to play Burt Reynolds's TV wife when he asked me to do *Evening Shade,* which turned into my second long-running prime-time comedy series.

Not to mention that I wouldn't have had lunch with Steve and his wife Victoria Tennant after we wrapped *L.A. Story;* and if I hadn't had that lunch, Rob and I may never have known about the tiny tobacco shop across from La Prefettura in Rome where you buy the little marriage stamp that permits foreigners to get married in Italy.

And if we hadn't known that, who knows?

Right after the pilot fiasco, I was about to have lunch with my agent, who spotted Steve and his agent, whom he knew. We were all introduced on our way into the restaurant, and we ran into one another again on our way out. "So what are you doing now?" Steve asked.

"Oh, I just left a project."

"Great," he said. "We're going to call you later today to come in on a project."

I was sent a script, which I liked. I wanted to read for the part of Ariel, a lesbian who owns a health food store. I met the director, Mick Jackson. I thought, Well, this might be interesting. I know a lot of stuff about health, and playing a lesbian would be a welcome stretch. Why not?

"Now, would you be able to come back tomorrow," Mick asked, "and read for the part of Trudy?"

I was confused, but went along. They asked me to come back and do three scenes with Steve. Trudy was much better for me. I loved her. She was like a quirky sitcom character, and it put me opposite Steve, which is an absolute gift. He is sensational to work with and a flat-out comic genius. I worked my butt off trying to impress, and bond with, Steve. He's the kind of actor whose respect you immediately want to earn, because he is so flawless, so on the mark. I felt I was able to create that character from scratch. Steve and Mick let me basically create my own dialogue as we went along. I could throw anything at Steve and have it tossed right back at me. It was thrilling to be around his wildly imaginative energy.

By the time we wrapped, things were beginning to liven up around our house. While doing the film, I had read in the trades that Burt Reynolds was getting a sitcom off the ground with the powerhouse writing-producing team of Linda Bloodworth-Thomason and her husband Harry Thomason, the Arkansas buddies of then-Governor Bill Clinton and Hillary Clinton. Despite having not even seen Burt in four years, I had a gut instinct that I'd end up working with him again.

Sure enough, in May, I got a call out of nowhere from my agent at Morris. Burt wanted me to play his wife on the sitcom, which was called *Evening Shade*—and which was to air at eight o'clock. I had always hoped to find another nine-P.M. show, because the later time slots are usually geared to a wittier, more urbane and sophisticated audience. Like *Taxi* and *Cheers,* they're usually without kids, they're not domestic comedies, there's an ensemble, and the themes have some sexuality to them. Most eight o'clocks are the kids, the dog, the wacky neighbors, and nobody's sexy. It's not my idea of a show.

But working with Burt again? No problem. I got psyched up to go in to meet with Linda, Harry, and him. They were all executive-producing. Linda would be writing the first bunch of episodes.

I hadn't seen a script before my meeting at Columbia. Even though I knew I wouldn't be nervous around Burt, I went nuts just getting dressed: Should I wear this, should I wear that? I don't want to look too this, I don't want to look too that. Should I show leg? Should I wear jeans? It's Burt—I'll just go casual. It's set in the South, I'd better look southern. I'll put my hair up, I'll let my hair down.

And then I thought: Do I really want to *do* a half-hour, eight o'clock sitcom?

I pushed aside whatever qualms I had, knowing the job was mine if we all got along. Working with Burt usually put me in a groove I loved. And I trusted him.

When I got there, I was still talking with Trudy's exaggerated Chicago twang from *L.A. Story.* I'm sure it sounded to suth'n girl Linda like chalk scraped across a blackboard. She apologetically asked me if I wouldn't mind just trying to sound a tad more Ozark.

Then Burt gave me the pitch. "Okay, how does this sound? We're married. Sounds good so far, doesn't it? We have three beautiful children. The oldest is a son, fifteen, a little girl is ten, and a little guy five. The first episode's about how I had a vasectomy, but it didn't take, and now you're pregnant again."

He ran down the terrific cast they were looking at: Hal Holbrook as my dad, Ossie Davis, Charlie Durning, Liz Ashley. Burt made it clear he wanted me on board. When we finished reading our lines, he made a big show of his affection for me in front of Linda. "I told you she was incredible, didn't I," he said, giving me a big hug.

I walked out feeling great, promising to think it over carefully.

I got on my car phone to deal with my agent. The informal negotiations had already proceeded to where I knew I was going to be in an expensive, first-class ensemble. I was not only a "22 out of 22" (my character, Ava, would appear in every episode); I had my five-year history in an award-winning hit show and a lot of other work to point to. I was in a strong position to swing a good deal.

But the subtext of the negotiations was clear: Either love it or leave it.

I was realistic, and willing to come down a bit. The salary structure in network TV had suffered since I had joined *Taxi*, owing to the emergence of cable and a steep drop in profits from the sale of shows to syndication, among other factors. My take was: I'd rather get less money for a classy show than a pile of dough for a turkey.

I instructed my agent in no uncertain terms, "Don't blow this over money. It sounds like a winner."

The other major thing going on that spring was that Rob and I decided to get married. Our dream was to have a small, intimate ceremony in Flavio's village, Carsoli, site of many of my personal milestones and lasting connections. My sister Christal and her fiancé, Roy, had been planning a spectacular wedding in the Cathedral of Chartres, two hours south of Paris, for early July, so we figured as long as everyone was headed to Europe, why not J.F.D.I.—and in my favorite place in the world.

Days before leaving for Rome, Rob and I met Steve and Victoria for lunch, where they shared with us the coincidence that they, too, had gotten married in Italy. They told us to make sure we avoided the red-tape nightmare of the marriage stamp. I couldn't believe this lucky tweak.

I'd learned all about marriage red tape with Freddie—but cross-cultural paperwork is far worse. We knew you needed to round up four witnesses for *each* of us and go to the Italian Consulate in L.A. Then, at the American Consulate in Rome, you needed three hours to process your papers from the States. Then it was on to La Prefettura, the building for administrative and legal processing, and the official marriage license.

"Then, you see," Victoria told us, "you stand in line for three and a half hours at the Prefettura, and it'll be summer and really hot and crowded. You'll finally get to the front of the line and hand all these documents to some little old lady who will immediately look at the back page and shake her head and tell you that you need *la stampa*. And the only place to get this stamp is at this little tobacco shop across the street from the Prefettura. Then, after you buy the stamp, you'll have to come back and wait another three and a half hours at the back of the line. I know. I did it. Please, do yourselves a big favor. Go to the tobacco shop first."

I got my TV series deal hammered out on Friday, June 22.

By the 24th, I was ready to nail down an even bigger deal. That day, we flew to Rome armed with marriage documents, witness signatures, and *molto* trepidation.

A week earlier, on my way to the Italian Consulate in L.A., I had gotten so worked up and anxious I had asked my niece Suzanne and friend Cynthia Wilkerson to pull into a restaurant. I recognized my symptoms as mild panic, and wondered if I could actually go through with it. I didn't need witnesses; I needed witness relocation. But after knocking back three glasses of white wine, I declared: "Okay, now we're ready."

Sort of. Once there, sitting next to Rob, I was nearly hyperventilating. My heart was pounding. When some guy came out and asked, "Who is the couple getting married?" I slid off my chair in a comedy pratfall. I knew I would spend the rest of my life with Rob. The question was: Do I want to go through all this again? I was still haunted by having fallen in love with Hammett and marrying Hank the first time around. Had we taken more time to get to know each other, Freddie and I probably never would have gotten married.

But Rob and I had been living together since March 1986—over four years. And a year earlier, I had taken three weeks of solo R & R at the Shangri-La to see how I felt away from him. I found out I didn't like it one bit.

Still, I was a nervous wreck—so terrified of getting married I considered praying for our plane to crash to avoid the whole thing. Thank God, I didn't.

What I had always loved about Italy was the way it felt so familiarly hamper. An entire nation held together by legal documents requiring tiny stamps sold at tobacco shops!

Sure enough, the tobacco shop was directly across from the Prefettura, and we bought the stupid marriage stamp first. Then we spent the three-plus hours on line at the Prefettura. The lady grabbed our bundle of documents and promptly thumbed her way to the last page, smugly expecting to inform us that the stamp was missing. When she saw it there instead, her face beamed. It was as if she had come across the Glowing Gem in the Space Quest computer game. She was now our best friend, exuding a vibrant Italian spirit as she helped us through the tangles of bureaucratic linguine.

We met up with Maria and Flavio and their family and went on to ancient, crusty Carsoli, where their family had their home in the Abruzzi Mountains. Getting married there, in a place associated in my heart with a time of self-discovery and change, was a dream of ours. Once again, a new journey was beginning in the quaint, one-phone mountain village.

Then a last-minute snafu nearly grounded us when we got to town, where we stayed in a tiny hotel. We had neglected to "post the banns"—the Church-required proclamation of the wedding, posted, according to local custom, in the public square two Sundays prior to the marriage. It gives anyone with objections to the wedding a chance to come forward. Back home, the local wedding banns were always posted—published, actually—in the "Parish Life" newsletter handed out at church.

Flavio finessed his way with the mayor and local officials, who waived the banns, probably because we had solved the mystery of the marriage stamp. Lunch with Steve and Victoria had indirectly saved our asses.

We got married on the 27th of June. Talk about hamper: I was so freaked out I left all my makeup back in Rome. I had to go to the local drugstore an hour before the ceremony and buy stuff. I had bought my wedding dress at a small bridal shop in Rome, but it was cut so poorly for me that I had to keep pinning and messing with it. All the little town kids followed our wedding party wherever we went. Young boys with shaved heads from God-only-knows what skin disorders kept asking about Tony Danza, whom they knew from *Who's the Boss?*

I had no idea what was going on; it was as if I had walked into an Italian wedding movie dubbed into some other language. Maria's command of English barely went beyond the phrase "photo opportunity," which I had taught her during wrap party week in L.A. I was meeting total strangers, members of Flavio and Maria's extended family, minutes before my wedding. The ex-mayor, who was presiding, was a Communist.

"You look beautiful," Rob said to me.

"You've got something in your teeth," I responded.

The ceremony was a riot. We all crowded into miniature Italian cars to drive from Flavio's family's house to get near to the tiny courthouse—about 200 feet away. We had to walk just as far from the car as we would have from the house.

I assumed the mayor would say something short in Italian, then Flavio would translate, word for word, and that we'd proceed back and forth like that. The problem was the mayor never stopped rattling on dramatically in Italian. We kept looking over for a translation, but the mayor didn't shut up for twenty minutes.

Finally, he ran out of steam and contentedly looked out over the hot, crowded courtroom. Poor Flavio, suddenly on the spot, was

barely able to hit the highlights: "Okay, he say you love, she love, you have duty, you also have duty, you leev together, you very very happy."

Somewhere lost in the translation, I was sure, was the mayor pronouncing us "signore e signora." Rob and I never got the chance to say our vows to each other. We couldn't help but notice people filing out of the courtroom and congratulating one another. It was over. We had no idea. We were dumbfounded. We never got to speak. We had to pronounce *ourselves* man and wife.

As we strolled out through the village, Lynnette signed autographs. Lorin took pictures. A bighearted, vibrant local woman brought out cake and wine for our wedding party.

Our reception for thirty-five people—which Maria, two months pregnant, pulled together—was held in the only decent restaurant around and involved many traditions: the handing out of sugar-coated almond sweets, a one-man band on a Yamaha synthesizer who had mastered "Mack the Knife" phonetically, and a pyramid of glasses delicately set up so wine could be poured from the top and made to flow down into each of the other glasses.

The food was unbelievable: Every dish had porcini mushrooms in it. The Santa Margarita pinot and corvo wines were delicious. I'd go back on dairy if every day I could have a piece of the torte they served. I absolutely loved these people. It was, in every way imaginable, exactly the wild, totally Italian wedding Rob and I had dreamed it could be.

As funky and ad hoc as our wedding was, Christal's, held two weeks later in the awesome Cathedral of Chartres, was pure elegance and spiritual pomp. Rob and I went from Carsoli back to Rome, then on to Florence and Lake Como, before joining my family in Paris.

The elaborate double-wedding jaunt to Europe had been six months in the planning, but had been indirectly triggered by what I call our family's "Black Christmas" in 1988.

Christmas had always been a precious family tradition—the one time of year when all six Henner kids and their children and mates would gather together, usually in Chicago, for two weeks. Christmas Eve was the best night of our time together—an eight-hour ritual of great food and funny personalized gift-giving. But that year things were off. What started one night as a heated discussion between Lorin and me ended the next evening as a verbal free-for-

all that left JoAnn and Melody barely speaking to each other for almost a year.

I hated that. I hate when things are left unresolved for so long. Before we faced another uncomfortable holiday season, I suggested we all set up family sessions with Dr. Sharon to pull us together again. Having lost our parents before their time, I couldn't bear the idea of our losing touch and drifting away from one another.

By Christmas 1989, the twice-monthly phone sessions had worked wonders and helped bring about a family revival. We were clearing the air, doing "maintenance" on one another; rediscovering one another as adults, communicating more honestly, getting more involved in one another's lives.

By the end of 1989, we wanted to retrieve the holiday spirit. Lorin and I took pledges from everyone (nieces, nephews, spouses, fiancés, etc.) for a Christmas fund. During one of our family sessions, we decided to pool our money and, instead of swapping gifts, travel to Paris on a $450-per-person ticket budget sometime in the summer.

By spring, Christal and her fiancé Roy Welland had planned a July 10 wedding at the Cathedral in Chartres and the Chateau d'Esclimont. This became the pretext for the family's ten-day Paris trip. Rob's schedule then got complicated by having to start shooting the TV series *Gabriel's Fire,* which our own company produced. He had to be back July 12, so we figured we'd go to Italy for a vacation *before* Christal's wedding, and join the family on July 5 in Paris. Once the planning got to that stage, our dream wedding made sense, though this meant that my family would largely be absent. Since Lorin and Lynnette had moved up their tickets to Paris, they came to Italy so Lorin could give me away.

Christal was a vice president at Merrill Lynch in charge of computer software technology, and on a volunteer basis she ran the New York chapter of a program that provides scholarships as well as mentoring and tutoring to inner-city children (she still does). Roy worked as an options trader on the American Stock Exchange. They have won several regional bridge championships. Their wedding was absolutely spectacular. Roy's sister, a concert cellist, performed throughout the ceremony. It's almost impossible to get permission to have weddings at Chartres, but they somehow managed to. The cathedral remained open to tourists; we just walked around them to the front, where a priest performed a beautiful ceremony, reading phonetically in English.

But no gathering of Henners—even in the awesome City of Light—would be complete without some hamper flourishes. Our penny-pinching travel agent got us a great deal in a hotel, except that when we got there it was way off in Paris's dreary, forsaken furniture *arrondissement,* ten blocks from the metro and two metro lines away from Paris's cool neighborhoods. The place was weird, with tiny rooms, fold-out beds, and a golf net downstairs. This was so not the brochure I wanted to be in.

I called the travel agent and bitched. She then recommended a Left Bank place off the Boulevard St. Germain. We checked the place out; it was a flophouse. One room they called "chambre à trois personnes" was a hovel with three mattresses on the floor. And it smelled like a *pissoir.*

We walked out the door, practically pinching our noses, and went down the tiny side street, where we stumbled upon a decent Left Bank hotel called Latitude. Incredibly, we were able to book eight rooms when there were no rooms anywhere in Paris.

My brothers contributed their own brand of hamper. Right before Rob, Roy, and the other men went off to Roy's bachelor party, Tommy and Lorin decided they needed to change money. This pissed Rob off, because it would hold things up; he and Lorin had a rare testy exchange. Rob said they'd wait. Lorin assured him they'd meet up with them. "And exactly how are you going to do *that* if you don't have the address?" Rob asked.

"Because you're gonna *give* us the address." That kind of thing. Not a minute later, as my brothers walked to the change bureau, Lorin turned to Tommy. "What was that address?"

"Oh, man, you didn't get the address?"

"I thought *you* were listening to the address."

"Oh, shit. I think it was a C street. It began with a C."

"No, it was a *sea*food place. I think it started with an S."

Somehow, they prayed hard and bumbled their way to a neighborhood that rang a bell in Lorin's head, walked down the first street they saw that started with a C, and walked right into Roy, Rob, and the others at the restaurant's bar.

"Didn't think you guys would make it," someone said.

"Guess it's our lucky night."

Right. Cut to six hours later, with Tommy and Lorin seriously pressing their luck. The guys had upgraded their bachelor activities from seafood to topless dancing at the Crazy Horse Saloon. Then, after everyone else had bagged it, Tommy and Lorin decided to stroll through the seedy heart of Pigalle at three-thirty A.M. and go for a nightcap.

A 50-franc ($10) nightcap, it turned out. They paid the cover, walked into a bar, ordered drinks, and the lights went out. "C'est fermé," they were informed by the thuggish manager.

"We just paid fifty francs," Tommy said belligerently. "You can't be closed."

"C'est *fermé.*"

"Let's split," Lorin said, sensing the worst. Before they could get out the door, they were greeted by five Gallic goons. Lorin tried to yank Tommy out fast, but they started whaling on them, kicking and punching my two baby brothers until they tumbled out to the street. Lorin was only scratched, but half of my other brother's face was Tommy tartare. He was covered in blood and beaten raw. Lorin started screaming, "GENDARME! GENDARME!" They could have been yelling "Jeanne d'Arc! Jeanne d'Arc!" for all anyone cared. Doors and shutters slammed closed, lights went out.

The cops showed up and Lorin calmly tried to draw on the recent French in Action lessons he had taken for his trip. "Mon frère," he said. The cops pieced the rest together at the nightclub. My brothers, the manager, and one of the thugs all went to a police station, and then my brothers went on to a hospital to bandage Tommy's wounds.

Tommy woke Rob and Joe Rowley, JoAnn's boyfriend, at the hotel to come get them in a taxi. This was an hour later, and they had just gone to sleep.

Soon, they were heading back to the hotel on deserted streets along the Seine. Exhausted, hurting, slumped over in the backseat, Tommy, his head swathed in bandages, and Lorin got a mood lift when they were treated to the uplifting sight of Notre Dame at sunrise.

By the time Tommy gave Christal away at the wedding, his bandages had come off, his shades had come on, and his condition had improved.

It was a fitting finale for a trip conceived as a way to help bring us closer together. Everybody seemed to be living up to our own flashcards.

Oldest sisters JoAnn and Melody had married, divorced, and become super single working mothers long before any of the rest of us had come even close to parenthood.

Tommy was still Accident-Prone, with an unerring instinct for dragging baby brother Lorin into trouble, though instead of merely sniffing spray enamel in the basement as teenagers, it had advanced to getting the shit beat out of them in a sleazy Pigalle clip joint.

Christal, the fair, blue-eyed angel, had a big-time Wall Street career, a great husband, and a wedding in one of the legendary cathedrals of the world.

As for me, my Quest for Perfection would now lead me back home, to a new life of marriage with a wonderful husband, a promising second sitcom—and an overwhelming urge to update, and upgrade, my own flashcard from Miss Personality to Mrs. Fertility.

21
Sex After Marriage

The timing was perfect: new series, new marriage. For the first time in years, everything seemed to be in its place.

In the same way that I told my agents not to blow my series negotiations over money, I was determined never to blow my marriage over sex. I wanted *both* the series and my marriage to work out, with one key difference: I was prepared to take less money for the series.

Sexual intimacy has always been nonnegotiable for me. It has to be right. I'll work hard to improve it, and fight to save a relationship. I'm not shy. So many people are hung up around sex, particularly those who find that marriage kills sex between partners. I even went on *The Tonight Show* and told Johnny Carson how marriage had *improved* my sex life. There's a spiritual bond between spouses that's never there between lovers before that commitment to forever is made.

Earlier in our relationship, just as I decided to move in with Rob, he said something lovely that meant so much to me. I had been living my breezy Holly Golightly life out of a suitcase, crammed into a one-bedroom place. "I'm going to make such a nice home," he promised, "that you're never going to want to leave."

Three months later, we were vacationing in Europe and I returned the favor—my way. Rob had gotten married when he was just twenty, to one of his first sexual partners. As a youth he had never had an older woman to teach him things, to experiment with, the way I always had older men. He stayed married for ten years. When I met him, he had just come out of an emotionally ugly four-year brawl with an actress. He was far more disposed toward commitment than conquest. Like me, he digs in; he chooses fight over flight. But he was clearly less experienced sexually than I was. I opted not to freak out, but rather to speak out. Just as I had proposed to him over dinner, I took the initiative and made sure I could get him up to speed. My speed.

We were in a hotel in Igles, Austria, and I handed him the magnifying mirror I travel with for makeup. But I wasn't removing splinters or plucking eyebrows.

"Here," I said. "You know what? I'm going to show you something." I lay back, peeled down my panties, and spread my legs. "Come over here and sit next to me. Okay. This is what women look like down here." And I proceeded to give him a rather clinical lay of the land, in what amounted to my own version of A Course in Miracles.

"This is what feels good, this is what feels best, this is what most men think drives us wild but doesn't do much at all," etc.

He loved that we could be so free with each other.

Rob's a quick study. He aced his first quiz, and that helped pick up the pace on vacation. "Can I just ask you one question?" he deadpanned after we made love. "Where were you when I was seventeen?"

Great line. Cracked us both up.

"Seriously," he said, "you just taught me so much I just didn't know. It all makes so much more sense to me now. Why don't more women do this for men?"

Exactly. Patience pays. Men are trainable. People should be smarter, more open, about sex. It's something that's got to be built into the process of developing intimacy and emotional depth. No one's more skeptical of first-sex excitement than I am. Sometimes you can put so much energy and attention on it in the early going, when it's unbelievably wild, scrape-me-off-the-ceiling sex, that you're doomed to not be able to come up with the goods three months later. There's a lot more to it than lock-and-key penetration. A strong connection is mandatory for great sex. It's what differentiates lovemaking from sport-fucking, which also has its place, provided you read all the warning labels. Sex may not be the most important thing in a relationship, but if it's off, it can turn into the focal point of all your problems and magnify them.

What I love about marriage is that sex is not like a one-shot benefit performance; it's a long-running show. The trick is making it interesting by changing the script, adding nuances, exploring, seeking adventure. The change I've seen with Rob is like day and night. My wildest, hang-on-to-the-headboard nights of Hall of Fame sex were always well into the relationships, not at the beginning. Making love simply becomes an easier dialogue, a more satisfying dance between two lovers willing to change and grow together.

It's one of the great male (read: sexist) myths that women crave sex less than men do. I was blessed with a strong libido, but I also don't know one friend who's been with a man who was lustier than she was. I find myself negotiating for sex with Rob. I'll exchange a daily double for a major frolic anytime, I tell him. I'll give you two weekdays off for a hot Friday night.

It doesn't even matter if I feel fat or depressed. There's always room for Jell-O. And that "headache" excuse? Bogus. That's a *great* time to have sex. Besides, I'd much rather treat a headache with a bare ass than a Bayer aspirin, any day.

I know the numbers—two, three times a week average. But those stats are, my mother would say, for "the public." The public is people who eat dairy, and it's absolutely known that if you don't eat dairy you can have more sex. Trust me. Dairy drags you down. You can't digest it. You have no stamina.

Rob, whom I wasted no time weaning from dairy, and I had dinner recently with married friends—a well-known musician-actress couple—and the subject of frequency came up in a lighthearted way. "I know *he* can have sex twice a day, no problem," she said, throwing her husband a glance.

"Yeah," Rob said, "that's how *she* feels," cocking his head toward me.

"Are you kidding?" she said, rolling her eyes at me with a look of surprise. "Me—two, three times a week, max!"

"Yeah." Rob shrugged. "I'm with you. Same."

It sounded like dialogue from a bad TV movie about groovy seventies swingers swapping spouses. It was amusing the way our libidos criss-crossed. She went on to say that her career distracted her sometimes; I know Rob succumbs to career depressions, too, and then he could care less about sex. The rocker and I: same tribe.

But even when Rob's got career headaches and I'm hating him, we can have sex at a moment's notice, and probably have a great time. The heat of the anger just makes it a little nastier, more intense. When Rob releases the floodgates of emotion, it's frightening. Rob used to say that our energies can be so intense together that when they meet over a landmass, they become a storm front and produce rain.

One key to improving sex is accepting each other at our worst. I've met men who got stuck in that prudish fifties "undress in the dark" mentality—the Little Woman who always makes sure she primps and looks like a bonbon, rather than the authentic, earthy woman she is. Rob and I are sexually comfortable with each other no matter how bad we look or feel. I can't imagine not getting past that superficial level.

Of course, as for many couples, the best option has been ingenuity, spontaneity, romantic gestures, and, of course, vacation sex. Maybe Rob's making up for all the "picnics" we missed in our peculiar courtship. He is, along with Freddie, the most effortlessly romantic man I've met in my life. In that sense both my husbands have reminded me so much of my father's spirit. Rob is great with the little gifts, the letters, the surprise notes when you wake up, and flowers for all occasions.

And leather. I loved the time he abducted me on my birthday to my favorite American city, San Francisco, and surprised me with a "Leather Birthday." He gave me a whole array of leather gifts, including a pair of very hot restraints. When I walked into our suite at the Sherman Hotel and saw the four-poster bed, I gasped, "Oh, my, this is so *fabulous.*" Everything has its place—especially with a willing partner.

That's the spirit I try to build into our married life. I've always used my imagination to great advantage, and see no reason why marriage should dull it. I once met a lover in a limo at the airport with nothing on but a trenchcoat, high heels, a bottle of champagne, and a sexy smile. I've made very discreet love on the beach, and one time on a Central Park bench in daylight. I once felt so proud of a TV writer-producer boyfriend of mine that when he won an Emmy I walked him outside to a remote, dark side street, backed him up against the wall of a carport, and presented him with an award of my own that left him, well, speechless.

And then walked him back in to meet the press.

A marriage can only improve with that kind of lusty abandon. Rob has caught on: There are times he and I are in the bathroom in the morning, preparing to work out in our little gym, but we'll suddenly be going at it up at the sink, giving our hearts a good cardiovascular workout before the treadmill and StairMaster.

Nothing beats getting Rob out of town, away from all his Hollywood *mishegoss*. We peak with vacation sex, which has been known to begin on our way *to* the vacation. We prefer DC-10s, because they offer the roomiest lavs for in-flight lovemaking.

Rob saved one of his all-time sexiest, most spontaneous moves for a quaint romantic restaurant in Venice. Service should be that slow in *every* restaurant; people would enjoy dining out so much more. We were in our favorite country, feeling intensely sexy and loving with each other. I was in a slinky dress with nothing on underneath but nylons and a garter belt. My devilish husband chalked one up for vacation dexterity under a candlelit corner table. Prix fixe or no, I tipped Rob big-time later that night.

It's not that every lovemaking session—on either the home or away schedule—has to be swing-from-the-chandelier time. But routine can be hazardous to your marriage's sexual health. I don't ever want to dampen the spark.

It amazes me to think that any two people can get along well enough to live under one roof together for most of their adult lives. What has really made our marriage grow and improve is dedicating enormous energy and care to hashing things out, clearing the air of lingering resentment and anger after we fight.

Neither of us has had illusions about how much maintenance is required to create an environment that supports and nourishes both people—not only as partners but as creative individuals with their own distinct goals. To make a marriage work by sacrificing your own personal growth makes no sense; it breeds resentment, or worse, breeds a corrosive, silent rage that destroys you with disease.

I brought Rob in on my therapy early on. We saw it as another "tool" for building our home. Dr. Sharon has helped us hear the unspoken messages in the "he said she said" miscommunications that go on with us, as in any marriage. Therapy speeds the process of digging down to the core of issues—where we attain a healthy understanding and acceptance. We've both got strong personalities; we're fighters. But we've gotten much better at weathering the stormy tensions that might have otherwise wrecked our marriage.

As Rob likes to wisecrack, "I've become a victim of all that improvement."

Rob and I both feel that insight-driven therapy can benefit any relationship. Rob has an amusing therapist-as-referee take on it. "I don't see how anyone can sustain a healthy relationship," he says, "without somebody in a black-and-white striped shirt and a whistle around the neck who can yell, 'Clipping! Fifteen yards. First down.'"

The key to our day-to-day maintenance is cleaning up as we go along. There's no waxy buildup of bad feelings. We don't sweep stuff under the rug. We hose and vacuum constantly. We are constantly in each other's face about everything. Therapy isn't a panacea; it isn't foolproof. But it can't help but improve communication, as long as both partners want the marriage to be enriched and to endure.

Typical irritants: Rob sees me as having a compulsion to be right all the time (he's *wrong!*), and to define, reduce, explain everything in terms of my "theories" (yin-yang, too much dairy, too little zinc, etc.). The Miss Smarty Pants/Goody-Goody in me provokes, irks him. But, as he sardonically admits, "You suffer from the standard female disease, which is having to be right. The fact that a great deal of the time you are right is just as irksome."

What makes me nuts about Rob: a crabby, sulky self-indulgence about career mishaps; a tendency to seem gruff (he often chooses not to be a schmooze, though he can be disarmingly adorable whenever he wants); and a dark, vaguely persecutory angst. Rob can turn a bad mood into performance art. The boy knows how to dwell, and wallow, when he sets his mind to it.

Of course, I've always been attracted to angst-ridden, depressive, artistic men; the more tortured the better. It's why Rob calls me a "Jew groupie." I see raw clay that I can mold, shape, lighten, play with. One of Rob's best lines about his temperament is: "If a Jew whines in his room, and no one hears him, is it a whine?" It can get to the point of "enough already."

When his terrific movie *Fire in the Sky* happened to open the same weekend as The Storm of the Century in 1993, it was a dumb-luck act of God. Who takes blizzards personally? Rob took it personally. He went into a long, deep funk. I understood his disappointment, given the incredibly hard work and discipline required to make the movie. But, unlike some of *my* movies, at least it got released, did fine, earned strong reviews, and did great in video. So it grossed $6.5 instead of $7.5 mil that weekend. I was, like, "People lost their lives in this storm, and you piss and moan about the grosses? Let it go. What do you want on your headstone —'Without the storm he'd have opened bigger'?"

Sometimes the harder I try to support him and tell him he has a wonderful career and life, the more defensive and angry he gets. In a foul, crabby state, he sees support as an attack. He wants to be nothing but an A-plus director of Oscar-winning films, and I'm trying, out of love and respect, to tell him it's okay not to be Stanley Kubrick.

This can kick in a classic cycle: If he's depressed, he pulls away sexually, which he knows I hate. In his eyes, I become even more critical and vicious. He then pulls further away and I feel like he's controlling me and the marriage.

I admit I've been harder on Rob than on anyone else I've ever been with. This is because I had previously kept one foot out the door. He said he wanted to make a home that was so nice I'd never want to leave. He did, and I don't. But I'm determined to make it as close to perfect as I can. I want to change, I want Rob to change, I want us to be better because I *am* so passionately committed to him. It's my compulsion, I know that. But I'm just as hard on myself. I'm constantly looking to improve myself. I am not a finished product, by any stretch of the imagination. Life is a work in progress.

Rob's got the best take on me: "You know what your sickness is? What's most obsessive-compulsive about you is your feeling that you're not obsessive or compulsive enough."

Therapy has helped us navigate through all these rough, murky waters. I kept a foot out the door as a way to be ready to split from his anger, his moods. It seemed easier to fix things that way, to know that I still wasn't completely stuck in place.

But I was holding out not only on marriage, but on family as well. As eager as I was to get pregnant, I didn't feel secure enough about him. There were times when I was sorry we weren't ready to start a family yet, because I thought it would be good for us. But it wasn't time. We kept on working at it, smoothing out the rough spots, finding our comfort zone.

It paid off. Since getting married, we've succeeded in building a rich, resilient, and genuinely loving life together on a foundation of devotion, shared goals and interests, ever-deepening communication, and great sex. We both feel free to "process" our stuff honestly—and without fear of losing each other for speaking up. Neither one of us is going anywhere.

A sitcom is probably the best kind of career to have in Hollywood—if you're also trying to maintain a normal, stable home life. The soundstage is a world of tight, almost unvarying, routine. Ensemble work tends to equalize egos, there are no prolonged dislocations to far-flung movie sets, the season is shorter than a school year, your weekends are your own, and you've got a five-month hiatus every spring and summer for movie or theater work. (I was able to make one of my favorite movies, *Noises Off!*, with Michael Caine, Carol Burnett, Christopher Reeve, John Ritter, and Denholm Elliott, and directed by Peter Bogdanovich, on hiatus after my first season of *Evening Shade.)* In these ways, the sitcom schedule can not only facilitate outside career goals, but can make having a solid home life a very real possibility.

Part of my excitement was working with Burt again, part of it was loving the rhythm of the week, with each day devoted to honing the work as we progressed toward Friday's live-audience taping. What originally intrigued me about my character Ava was how much I thought she could resemble my own mother in some ways, and myself in others. I had always felt Elaine Nardo was more my sister JoAnn—older, divorced, raising two kids, struggling to give expression to her creative, artistic side.

Ava, on the other hand, was happily married, the sensible spouse, and she had the kids but kept her figure and sexy spirit. Ava and Wood's kids were, like Burt and me, spread out over fifteen years. I remember feeling so close to home that I joked to Burt early on, "If I have any more kids, we're opening a dance studio out back. Forget this prosecutor bit."

I liked that the show was rooted in small-town Arkansas life, a throwback to homespun fifties, early-sixties values. But it had, in Ava, the veneer of nineties political correctness—a successful prosecuting attorney with four kids. I saw enormous opportunities to grow into her and run with it.

I loved my new job. The mood of the set was a far cry from the wild, edgy New York energy of *Taxi*. Both Burt and I were married, the cast was older and more settled, and so there was none of the youthful wildness that drove the *Taxi* set. But if I loved *Taxi* more as a show, *Evening Shade* found me in a far more contented era of life. I had really grown up—and I could roll with the punches of a very different work detail.

Putting together *Evening Shade* was much looser, more chaotic and tense, and, in many instances, far less disciplined than the *Taxi* drill. I'm not even referring, for now, to the vast creative and personality differences between Jim Brooks and the Burt Reynolds/Harry and Linda Thomason camp. The two shows had utterly different creative cultures.

It's just that there were times when our *Evening Shade* writers hadn't even finished a script by Monday morning and we were told not to bother showing up yet. Or when the script awaiting us for a cold reading on Tuesday would run sixty pages—some 33 percent too long. With too little time to cut and shape, we would just deal with the long version (which obviously requires far more shaping); if it wasn't working, it would be tossed out and a new one would be created overnight for another shot at it Wednesday. Then, we would shoot it, often as written, however long, and it would then be edited down over the weekend by eight to twelve minutes for airing.

It's interesting to notice how *Evening Shade* has always had many more close-ups of us talking than *Taxi* ever did. When you think of *Taxi* you see movement, action; you see people walking across the garage set doing their actorly "business." That's because if *Taxi*'s writers ever lost thirty seconds of material, it would have killed them. On *Taxi,* we didn't see a script until it was already polished and tightened through a half-dozen drafts, and we'd work through two more before shooting.

Both methods obviously work, and I'm lucky to have had nine seasons of prime time to show for them.

As with *Taxi,* every season of *Evening Shade* was different for me. My favorite season, with some of my best work, was the fourth, in 1993–94. The writing staff finally *got* my sense of humor and found my character at last. I was given a lot more to do.

But it had sometimes been a long, often frustrating struggle. I don't actually know how it happened, but somewhere along the way, Ava became predictable, almost generic. Her statements flowed from her like slogans. She said the right thing. She had perfect opinions, exactly those you'd expect. What she lacked was a gritty, wild-card human quality: She lacked being me! You rarely saw Ava get mad or testy or obnoxious with anybody—until the fourth season. Then I finally got to say feisty things to Burt's Wood and really tell him how I felt.

Was I acting out the role of Linda's tame southern alter ego (because in real life she is a dynamo of a wife and partner to

Harry)? Or was it Burt who never wanted any Ava back talk? I'll never know.

I lodged my complaints a couple of times in each of the first three seasons, telling the writers, "You know, guys, it's weird: I'm out there on all these talk shows talking about how wonderful our show is, and there's not even a clip they can run because I don't have a funny punch line to show off the episode. Let's get with the program."

For many episodes, Ava had mostly what I call "p.p. lines"— plot-pushing lines: innocuous, pipe-laying "exposition" that moved the story forward without providing any emotional content. The big cast had plenty of mouths to feed and story lines to set up with p.p. lines. But I'd rather have three lines that are true to character than 20 p.p. lines.

I felt fulfilled, and challenged, in only a couple of episodes in each of the first three seasons. Often, I had only three to six lines a week. Still, for me it was never about quantity, but point of view. In my fourth season, Ava got some bite to her, and my gags got sharper. As Burt said to me, "Well, they finally realized you've got a sense of humor, that you're funny."

The irony was that I was so much more confident and easygoing, so much less insecure about my craft, on *Evening Shade* than I had been on *Taxi*. I was constantly asking myself on *Taxi* if I was doing a scene just right. I felt, from day one, on more equal, self-assured footing with the gang on *Evening Shade*.

Doing the series while working out the first years of marriage was an ideal manifestation of yin-yang harmony—expansion and contraction, day and night. I already had enough drama and uncertainty at work. The less drama the happier I was, the more balanced my life.

That delicate harmony finally fell apart by the spring of 1994, as we neared the end of season four, in the aftermath of Burt's very messy, very tabloidy split from Loni. Until then, it had been a controlled, low-key soundstage.

The one exception was when Burt caught on fire in our second season. That was scary.

Friday the 13th of September 1991—an inauspicious day for special effects. In the scene Ava's driving our RV next to Wood, with our baby asleep next to us. Herman, played by Michael Jeter, is back in the little galley, trying to make breakfast. Wood asks him to heat up the baby's bottle. Herman does all kinds of klutzy Buster Keatonesque physical gags, with stuff spilling and popping everywhere. When he starts a small fire on the stove, Burt goes back and tamps it out with his hands (which were covered with fire-retardant gel). The scene ends with Herman dousing the fire with a small extinguisher.

Burt had asked that the extinguisher be filled with baby powder instead of foam, because he had once had a bad experience with foam. I couldn't see him or Michael, but I heard their lines, the commotion, and the audience laughter.

Suddenly, I heard the *whooosh* of the extinguisher, followed by a terrifying, unscripted *poooof!* of an explosion, then the thud of a body hitting the floor right behind me. I heard bloodcurdling shrieks from Loni, who was in the audience. I had a camera on me, but I turned and saw people rushing the stage and went, Oh, my God!

I thought Burt had had a heart attack.

He had been completely torched. His body was inside a flame. It was horrifying. Drawing on his experience in stunt-filled action movies, he had the presence of mind to put his gel-covered hands to his face and roll over on himself to snuff the flames, which were quickly extinguished by crew members.

Burt was in shock. He was white. His eyebrows were singed to ash; you could flick them off. He had soot in his lungs.

And he wanted to do another take! I couldn't believe how macho he was being. He must have thought he was still doing *Sharky's Machine.* They rushed him to a hospital, and he came through it.

What happened was that the effects guys, as Burt had requested, had packed the extinguisher with baby powder, which contains highly flammable cornstarch. When Michael sprayed it, a spark from the stove ignited the powder around Burt, engulfing him in flames.

The next time we saw Burt get burned that badly was in the second half of 1993. This time the flames came shooting from the supermarket rags, and no one could snuff them out.

Burt had not seemed too happy the year before he and Loni split, though I was hardly privy to what was going on. Loni had always seemed quite devoted, wiping little beads of sweat off his brow or straightening his tie at awards shows. He never seemed to be pushing her away. If they had problems, they seemed no different from anyone else's.

But I did sense a sadness from Loni as time wore on. Burt worked like a machine. He was the first to arrive at dawn, the last to leave after dark, pumped up on caffeine from iced tea and coffee. I'd see Loni, whom I grew to like very much, at Friday tapings, and say, "He must crash all weekend long."

"I don't see him from Friday night to Sunday night," she'd say. "He sleeps through the whole weekend."

The tabloids went berserk with this story all through the summer. I knew absolutely nothing of Pam Seals, the cocktail waitress in Florida, where Burt spent his months on hiatus. She was named in the papers as his longtime girlfriend on the side.

By the time we went back to work, the headlines had died down, the divorce was under way, and Burt seemed a little mellower. The worst was behind him. His opening line to us at the first read-through was classic raised-eyebrow Burt: "So, anything interesting happen this summer?"

The season turned into a strong one for me. But while I was just beginning to "find" Ava—with the help of better writing—the show was beginning to lose its audience. As we moved toward the final few episodes, the series simply seemed to be running out of gas. It was an extremely costly show to produce and ratings were down, generating less advertising revenue. And the previous year had taken a toll on Burt.

On March 11, he showed up for the Friday taping looking awful—drawn and depressed. I wondered if he had been up all night. He had. He whispered to me that he and Pam had broken up that night, that she had left him that morning. He was heartsick. And his dear friend Dinah Shore had passed away just days earlier.

We were working that week with John Ratzenberger, the actor who'd played Cliff on *Cheers* and who had directed several episodes of that show. He's a veteran of what Burt called "East Coast Shows." Burt has always had a real southern thing about "eastern" shows. Two distinct attitudes, different styles. Burt was upset that week, complaining that John had been "curt." It was clear the two men rubbed each other the wrong way.

To me John was a no-nonsense, cut-to-the-chase type who could easily have directed *Taxi*. No schmooze time, just a hall-monitor type who liked to get down to work. John came on the set needing to establish his authority—like a substitute teacher—with an ensemble that had worked together for four years. Not easy.

It was a more complex show than usual, with three story lines, and we were a little behind. I had had a great week with my costar and new best friend, Kathie Lee Gifford, whose last regular work on a prime-time comedy show had been in *Hee Haw Honeys* back in the late seventies. This time, she played my old college roommate who comes to visit. She and our oldest son (Jay Ferguson) develop a crush on each other, have a date, and end it with a little kiss. And I'm outraged.

It was a cute and poignant episode. Kathie Lee was wonderful to work with. She displayed a natural and impressive gift and energy for the rhythms of comic delivery. Her talk show with Regis Philbin has been the perfect showcase for her amazingly quick, well-informed wit and biting sense of humor; but that week proved she can also act. It was one of my all-time favorite work weeks, out of 101, on the show. (Kathie was, in fact, working, most deservedly, on her own series pilot.)

John got the ball rolling early and, during one of Burt's lines, came over to reposition Kathie Lee, Jay Ferguson, and me. This pissed Burt off. He thought John was being rude and inattentive, walking in front of him to reblock the shot.

Burt mumbled something, and John said, "It's okay, fine, let's just go on."

"Well," Burt snapped back, "maybe I don't want to go on."

"No, really. Let's just go on."

"Maybe I don't *want* to go on." With that, Burt pushed over a chair, and we thought: Oh, shit, what's this going to turn into?

Burt then got ready to start up again when Jay, who is nineteen, said, "You know, I can't put up with this shit anymore. I can't work like this." I couldn't believe Jay was copping an attitude.

"All right," John yelled, "everybody take five." Kathie Lee grabbed my arm and said, "Let's go to makeup." It all seemed so silly, so crazy. At least it threw Kathie Lee and me into a memorable "bonding" moment.

Then, from the makeup room, we heard a noisy scene going down between Jay and Burt. Burt was confronting Jay, taunting him, pushing him back slightly. "Oh, so you think you've had a tough week? Let me tell you about a rough week. My best friend in the world died, I'm getting a divorce, I'm fighting for my child, and now my girlfriend left this morning. This has been the worst goddamn year of my life. And what's *your* problem, kid?"

I'm not exactly comfortable around father-son confrontations to begin with—having witnessed one at seventeen that directly preceded my father's fatal heart attack. When Jay and Burt got into it, I pulled away. But I felt so bad for Burt. I knew he was hurting.

When things calmed down, Burt came over and sat next to me. He was sobbing quietly, and he sort of leaned on my shoulder and expressed something that deeply moved me. "I don't think you realize," he said wearily, "how much I need you to hold me once in a while and to tell me everything's okay."

Burt then had to shoot a fight scene with the father of a young girl who has challenged our younger son at school. The actor, Joe Griffo, was a little person. As scripted, he came in the door, he and Burt argued, and Joe threw a stunt punch. But when Burt ducked, he fell back wrong and landed on his hand, breaking a bone. He needed a cast up to his elbow.

By the time I got home from this withering series of psychodramas, I had dozens of messages from tabloid reporters and friends trying to get the scoop. Scoop? These reporters didn't need a scoop—they needed a shovel for all the horseshit they were so determined to print.

The story had snowballed into: Burt fractured his hand during a violent duke-out with director John Ratzenberger and/or Jay Ferguson (depending on whose bogus account you heard), with sets being smashed, props flying, and me and Kathie Lee fleeing for our safety in tears and smudging mascara.

The tabloids had struck again, with insane inaccuracy. They had everything but Kathie Lee and me as Wild West barmaids, jumping off the saloon bar onto guys' backs and cracking whiskey bottles over the villains' heads.

By the time the stories came out, it felt like the end was near. All the networks were preparing their fall lineups, and rumors were circulating that we were among the expendables. Bad press like that could only speed our demise. We were all pretty burned out and frayed. We ended the season with a new kind of series cliff-hanger: Would we be back for the next season?

We went into our last episode anticipating the worst. At other times in my life, this might have been a sad, unsettling sensation—

basal thermometer readings are a must. For me, they're all but
impossible, since you're supposed to lie at rest for five hours
beforehand. I don't necessarily even sleep that long; awake I'm way
too hyper. Five hours? Forget it.

Other tips from the Shettles owner's manual: Females should
avoid orgasms (boy sperm swim too fast upon lubrication);
vinegar-douche after sex to favor baby girls (the acidity kills off
boys); douche with baking soda for a boy. I did neither; no way I
was going to bed smelling like a salad—not even one with balsamic
vinegar in it.

I also learned how the missionary position deposits boy sperm
farther away from their target, thus making it less likely they will
survive the rough seas. (For the record, to have a boy, sex from
behind is better. On top for a woman is never recommended for
conception: It may be great for its gratification, but not its
gravitational pull.)

With all our fabulous new knowledge, after a year and a half
nothing had come of our efforts. My feeling was that any baby we
made would be the one we wanted. Now that I see how hard it is to
have a baby, every human being walking this earth is a winner, just
for getting here.

We both then had a complete fertility workup that included what
is known as a percol wash. Rob was asked to ejaculate, and I let him
have this date on his own. They'd take him to a small room
equipped with girlie magazines and soft lighting to get him in the
mood. The "wash" filters out the inferior two-headed, twin-tailed
varieties, leaving a purified, stronger sperm concentrate. When
Rob scored huge sperm-count test results, it was like he'd gotten an
800 on both SATs. He was really puffed up.

Then they put the sperm in with hamster eggs, which have a
membrane coating similar to those of human females, to measure
penetration. All our scores—sperm, sperm type, penetrability, my
FSH levels ("like those of an eighteen-year-old girl")—were sky-
high. I took a test called a hysteroencephalogram, where they inject
you with iodine dye and then take pictures to determine if your
tubes and ovaries are blocked. Nothing. Flying colors. Clean as a
whistle. The more we knew, the more we were mystified.

Rob and I were also keeping track of my ovulation with a sex
calendar, making sure we hit our marks with perfect timing. We

used Van Morrison CDs, candles, the works—figu
great babies. A quickie during ovulation (or having
metal) seemed a surefire formula for creating a neur
no go.

The calendar was actually used as much to keep scor
track. Rob first used it to chart his workout progress. W
using it to jokingly mark sexual activity—and, ultim
monthly timing when we were apart so much. We did go
period where I was busting him for too little sex. I wasn
enough.

He teased me that I should keep a list of all his bad an
qualities on the bathroom wall, so he'd never lose sight of
Good qualities: good cook. Bad qualities: not enough sex.
kind of thing.

In January 1991, I told him we were lagging. I gave him Febr
to pick up the pace or I was leaving him. I was, of course, jok
though sex has always been the dramatic B-story of our love aff
I've always been amazed how men can think of only one thing a
time, while women can think of twenty things at a time. If men a
on the sex track, great. But if they're on their career track, that's it
forget about sex. Women can think about sex, shopping, food,
work, kids—all at once.

Rob won the February sweeps. When I was on *The Tonight Show*
with Johnny Carson on April 5, 1991, I talked about the calendar
—we draw little tongues and lips to note extra credit—and how
our sex life had improved after marriage. I said there was hope for
couples, that my husband and I had had sex sixteen times in
February, noting that it was a short month. Johnny didn't know
what hit him. This cracked him up. Rob was only too happy: Now
he was really strutting his stuff.

By the end of '91, our infertility situation got complicated by
long separations due to work. Over one fifteen-month stretch, we
were together only five ovulating periods.

Through the spring of 1992, we investigated intrauterine insemination (IUI). When my gynecologist made sure I was ovulating, we
went down a couple of flights in the same office building and visited
a clinic. This time, instead of letting Rob go off alone into a tiny
room with magazines, soft lights, and an aquarium, I asked for an
examining room—with a view—and went in there with him. We
turned off the lights, bolted the door, and had sex. Of course, Rob

being cut loose, having to go out into the crazy Hollywood marketplace to nail down a new project.

But I wasn't letting anything upset me, and for good reason: When our final episode wrapped on April 5, 1994, I was eight months pregnant with a miracle baby Rob and I had thought I would never be able to have.

22
In the Nick of Time

~

After Rob and I had been dating about two weeks, I not only started thinking real estate; I started thinking family. And my approach was a full frontal assault. The usual.

"Okay," I said, "I know you have two kids. I have to ask how you'd feel about a second family, about having more children."

I was ready for some backpedaling avoidance, or at least an evasive speech about not wanting to go through it all over again. Instead, he stunned me, and he thrilled me.

Without hesitating, he said: "It's mandatory."

I was tempted to figure, Sure, he's going to tell me exactly what I want to hear; he knows that otherwise, it's over. But Rob had already struck me with his sincerity, honesty, and directness. I believed him.

Mandatory was what we wanted. Miraculous was what we got.

I had always taken my ability to get pregnant for granted, figured it would be a snap. The truth is, I had gotten pregnant as a younger woman, in the context of a strong relationship with a man I was crazy about, but whom I would never marry. It was a brutally painful decision to terminate the pregnancy, but I knew it was the right thing to do. Searching for the silver lining in my loss then, I had focused on the ease with which I had conceived—and took no small comfort in vowing that the right man would someday come into my life and create a beautiful family with me.

But then he never came along. Until Rob.

A few months before Rob and I got married, I assisted my best friend Cynthia in the birth of her daughter Gabrielle. As I cut the umbilical cord and watched life breathe into her beautiful little face, I said to myself, *This is what I want. This is what life's all about.* I knew it was time for Rob and me to get serious, and I had my IUD removed.

We had delayed any decisions about children until we were married, and I had delayed our decision to get married until I was absolutely sure about us. We had started off so hot and so heavy I needed time to get my bearings, to see if we had legs. We were working out the kinks in therapy. A child out of wedlock was out of range.

I also wanted to be more secure in my career, since things hadn't come together the way I had wanted them to. I didn't want to have to turn down a terrific new series or movie because I was pregnant. I was hedging my bets all around—on Rob and marriage, on my career, on babies—and time was flying.

Then, almost overnight, things came together: I was married and signed to a new series. Soon, we stopped using protection, figuring we'd strike paydirt right off the bat. It was naive of me, if true to form, to assume I had that much control over it.

As months went by without success, my feelings ranged from relief and concern to ambivalence. We were often separated by work, so there wasn't a constant energy put into getting pregnant. If we were fighting, it gave me some leverage. I'd tell Rob, "I'm not making a baby this weekend. I hate you this weekend."

But after a year of marriage, it occurred to us that maybe we had a battle on our hands. Nothing was happening. As I did years before, with nutrition and health, I read everything I could about fertility, and learned about the Shettles Method, which is used for couples determined to have a baby of a certain sex. Neither of us was partial—Rob may have wanted a girl—but if Shettles upped the odds of having a baby, we were game.

The Shettles literature includes fascinating details on the difference between male and female sperm: Boys are bullet-shaped, swim faster, and die sooner, usually within twenty-four hours; girl sperm are rounder, move at a more leisurely pace, and live up to seventy-two hours.

Consequently, the ideal way to conceive a girl is to stop having sex two days before ovulation—by which time the vast majority of live sperm are female. Knowing precise times is key—and precise basal thermometer readings are a must. For me, they're all but impossible, since you're supposed to lie at rest for five hours beforehand. I don't necessarily even sleep that long; awake I'm way too hyper. Five hours? Forget it.

Other tips from the Shettles owner's manual: Females should avoid orgasms (boy sperm swim too fast upon lubrication); vinegar-douche after sex to favor baby girls (the acidity kills off boys); douche with baking soda for a boy. I did neither; no way I was going to bed smelling like a salad—not even one with balsamic vinegar in it.

I also learned how the missionary position deposits boy sperm farther away from their target, thus making it less likely they will survive the rough seas. (For the record, to have a boy, sex from behind is better. On top for a woman is never recommended for conception: It may be great for its gratification, but not its gravitational pull.)

With all our fabulous new knowledge, after a year and a half nothing had come of our efforts. My feeling was that any baby we made would be the one we wanted. Now that I see how hard it is to have a baby, every human being walking this earth is a winner, just for getting here.

We both then had a complete fertility workup that included what is known as a percol wash. Rob was asked to ejaculate, and I let him have this date on his own. They'd take him to a small room equipped with girlie magazines and soft lighting to get him in the mood. The "wash" filters out the inferior two-headed, twin-tailed varieties, leaving a purified, stronger sperm concentrate. When Rob scored huge sperm-count test results, it was like he'd gotten an 800 on both SATs. He was really puffed up.

Then they put the sperm in with hamster eggs, which have a membrane coating similar to those of human females, to measure penetration. All our scores—sperm, sperm type, penetrability, my FSH levels ("like those of an eighteen-year-old girl")—were sky-high. I took a test called a hysteroencephalogram, where they inject you with iodine dye and then take pictures to determine if your tubes and ovaries are blocked. Nothing. Flying colors. Clean as a whistle. The more we knew, the more we were mystified.

Rob and I were also keeping track of my ovulation with a sex calendar, making sure we hit our marks with perfect timing. We used Van Morrison CDs, candles, the works—figuring great sex, great babies. A quickie during ovulation (or having sex to heavy metal) seemed a surefire formula for creating a neurotic kid. Still no go.

The calendar was actually used as much to keep score as to keep track. Rob first used it to chart his workout progress. We ended up using it to jokingly mark sexual activity—and, ultimately, my monthly timing when we were apart so much. We did go through a period where I was busting him for too little sex. I wasn't getting enough.

He teased me that I should keep a list of all his bad and good qualities on the bathroom wall, so he'd never lose sight of them. Good qualities: good cook. Bad qualities: not enough sex. That kind of thing.

In January 1991, I told him we were lagging. I gave him February to pick up the pace or I was leaving him. I was, of course, joking, though sex has always been the dramatic B-story of our love affair. I've always been amazed how men can think of only one thing at a time, while women can think of twenty things at a time. If men are on the sex track, great. But if they're on their career track, that's it, forget about sex. Women can think about sex, shopping, food, work, kids—all at once.

Rob won the February sweeps. When I was on *The Tonight Show* with Johnny Carson on April 5, 1991, I talked about the calendar —we draw little tongues and lips to note extra credit—and how our sex life had improved after marriage. I said there was hope for couples, that my husband and I had had sex sixteen times in February, noting that it was a short month. Johnny didn't know what hit him. This cracked him up. Rob was only too happy: Now he was really strutting his stuff.

By the end of '91, our infertility situation got complicated by long separations due to work. Over one fifteen-month stretch, we were together only five ovulating periods.

Through the spring of 1992, we investigated intrauterine insemination (IUI). When my gynecologist made sure I was ovulating, we went down a couple of flights in the same office building and visited a clinic. This time, instead of letting Rob go off alone into a tiny room with magazines, soft lights, and an aquarium, I asked for an examining room—with a view—and went in there with him. We turned off the lights, bolted the door, and had sex. Of course, Rob withdrew and ejaculated into a cup. We emerged smiling. The MD showed us the sperm in maximum motility, before the wash. It was all those double-headed, twin-tailed things, like rush-hour traffic in Tokyo.

This happened a few times, always the same way. We'd have lunch, take the sperm (preserved in some kind of cooling vapor) up to my gyno, and be instructed to "bond" with our sperm.

The doctor would then inject the sperm into me through a long stick with a push-up extension that could deposit them near the egg. Intercourse was like trying to get sperm to arrive in Seattle, but from the starting point of L.A. Doing IUI was like starting in Portland; you're already in Oregon, and past the worst freeways.

This method failed. We were baffled.

I saw a fertility specialist in Beverly Hills, but his office had a plant and a leak—and I don't mean a hanging fern and a plumbing problem. I mean a tabloid informant. A story came out in some rag claiming I was there to have some sort of operation. As usual, they got it all wrong and spread it all over town.

In my frustration, I decided we should just relax and try to get pregnant the old-fashioned, fun way. Unfortunately, Rob was gearing up to go off to Roseburg, Oregon, near Eugene, to shoot *Fire in the Sky,* his film about an alien abduction. I was mulling over doing an exercise video. It was a terrific career break for him, and I was happy over the prospect of making a fitness tape; but we would now be apart for weeks on end. I figured doing the video was meant to happen while I still wasn't pregnant, so in April and May, we took it easy and stopped worrying about fertility.

While I was doing my video, a friend on the shoot referred me to a wonderful specialist at UCLA named Dr. Joseph Gambone. Rob was scheduled to go away June 27, I was going back into *Evening Shade* in August, and Rob wasn't coming home until November. So timing was critical. The doctor wanted Rob to bank eight sperm deposits before leaving, which could then be frozen and used for insemination in his absence. Rob spent so much time at UCLA coming into cups I hardly saw him before he limped off to Oregon.

Even with Rob's frozen bank assets, I missed the real thing. So in mid-August, during ovulation, I met him in San Francisco. Somehow, a tryst there seemed nicer than IUI; no one has ever heard Tony Bennett singing "I Left My Cup in San Francisco."

We each flew about an hour, met at nine A.M., and checked into our favorite hotel, the Pan Pacific, not far from where a Peeping Tom had once crouched on Dashiell Hammett's fire escape to watch Freddie and me make love. We were both exhausted (Rob had had a night shoot), but this was worth it.

Rob and I wasted no time getting down to business. Then, we both fell into a deep sleep. We got up, went out to a great meal, came back, made love, fell asleep, woke up, had another great meal (Wolfgang Puck's PosTrio), made love, fell asleep, woke up, and had another meal. It was an incredible twenty-four hours: three hedonistic cycles of sex, sleep, and great food crammed into one day.

But no baby.

With almost half the sperm losing their tails in the freeze, the doctor recommended I take Clomid, a popular fertility drug that creates multiple eggs, for one month.

I hadn't taken an aspirin in over a decade. I hated fertility drugs because I felt—and I could be completely wrong—that a lot of women who put themselves through them end up with ovarian cancer. But I went along for one month.

As I'd predicted I would, I felt psychotic on Clomid. I couldn't sleep, I was alone and far from Rob, and I was bonding with frozen sperm. I figured if I was going to put my body through the Clomid, then I should be with my husband, and we would at least use Rob's warm sperm.

I tried hard not to get obsessed about missing out on motherhood. Out of 365 days in the year, there are only 13 when you can get pregnant. Of those, Rob and I managed to be together for half. That's seven days of major focus, which leaves an awful lot of living to do. We went about our lives without getting crazy. Instead of obsessing about my biological clock, I looked at it more as a biological stopwatch. When I punched it off, I went on with my life.

I did try one very hip L.A. thing to get pregnant. A woman who asked me if I had any pregnant women friends suggested something that sounded like a *Saturday Night Live* spoof of New Age quackery: "Tell a pregnant friend of yours to dry out the petals of six dozen roses and put them in a bathtub filled with water. Tell her to get in the tub, relax, and at some point urinate in there to get her hormones on these petals floating in the water. Then, have her husband dry out the petals again and give them to you. Then, you take a bath with these petals in your tub."

I don't know if this technique was supposed to leave me smelling like a rose or feeling pissed off. At least I got a sexy bath out of it—if no baby.

The topic of laparoscopic surgery came up through the holidays and early months of 1993. I was holding out. This is a look-see fiber-optic surgical procedure through the navel to check if anything such as scar tissue from an IUD might be obstructing the fertility process. We decided to wait, lay back, and reassess. One thing never failed me—the crystal-clear vision of myself having a baby grow and pass through me. It wasn't just holding a baby I might adopt, it was seeing myself pregnant. I just always believed in my heart of hearts that it was meant to happen.

Before I would commit to the laparoscopy, we went through "mucus compatibility" tests with another fertility specialist in New York. This checks whether a woman who has waited so long to conceive has developed a resistance to her partner's sperm as a sort of "muscle memory."

We passed the test; I made a July appointment.

"You watch," a friend said, "it sort of cleans out your tubes. The next month you'll get pregnant. Happens all the time."

I went in for the laparoscopy, and I checked out fine. No problems. No scar tissue. Our case was being filed under "Unexplained Infertility."

The following month, on the morning of August 19, I had a ten A.M. call for *Evening Shade*—later than usual because of a football scene being shot. Rob and I got up and had a great, sexy, leisurely morning together. I knew I was very early in my cycle and wouldn't be ovulating for a few more days, so we had carefree sex without thinking much about it.

When I got to work, a Thursday, Burt gave me a stunt to do where I'm at our son's football game and I have to grab on to the railing in the bleachers and leap over the railing onto the field. I don't know if something got knocked into place or what, but that night we were at a restaurant and something felt strange: "Rob, I know I'm ovulating today. It's so weird. It just feels like it, though I'm not supposed to start until Sunday."

We went to London for a vacation—determined to press on in September with the baby quest. I blamed my prolonged lethargy in Europe on jet lag. But by the time we returned on Sunday, September 5, my period was four days late.

Curiosity was eating away at me. At the Tuesday read-through, I was in my dressing room, and Rob was at home with my brothers, when my niece Lizzy went out and got four home pregnancy test kits. My friend Sharon Feldstein, a mother of three children, was with us. During a break, I urinated, as directed, on the pink stick. A pink dot means you get a baby.

"You want me to go look?" Sharon said.

"Okay." She went into the bathroom and came back with some unbelievable news. "It's pink. There's a definite dot. Trust me. I've seen a million of these."

It looked only vaguely pink, and I wasn't buying it: "It's not pink. I don't think so. I'll try peeing on the blue stick." The blue indicator was more visually definitive. I didn't want to get my hopes raised again, only to have them dashed.

I tried it with the blue stick, and Lizzy, Sharon, and I gathered around in utter amazement. "That is a blue line, no doubt about it," Sharon said.

I had to be dreaming. My heart was racing like crazy. This was surreal. No way it had happened so easily, so naturally, when we had least expected it. I had been jogging every day, drinking every night. I had eaten cookies loaded with sugar one night in London, which was like a giant mortal sin. I'd never have eaten sugar had I known I was pregnant. And to get pregnant when you're sure you're not even ovulating—*impossible!*

Plus, I had come to believe—no pun intended—that I had had way too much fun during sex to get pregnant. That Thursday morning, I had a ball, and I figured we'd blown it.

I called Rob to give him the tentative update. Neither of us wanted to be set up for another heartbreak, or the agony of a false positive.

I met Rob at home for lunch. We were in a weird kind of iffy ecstasy. I went back to work and afterward I rushed over to my doctor. He examined me, shook his head, and grinned. "Yep. You're pregnant." We screamed and howled and I jumped up and down with the news. I called Rob with the announcement I thought I'd never be able to make.

"We're having a baby, sweetheart," I said, and with that we both broke down in tears of joy over the phone. Three years of tests and worry, uncertainty and fear, had suddenly been blown away and replaced by a dream that was now within our grasp.

As you might expect, I threw myself into new motherhood 200 percent, stocking up on about fifty books from bookstores and my health food store in my quest for pregnancy perfection. I held off informing Burt, Harry, and Linda until the doctor could see my baby's heartbeat.

On September 22, we went to his office for a sonogram. It blew my mind. We could barely make out a tiny flicker that made me think back to the Pentecost Sunday Holy Cards we used to get as kids. They had pictures of the Apostles with "tongues of fire" over their heads. It was all I could make out on the gray, grainy screen—my baby's own tiny tongue of fire beating inside me. This was a delirious spiritual moment, and Rob and I just fell apart, sobbing and laughing and hugging each other as we watched in teary awe. I looked at Rob and knew he would be a dedicated, energetic, and loving father.

In our miracle's aftermath, I heard all sorts of speculation about why it happened the way it did. I had always miscalculated my ovulation, and the mis-miscalculation hit it just right for once; the laparoscopy had cleaned my tubes out; we were more relaxed.

Maybe jumping over and over from the bleachers outside the soundstage had just knocked everything perfectly in place for one flawed, freaky tick of the biological clock. Perhaps in that jarring instant, a daring and determined boy sperm was sent hurtling through the egg membrane to score the Hail Mary touchdown that answered our prayers after we'd waited so long.

Talk about tweaks: The day we saw the baby's heartbeat, September 22, 1993, was eight years to the day after Rob and I had fallen in love at the Raiders game.

It was perfect karma for a control freak like me: When we were least conscious of controlling our (unsuccessful) efforts, we succeeded. Having a family with Rob was meant to be; but it was not meant to be revealed until our time had come.

I had the easiest pregnancy in history. There was not one day, one second, I did not want to be pregnant. It was a glorious, magical, and sweet time for Rob and me that marked a deep line in our lives between the people we had been, and the ones we were about to become.

I was so sure it was a boy that I staked $1,000 on it in a bet with Rob, who was sure it was a girl. We went for my amnio and sonogram on December 6, in my second trimester. That day was the Feast of St. Nicholas, and we knew we would name our baby Nicholas or Nicoletta (my Greek mom's name was Nikoleta before it was Americanized to Loretta). The sonogram showed quite conclusively that that teeny penis was attached most definitely to a Nicholas. We were thrilled and again hugged and sobbed in our joy.

Except that Rob was out a grand.

The first call we made from the car was to my business manager, requesting a funds transfer. Then I decided cash was cold; I wanted a gift instead.

Yet nothing Rob could give me from the material world could come close to matching the precious bundle growing inside me.

Having spent three years getting pregnant, instead of three minutes, I never once worried if the time was right, if it would make me lose jobs, what movies might come up, what outfits I couldn't wear to what events, if it would fit into our lives, if I would get my body back or lose my figure. Never once. No baby came into this world more appreciated than Nicholas Morgan Lieberman, and nothing else ever mattered as much as he did from the moment I knew I was carrying him.

I never got morning sickness. I had learned from one of my obscure health-food-store books that sickness comes from a drop in calcium in the middle of the night. It's why people want to have orange juice first thing in the morning—to release the calcium. Every night before bedtime I drank O.J. with a supplement composed of 1,000 milligrams of calcium and 500 of magnesium. The one night I tried not taking it, sure enough, I awoke at two-thirty A.M. almost shaking for my cal-mag fix.

I ate the same, but the smell of garlic suddenly made me ill. So for three months I had to avoid Italian restaurants, which was no small feat. I gained twenty-eight pounds, and it was all baby-in-front weight. Right up to the end, I didn't look pregnant from behind at all.

I did, of course, keep lists and charts of everything throughout my nine months: what I weighed, what I ate, how much I exercised (I stopped running and walked on the treadmill), how many hours I slept.

And I never drank alcohol. I had always imagined Rob and I would knock off one of our two bottles of 1979 Cristal as soon as I found out I was pregnant (the other would be for the delivery room). But we didn't. Nothing could make me risk harming or losing this baby.

I did decide to work through the series shooting schedule, which would wrap at the end of my eighth month, on April 5. But the producers decided not to write into the show another baby for Ava and Wood on *Evening Shade*. They didn't want to bother with adding another baby to the cast next season. It could have been a boy-girl cliff-hanger.

Instead, they had me sitting down a lot toward the last few episodes. Looking back, I'm sorry they didn't write the pregnancy in. All those cute outfits!

I always had a fantasy that when I got pregnant, work would slow down and I'd finally organize a Rolodex that had always existed only in my head.

That never happened. Though I went down for naps in my first trimester when I got tired, my workload seemed to double. I had the series to shoot, I began work in preparation for my new syndicated talk show, *Marilu*, I was writing this book, we got a green light for me to star in a TV movie Rob and I would produce, I had meetings to get TV movies and a pair of series—*Under Suspicion* and *Medicine Ball*—off the ground for our production company, Crystal Beach.

The middle trimester was a breeze. We spent the holidays in Aspen, at the gorgeous eight-bedroom, 6,000-square-foot home we'd recently bought there. I know a lot of women have their husbands take pictures of them naked around that time. I never did. Instead, I went on talk shows to chronicle my pregnancy progress.

Then, on January 17, 1994, the Los Angeles area was rocked by the terrifying Northridge earthquake, which was followed by hundreds of aftershocks so powerful they felt like earthquakes.

I was half-asleep, having just gone to the bathroom, when the giant tremor struck in the predawn darkness of the 17th. Our house, up in the hills over Hollywood, sits on its own small, but steep, crest of land, so much of the seismic shock gets absorbed by the earth beneath it.

But this was a big one that rumbled and rocked our house. It's an amazing sound, deeper and scarier than anything else imaginable. Yet I didn't feel any great adrenaline rush. And thank God, we sustained very little damage. Nothing fell off the walls or from counters; ceilings didn't collapse. Though the top of one pretty jar in the bathroom fell to the floor and cracked in half, I didn't even have to straighten a frame or sweep up a shattered glass. An entire row of wine bottles and glasses on a shallow shelf was still there afterward.

Through it all, I never panicked. I felt my baby was safer being inside me than out, and I was so committed to remaining calm for him that I just refused to go nuts with fear. You feel a new kind of power when you've been able to create this life inside you. I simply wasn't letting stuff bother me and trickle down into his safe, insulated world. I was dealing with everything—moving it along and letting it go. I'm sure I would have freaked for his safety if he had been an infant.

Plus, I had all this testosterone surging within me, so I was more macho about everything. Ask Burt—he was always joking on the set that pregnancy had turned me into a tough guy.

One major aftershock occurred at an inopportune moment—at the tail end of a fabulous baby shower at my house, with eighty-five women milling around, getting ready to eat. "My God, everybody's still hanging out in the front foyer," I had just whispered to my friend Mary Ann. "How are we going to get people outside for brunch?"

With that, all of Southern California started to tremble. Everyone froze, not knowing if this was The Big One, truly scared. I froze, muttered "Oh my God," and waited for the rattling to stop. Thank God, things settled down. Nothing'll clear a room like a 5.1 aftershock. My friend Marci had the best line: "You know," she said, "you just tripled your liquor bill." By spring, we were all so used to the shocks it was a nonissue.

Finally, at three o'clock in the morning of May 12, the day I was due, I woke up with cramps in, and down, my legs. The baby felt different inside me. I knew: This is the day.

By three-thirty I was getting my first contractions. I woke Rob, and told him this was it. When they began coming every twenty minutes, I started popping ginseng royal jelly, which my nutritionist had given me for strength. It also took the edge off the pain at the end of the contraction cycles, though it isn't a painkiller.

Rob and I had studied the Bradley Method of birthing for about four hours. Whereas Lamaze is all about distracting yourself with breathing and focusing on some object, Bradley is more tied to animal birthing. Animals go off and breathe through it, focusing inward. I drew in deep singing breaths to relax my diaphragm, making a low, comforting moaning sound.

By late morning, the idea of a car trip down La Brea to Cedars-Sinai seemed overwhelming. A hospital seemed cold and impersonal—not to mention the bad lighting. But it was now or never; I was beginning to fantasize staying home and having the baby right in the soft lighting of my beautiful Tuscany Italian bedroom with a view of the Pacific.

I snapped out of it. With a first birth at forty-two, I wasn't into taking any chances. Off we went—my brother Lorin at the wheel and me clutching Rob in the backseat. My sister-in-law Lynnette and nieces Suzanne and Lizzy were to meet us there. The contractions were now about three minutes apart, but, curiously, they spread out when we traveled. That often happens; the body goes into some sort of shock with the motion. In nature, animals don't ride in cars just before birthing their young.

Don't let anyone ever say contractions aren't painful. I felt his little head moving around as my pelvic bones seemed to be breaking apart. That hurt big-time. You take some comfort knowing it's finite—that you've got "only" some 500 contractions. I was about to break into "Ninety-nine bottles of beer on the wall." I looked at Rob at one point, laughing through my pain, and said, "Only four hundred sixty-seven to go."

They wheeled me straight into LDR No. 1—the labor-delivery-recovery room with the best view. I guess my doctor had pull. My doctor-associate checked our heartbeats, and they were fine.

So was his. It happened that four years earlier I had fixed him up on a blind date with my stunning niece Suzanne, who was now in the room with me. It had never gone anywhere with them, but he'd always had a thing for her. The moment he saw her, I could see he went *Whoooaaa!* and canceled the rest of his day to stick around.

What a perfect "figures prominently": My son would draw his first breath in a delivery room reeking of PF.

Rob wanted Lorin to man a camera and stay on through the birth, but I wasn't entirely comfortable with that. So I let Suzanne and Lynnette stay in the LDR through the labor. This allowed Rob to have a two-camera birth—one on a tripod trained on me, the other used for "coverage," or reaction shots, of Rob and various doctors and nurses. You'd have thought the Bradley Method also included storyboarding of shots the way Rob the director ran the LDR location. Mary Ann was also on hand with her cinematographer husband David, who set the lighting for the cameras. I wasn't messing around.

By the time I dilated to five centimeters, I was in such overpowering pain I was almost levitating off the bed. My legs were quivering uncontrollably. "I'll take that epidural now," I said. "Trust me, I want it. If I still have five more centimeters to go, I want it."

It was amazing. Ten minutes after I got the epidural, I went from white-knuckle agony to, "Say, does anyone have a nail file?" I phoned people, laughed; people brought food in. It was a party.

And I did group. Being a bit compulsive, even with the epidural, I realized that it was Thursday—time for a group phone session with Dr. Sharon back in Princeton. It was like we were shooting an AT&T spot: the "Reach Out and Birth Someone" ad campaign.

The group was amazed I was doing so well, but then they kind of busted me for trying to be a hero and gut it out without painkillers. They thought that was crazy. But no one thought it was unusual that I was on the phone during contractions. They knew me by then.

As the drugs wore off, it was time for me to push. I was lying on my left side. It was four-twenty P.M. With 14 people on hand, it was time to clear the set. Everyone left except for Rob, Lynnette, Suzanne, Dr. George Weinberger, and the associate, Dr. Stuart Fishbein.

Once I got into the pushing, it was over in less than forty minutes. Nicholas's head was twisted a bit from my lying on my side—though I didn't hurt from it until the next day. I felt him right himself inside me just as I pushed. It was unbelievably intense, but awesome, when you realize there is no turning back. A certain number of pushes and, no matter how much it hurts, the pain ends, a life begins. One incredible journey was ending for us; another was beginning.

Baby Nicholas crowned for a few moments and relaxed, as the doctor massaged me to make me soft. He suddenly said, "Look," and held a mirror as this little furry coconut head popped out, covered with hair. That was a moment I will never forget—no birth mother can ever forget.

They held the mirror for me so I could see his face, which was looking down and away. You just cannot believe this is happening. It was eerie: He looked exactly as I had imagined. He looked just like my baby.

Having this head poking between your legs is not the most comfortable feeling. And you know the shoulders are next, and you simply cannot believe you are about to open up that wide to let that life come through. It's a state of excruciating pain, combined with joy, wonder, and awe.

When he was out, they immediately put my crying baby on me, and he took my breast. I didn't want him all cleaned up first. It was a moment of pure joy: We were all sobbing. Giving birth is an indescribably weird sensation I can describe only as like having a giant vacuum sucking an enormous weight out of you, as if your stomach is emptying itself out—followed by a euphoric flush of joy when you first hold your baby in your arms.

That night was like an Italian festival. People were coming in and out of the waiting room, bringing sandwiches, swapping stories, making more videos. The doctors came by the next day to say how lovely a birth it was because everyone had been so attached and involved and full of love.

One of my first questions for the doctors was, How soon can we have sex? They said six weeks. That didn't sound right, so I got a second opinion. My nutritionist Dr. An Than said three, and he gave me an herb-based lotion to speed things along so I'd heal quickly. I went with his take on the situation.

In our postpartum party, before Rob and I sacked out for the night, I had my first drink in nine months, a glass from our magnum of precious Cristal. It kicked up my temperature a degree—and kicked in my maternal instincts. The nurses had just brought my baby in when they noticed my "fever." Now, they insisted, they had to keep him away from me.

"Give me my baby," I said.

"We have to keep the baby away."

"No way." I called my doctor and explained. "Tell them to come back in an hour and check," I said to him. They did, and, sure enough, I was back down to normal.

If I didn't love the way the nurses worked, I soon had another reason to hate hospitals. The next morning it was time to leave, and I became suspicious when a hospital worker offered, almost obsequiously, to help wheel me out. I went along. As we went through the lobby, he wheeled me straight at a guy armed with a point-and-shoot camera.

"May I take your picture?"

"No, I'd really rather you—"

Click. Click. Click. He fired off a roll as I looked away in disgust. Then I pointed my finger at him.

"That's incredibly rude."

"Oh, I'm so sorry," he said—and snapped off another frame or two from the camera dangling at his hip.

Rob went wild. He took off after this creep, but, having not been on his treadmill lately, gave out a couple of blocks away. Then Lorin got into this relay race, and tracked the guy to a restaurant near the Beverly Hills Hard Rock Cafe.

Before the guy could even read the day's pasta specials, Lorin went up to his table and snatched off his eyeglasses, demanding the film for the glasses. They had some words, and then negotiated as they walked outside. He would go apologize to me, but not hand over the film. Lorin then made a counteroffer the guy couldn't refuse: He threw a shit fit.

"Give me the *fucking* camera, goddammit!" he screamed. He went berserk on the guy. That settled it. The film for the glasses.

With that little tabloid hassle behind us, we drove home in peace, in love with our little miracle baby, who was snuggled in his car seat as we listened to a beautiful children's album given to us by our friend Kenny Loggins. It was hard to believe I had given birth barely eighteen hours before.

As we got out, Rob's daughter Erin rushed out to greet her new brother. Lorin and Lynnette pulled up behind us, with all the flowers. Rob handed the baby over to Erin, saying, "Here's your little brother, honey."

Just then, in the middle of this magical family moment, I heard a commotion from above. "Marilu," Lynnette said with some urgency, "go on inside. They're videotaping us!" Now Lorin the Enforcer was yelling and running after a couple of goons hiding in our bushes with a video camera aimed at the driveway. He flushed them out and confronted them by their car, demanding they leave. There was a verbal exchange as one goon continued to video the hassle. Finally, they tossed their gear into the trunk of their Lexus and took off. We never saw anything air.

What an omen!

When Nicholas was just five days old, I called into the *Evening Shade* production office to speak with Linda and Harry and fill them in. I had left a message with Burt the day after giving birth, but he hadn't gotten back to me yet. The networks were all presenting their fall lineups to the press that week, and there had been plenty of speculation about the fate of our show. With everything that had been going on with me, I didn't have the latest word. More important, I couldn't wait to share my big news with them.

Harry and Linda were out, but the secretary had some big news of her own to share. "CBS isn't picking up the show," she said. "It's not in the fall lineup. You've been canceled."

The irony was remarkable: For four years I had enjoyed what so few women in Hollywood ever find—a second hit series—but had craved what so many women effortlessly have: a first child. Now, in the same week, I had lost one—but finally found the other.

Great roles for women in their forties?

I had just landed the most extraordinary role I'd ever have in my life, the one I had waited the longest for, and worked the hardest to win.

Epilogue
By All Means
Keep On Moving

~

The Lord giveth; the network taketh away. What are you going to do? I would have been more upset about the show had I not seen it coming. But I had been saying to Rob all through the spring that we were on our way out.

We gave the network all the excuses it needed not to deal with us anymore and to pull the plug. Bottom line: If the show had stayed in the Top Ten and been a moneymaker, we'd be in production right now. Money talks.

But so do baby boys. There's nothing sweeter than being at home listening to our son babble, gurgle, burp, and drool. Nicholas Morgan was definitely meant to be my firstborn. I was out there working for that sperm and egg to mix and match, waiting for him to come into our lives. I look at him now and think, There could not have been any other child.

Maybe losing the show when we did was my wake-up call, reminding me of how hard we had worked to bring him here. At least I had part of the summer to spend some serious time with Nicky so we could get to know each other.

My one real sadness was that I didn't get to bring him to the set every day to show him off—and show myself off as a mommy—to all my dear friends at *Evening Shade*.

At first I had fretted that it would have been nice to have had the financial security of a prime-time series during Nicholas's first years. But today, as I sit here in the morning with him on my patio, with most of L.A. spread out before us, I have a real meant-to-be feeling about it. It all happens for a reason; everything seems more connected to everything than ever.

That Rolodex is going to have to wait. As soon as Nicholas came along and the series was canceled, other work started popping all over. There was *Marilu,* which will be an enormous challenge and, I hope, the highlight of my career. This, my third show, will undoubtedly demand more of me than my previous two TV ventures, and push me in exciting new directions as host of a daily talk show.

Then, Rob and I learned that our production company's two series in development, *Under Suspicion* and *Medicine Ball,* both hour-long dramas, had been picked up for the fall season by the networks. This was something Rob and I had been working toward for years—to get Crystal Beach off the ground, to make our own movies and create and produce our own series. With a pair of potential hits on our hands, we'll have so much more visibility and stature, and that will open up all sorts of new possibilities.

I'm hopeful that *Marilu* will become the wide-ranging showcase for me that *Evening Shade* never could have been, even though it will be a "reality" program, not a dramatic or comedy series. I hope it can help get my theories and messages across about health and fitness and marriage and motherhood and society and living in the nineties.

It reconnects me to my very first "work" on TV—when Uncle and I would create make-believe segments of *The Tonight Show* as we took turns being Johnny and his guest. The guest part of that experience has already been put to good use dozens of times; now I get to try out the Johnny part as host. Thank you, Uncle.

Having a baby also puts you in deep contact with your own parents, because you suddenly see the world and your own child the way they saw you. I often feel, the way that Nicholas has already become such an organic part of my world, that I have stepped back into my mother's life. Seeing myself mothering him has given me a wide and clear window into my mother's heart that I never enjoyed while she was alive.

Even with six kids, she never missed a beat, never stopped being who she was. We became part of her world. My parents were always packin' us up and takin' us along for the ride. We were part of her dance world; part of my father's showrooms. We were never sequestered and closed off from who they were.

Now I understand, when I hold my son, the unconditional love they had for us. I now see why my parents had this driving passion to create a bustling home life where we could all be around one another. I also now see how it made sense that they never went anywhere without us. That's all coming into focus. I can't imagine ever wanting to leave Nicholas behind. He waited a long time to get here, and now he's coming along for the ride.

Nicholas has already had lots of people in his world, from the moment he arrived here. He started taking feedings and meetings at about the same time. He was born at 5:07 on Thursday, and twenty-four hours later I had a talk-show-related meeting at the house, with him in my arms. Over that weekend, I was still finishing up the manuscript for this book, holding him as I worked, stopping only to take nursing breaks. Rob and I suddenly had all sorts of projects popping—a TV movie for me to star in, our production company's two series being picked up, my new talk show, and a bunch of TV pilots. At barely three weeks old, Nicholas had already been to all three networks, a number of production bungalows, and backstage at *The Tonight Show*. As my life begins to move on in so many new and exciting directions, Nicholas moves with me because he *is* my life now.

When he was a month old, we packed up his equipment—he has more *stuff* already than anyone else I know—and took him to Aspen. That was the way my mother and father were. I have friends who decided that for the first forty days of their newborn's life, he would be isolated and not be allowed around anyone but his parents. I felt that was overindulgent, not good for the immune system. I threw Nicholas right into the mix, and within no time flat he was an overwhelming presence in our life. And it feels like we have all made a healthy, happy adjustment to parenthood.

Rob, naturally, felt it was almost too thorough, too quick. "You can't take a day off?" he asked when Nicholas was less than a week old. He sounded slightly irritated.

"What do you mean?" I said. "I took a day off. I took Thursday off."

"You gave *birth* Thursday."

"That's what I mean. I didn't work. I had the baby."

I know having this baby—and we're already talking about a brother or sister for Nicholas—will profoundly change me and my life. Rather than wanting to pull back and ease up, now I want to succeed even more. We naturally want to be able to give him everything he needs, to give him the best education he can get, and to go on fun, exciting adventures. We want him to have a *great* childhood. I haven't lost any ambition. On the contrary, since I got pregnant, it seems I have never been busier.

If I have always been a bit detached and wary of the collective "values" of the Hollywood culture, motherhood has already taken me a little bit further from the rat race of filmmaking and TV. I'm not trying to be cavalier about it, because I still make my living as an actor, and my husband is a director, producer, and screenwriter. And I definitely feel my best work is still ahead of me.

But more things from that world now just seem silly. I already see a shift in my priorities and interests.

But it's more complicated than that. As Rob has said, "Once you become a parent, you've bought into all the fears and worries and considerations you could so easily avoid as a single adult. There's no turning back." Things like the environment, crime, child abuse, schools, TV and movie violence—they were interests of mine before; now they're obsessions, if not fears. And now they can all become topics on my show!

But it's frankly a relief to have something else, *someone* else, to worry about. I'm all for having something take me out of myself at this stage of my life. I've had a lot of years of me, me, me. Now, it's him, him, him—and I can't believe how powerfully protective my love for him is. I can't believe how every second of the day is filled with Nicholas, with taking care of him. I used to have routines; my life required them. They're all shot now, history. Now I have new routines. And life goes on. Amazing.

Being a mother has already brought immediate changes in the way I live. I can't believe I want to spend more money on his wardrobe than on my own. That's a big step for me. That's major.

He's already got baby hangers. A month before he was born, I had all his identical, custom-ordered hangers ready. (Of course, I have always had matching hangers in *my* walk-in closet, ever since I called up a boutique supply place and told them I had a retail outlet and needed hundreds of identical hangers. All my dresses and suits hang on perfect, double-hung racks, arranged by color, pattern, and style. This is what I call obsessive-compulsive order—finding a way to make your neuroses work for you. Lorin was being facetious when he said the only reason I wanted a child was to have another closet to arrange. But he's not entirely off-base.)

It's also a major step that my house is a major mess most of the time now—well, by my standards. A couple of sweaters that need folding and filing away—that's a mess. And things like my stocking and underwear drawers are in a state of virtual chaos. Stuff isn't in neat piles, colors are out of place.

Oh, well. I'll get around to them, and to that updated Rolodex, when he goes off to college. Until then, I'll live.

My lifelong maniacal need for order and control has already been demolished by this tiny little being we call Nicky. I have to learn to relax and accept that baby stuff doesn't always match. We haven't gotten around to painting the large, built-in, raw-wood wall unit in Nicholas's room yet, because of the fumes. It'll get painted when we take our next trip. So it's pretty hamper in there now—a room half done, with half-unpainted wood. But the great thing is, I don't care. He won't remember, he won't be scarred by this. And neither will I.

Besides, a touch of hamper is good for your health. That much I know.

No great roles after forty? Forget it. I don't need a TV series to tell me I'm in prime time. I love the way things are turning out. I love the story arc Rob and I have going for us. We each needed to take a long journey on our own before we found each other, but we're moving ahead together now into the most wonderful and exciting time of our lives. It wasn't always easy, and it didn't happen without some painful lessons and losses. And we both know there will be all sorts of other challenges to face, setbacks to survive, victories to savor.

But wherever this journey takes me, I know I'm going to love getting there, because I'm just hitting my stride.